Studies in Mobilities, Literature, and Culture

Series Editors
Marian Aguiar, Department of English, Carnegie Mellon University, Pittsburgh, PA, USA
Charlotte Mathieson, University of Surrey, Guildford, UK
Lynne Pearce, English Literature & Creative Writing, Lancaster University, Lancaster, UK

This series represents an exciting new publishing opportunity for scholars working at the intersection of literary, cultural, and mobilities research. The editors welcome proposals that engage with movement of all kinds – ranging from the global and transnational to the local and the everyday. The series is particularly concerned with examining the material means and structures of movement, as well as the infrastructures that surround such movement, with a focus on transport, travel, postcolonialism, and/or embodiment. While we expect many titles from literary scholars who draw upon research originating in cultural geography and/or sociology in order to gain valuable new insights into literary and cultural texts, proposals are equally welcome from scholars working in the social sciences who make use of literary and cultural texts in their theorizing. The series invites monographs that engage with textual materials of all kinds – i.e., film, photography, digital media, and the visual arts, as well as fiction, poetry, and other literary forms – and projects engaging with non-western literatures and cultures are especially welcome.

More information about this series at
http://www.palgrave.com/gp/series/15385

Roger Bromley

Narratives of Forced Mobility and Displacement in Contemporary Literature and Culture

palgrave
macmillan

Roger Bromley
University of Nottingham
Nottingham, UK

Studies in Mobilities, Literature, and Culture
ISBN 978-3-030-73598-2   ISBN 978-3-030-73596-8 (eBook)
https://doi.org/10.1007/978-3-030-73596-8

© The Editor(s) (if applicable) and The Author(s), under exclusive license to Springer Nature Switzerland AG 2021
This work is subject to copyright. All rights are solely and exclusively licensed by the Publisher, whether the whole or part of the material is concerned, specifically the rights of translation, reprinting, reuse of illustrations, recitation, broadcasting, reproduction on microfilms or in any other physical way, and transmission or information storage and retrieval, electronic adaptation, computer software, or by similar or dissimilar methodology now known or hereafter developed.
The use of general descriptive names, registered names, trademarks, service marks, etc. in this publication does not imply, even in the absence of a specific statement, that such names are exempt from the relevant protective laws and regulations and therefore free for general use.
The publisher, the authors and the editors are safe to assume that the advice and information in this book are believed to be true and accurate at the date of publication. Neither the publisher nor the authors or the editors give a warranty, expressed or implied, with respect to the material contained herein or for any errors or omissions that may have been made. The publisher remains neutral with regard to jurisdictional claims in published maps and institutional affiliations.

Cover credit: Jerome Cid/Alamy Stock Photo

This Palgrave Macmillan imprint is published by the registered company Springer Nature Switzerland AG
The registered company address is: Gewerbestrasse 11, 6330 Cham, Switzerland

This book is dedicated to Anita and our grandchildren, Jonah and Emma, and to the memory of Virginia (Ginny) Bromley (1936–2021)

Acknowledgments

At the time of the power workers' strike in the United Kingdom in 1970, someone wrote to *The Times* newspaper, starting the letter with "Sir, Writing by candlelight ..." and I feel that I should start my acknowledgments by saying "Writing in the pandemic ..." as this has dominated my life, and those of millions of others worldwide, throughout the whole period of writing this book.

I have been researching and writing about asylum seekers and refugees for some years now but my most valuable experience was in volunteering with the Nottingham and Nottinghamshire Refugee Forum as foodbank helper, café assistant, conference organiser, and trustee. I was also director of the Refugee Week festival for a number of years. This experience gave me insights which no books or internet searches could have provided and many of the refugees became friends as did some of the people who helped with the festival and other activities: Farouk Azam, Fiona Cameron, Chris Cann, Caroline Hennigan, Jane and John Henson, Skinder Hundal, Peter Lowenstein, Helen O'Nions, Rob Peutrell, Sooree Pillay, Sr. Philomena Rooney, and Patricia Stout.

Apart from my volunteering experience, the initial ideas for this book came when I was invited to give a lecture at the launch of the AHRC project "Responding to Crisis: Forced Migration and the Humanities in the Twenty-First Century" at Keele University in October, 2016. I should like to thank Mariangela Palladino and Agnes Woolley for involving me in this project as a member of the Advisory Board. Thanks to Mariangela also for inviting me to give a seminar paper at Keele on one of the topics in Chapter 5, a month before lockdown.

With increasingly restricted access to libraries, much of the research for this book has been carried out online. Having been retired for some years now and without any immediate colleagues, I am thankful for the support of the following in assisting with the development of this book: Alexandra D'Onofrio, Eva Giraud, Lindsey Moore, Peter Morey, Annalisa Oboe, Maggie O'Neill, Teodora Todorova, Patrick Williams, Hicham Yezza and Robert Young. Special thanks also to the film directors, Fernand Melgar, and Antonio Augugliaro, Khaled Al Nassiry, and Gabriele del Grande, for graciously allowing me to use images from their films at no cost. Thanks are also due to Lilia Laura Stankiewicz Gonzalez at the Galeria Peter Kilchmann, Zurich and to the artist, Adrian Paci for their generosity in allowing me to use the image in the Introduction.

For the three years from 2015 to 2018 I had the pleasure of being part of the four universities Postmigration Research team in Denmark and thank Sten Moslund, Anne-Ring Petersen, and Moritz Schramm for inviting me to give lectures and take part in conferences in Copenhagen and Odense. I should also like to thank Carmen Concilio and Pietro Deandrea for asking me to give lectures at the University of Turin and to contribute articles to journals which they edit. Another debt is also owed to Fadwa Kalam Abdelrahman at the faculty of Alsun, Ain Shams University, Giza, Egypt for her warm hospitality offered when inviting me to give a keynote lecture at their annual conference where some of the ideas in Chapter 5 were presented.

As one of the few remaining academics still writing in longhand, I was fortunate that Amanda Graham was able to do an excellent job in transcribing my scribble into something resembling coherence. As someone whose IT skills are the historic equivalent of the quill pen, I was similarly fortunate in having Paul Poplawski as a meticulous and patient copy editor who did an exceptional job in not only transforming my manuscript into publishable shape but who also made a number of constructive criticisms which improved the quality of the argument at different points. My son, Carl, gave his time and years of publishing experience in New York to help curb some of my excesses and keep the analysis in focus. Lynne Pearce, long-time friend and series editor, mentored the book project throughout and gave prompt, invaluable advice and continuing encouragement. My editors in New York, Allie Troyanos and Rachel Jacobe, showed great forbearance in waiting for me finally to produce this book after several delays, and also answered my numerous queries promptly.

The pandemic has made life difficult for all of us, especially during periods of shielding and I am especially grateful to my daughter, Catherine, who has helped throughout and to friends like Gill Barber, Kim O'Neill, Lauren Johnston-Smith and D J Johnston-Smith who ensured that we were fed and kept sane. My bowls friends, Caroline and Rob Fairnie, Alasdair Hutcheson, Dougie Hutchinson, Brian Thomson and Eric Walker helped distract me from the demands of the book at times, and my acupuncturist and laser therapist, Jill Buchan, kept me fit enough to keep on typing. On a sad note, my good friend, inveterate peace campaigner, and armchair politics and football sage, Ken Fleet, died from the virus in the early part of the pandemic and will not see the outcome of some of our discussions. His memory is treasured.

Finally, my deepest gratitude is due to Anita who, for fifty-four years of companionship, love and wisdom has, despite her own busy legal career, always been there for me as reader, guide, and support.

Although substantially rewritten and revised, sections of some chapters have appeared in earlier forms. Part of Chapter 2 was published in *Working and Writing for Tomorrow: Essays in Honour of Itala Vivan*, CCCP, 2008. Versions of the first half of Chapter 3 appeared in "Asylum Accounts", *Moving Worlds* (2012) and *The Culture of Migration: Politics, Aesthetics and Histories*, I.B. Tauris, 2015. A section of Chapter 4 was published in *Recognizioni: Rivista di Lingua, Letteratura e Culture Moderne*, 2016 (1). Versions of parts of Chapter 5 were published in *From the European South*, 2018, and *Le Simplegadi*, 2019.

Praise for *Narratives of Forced Mobility and Displacement in Contemporary Literature and Culture*

"In his outstanding engagement with the recent literatures of enforced mobility and displacement, Roger Bromley assembles a significant range of resistant cultural responses to today's expanding regimes of checkpointing, border control, and forced displacement that constitute our global coloniality. Resourced by an exceptional literacy in cultural studies, political theory, postcolonial critique, and decolonial thought, Bromley's consistently dazzling analyses formulate vital new ways of thinking which steadfastly refuse the pernicious demonisation of precarious dwellers and refugees."

—John McLeod, *Professor of Postcolonial and Diaspora Literatures, University of Leeds, UK*

"Roger Bromley's wide-reaching book takes an incisive and theoretically rigorous look at how cultural practitioners are responding to the central geopolitical phenomenon of our times. Taking in multiple genres and geographical contexts, it is an invaluable resource for students and researchers alike."

—Agnes Woolley, *Lecturer in Transnational Literature and Migration Cultures, Birkbeck, University of London, UK*

Contents

1 **Introduction** 1
　Political and Theoretical Context 3
　Textual Methods 10
　The Im/Mobilities Paradigm 11
　Refugee Journeys 13
　Borders 15
　Decoloniality 19
　Global Context 19
　Chapter Outline 22
　References 24

2 **People on the Move: Narratives for a Journey of Hope** 27
　Not Belonging and Unwanted 32
　Somewhere in the EU 37
　No Longer in This World 40
　The Longest Journey 45
　Reversing the Appearance of the Frontier 48
　References 57

3 **Policing Displacement and Asylum: Giving Voice to Refugees** 59
　Crisis at the Border 60
　The Liberal Dilemma 62
　Mapping Separation 63

	Storying the Stranger	66
	Telling the Story Differently	73
	Into the Abyss	78
	Writing the Migrant into the Narrative	80
	Writing a Name in the Sky	88
	Leveraging the Queue as a Technology	90
	References	97
4	**Out of Focus and Out of Place: The Migrant Journey**	101
	Telling a Story with a Voiceless Pencil	105
	In the Labyrinth	112
	The European Middle Ages	119
	Calais Context	120
	Framing the Dispossessed	121
	In the Grey Zones	132
	References	138
5	**Restaging the Colonial Encounter: Far-Right Narratives of Europe and African Migrant Responses**	141
	White Genocide	144
	The Southern Gaze	151
	Elsewhere and Here: Revisiting the Colonial Encounter	156
	Silenced Deaths	166
	Unequal Mobility Regime	174
	References	177
6	**Fragmented Spaces/Broken Time: Restoring the Absence of Story in the West Bank of Palestine**	181
	Time, Space and Mobility	183
	Naziheen, the Displaced Ones	188
	The Architecture of Occupation	193
	Here Distances Always Measure the Same	200
	Plan Dalet	204
	Tracing History	207
	An Infinity of Traces	212
	A Jar in Ramallah	219
	Postscript: An Incurable Malady	226
	References	228

Index 233

List of Figures

Fig. 1.1 Migrants wait endlessly to board a non-existent plane as a fighter-bomber passes by. ADRIAN PACI. Centro di Permanenza temporanea, 2007. 16:9 video projection, 5.30 min., colour, sound. Video still (Courtesy the artist, Galerie Peter Kilchmann, Zurich and kaufmann repetto, Milan) — 2

Fig. 2.1 *On the Bride's* Side (2014). The bride and groom crossing the border between Italy and France at Grimaldi Superiore (Reproduced by courtesy of Antonio Augugliaro, Khaled A. Nassiry, and Gabriel del Grande. *Photo* Marco Garofalo) — 52

Fig. 3.1 Refugee excluded and waiting in La Forteresse, Switzerland (Reproduced by courtesy of Fernand Melgar [director]) — 74

Fig. 4.1 An aerial view of the Jungle Refugee camp, Calais (Reproduced by courtesy of Daniel Vernon/Alamy) — 121

Fig. 5.1 African migrants climb a border fence between Morocco and Spain's North African enclave of Melilla (Reproduced by courtesy of Reuters/Alamy) — 157

Fig. 6.1 Cultural resistance in the form of graffiti on the annexation wall in Bethlehem (*Photo* The author) — 198

CHAPTER 1

Introduction

This century, and the past decade in particular, has been characterised by the massive global displacement of people whose lives have been altered or destroyed by geopolitical events. Displacement of peoples within, and across, borders is not, of course, a new phenomenon but, arguably, the fall of the Berlin Wall, the bombing of the Twin Towers in 2001, the 2007–2009 great recession, and wars and conflict in the Middle East and Africa, have produced new and different forms of mobility and immobility. In thinking about this project from the perspective of someone whose research is in the Humanities, the first challenge which came to mind was to consider the adequacy of existing criteria which refer to the situation of the refugee/migrant (for reasons outlined below, these terms will be used interchangeably). This was followed by attempts to locate the ideological underpinnings of current European attitudes towards refugees, encapsulated in the concept of *racialisation* as the primary logic of global capitalism. Finally, I considered how to find counter-narratives to subvert, or at least question, negative, populist representations of refugees as 'dangerous invaders'. These representations echo the long-standing colonial violence of historical and cultural representations of the Global South. As Lucy Mayblin argues, "The logics of excludability not only *result* in dehumanisation, but also *emerge from* long-standing modes of thinking

© The Author(s), under exclusive license
to Springer Nature Switzerland AG 2021
R. Bromley, *Narratives of Forced Mobility
and Displacement in Contemporary Literature and Culture*,
Studies in Mobilities, Literature, and Culture,
https://doi.org/10.1007/978-3-030-73596-8_1

Fig. 1.1 Migrants wait endlessly to board a non-existent plane as a fighter-bomber passes by. ADRIAN PACI. Centro di Permanenza temporanea, 2007. 16:9 video projection, 5.30 min., colour, sound. Video still (Courtesy the artist, Galerie Peter Kilchmann, Zurich and kaufmann repetto, Milan)

about the world, and the various people in it, in colonial/modern hierarchical terms" (Mayblin 2017, 175, italics in original). My own approach will start from similar "long-standing modes of thinking about the world" in order to situate ideological attitudes, at both elite and popular levels, which make dehumanisation of 'people out of place' possible (Fig. 1.1).

Given the scale of mass displacement and the vastness of the topic, combined with the increasing amount of legislation around detention, deportation and dispersal, the crucial question which arose was how to produce a viable project which might contribute to an understanding of the cultural impact of involuntary, or forced, mobility on the lives of those displaced by war, persecution and conflict as well as by famine, climate change and poverty. Coming from the discipline of Cultural Studies, I decided to focus on the evidence of the effects of displacement as seen in narratives—cinematic, testimonial and literary—produced by, with, or about refugees and migrants. Outlined below are the core components of the theoretical resources which I shall use in order to shape and inform the cultural/textual analysis of representational forms which constitutes the methodological approach of the book. Each chapter will focus upon at least three narratives, of a contrasting nature, and, in the process of critical analysis, it is hoped to generate an alternative 'map' of texts for understanding displacement in terms of affect, subjectivity, and dehumanisation with the overall aim of contributing to a re-direction of the current stream of anti-refugee rhetoric or, at the very least, opening up new dialogues.

The next three chapters are based primarily upon refugee journeys, asylum seeking, trafficking and detention; the final two, Chapters 5 and 6, while inevitably raising some of the same issues as the previous ones, will focus upon territorial displacement, the architecture of occupation and settlement, and border separation. Borders are everywhere, and in the words of Gloria Anzaldua: "The US–Mexican border *es una herida abierta* [an open wound] where the Third World grates against the first and bleeds. And before a scab forms it hemorrhages again, the lifeblood of two worlds merging to form a third – a border culture" (Anzaldua 1999, 25). Although part of my title is "Forced Mobility", in fact it is at borders where the most common experience of the displaced is 'forced *im*mobility', so the book will pivot on this contradictory oscillation between movement and the arrest of movement.

POLITICAL AND THEORETICAL CONTEXT

In the popular imagination, distinctions between asylum seekers, EU migrants and 'irregular' economic migrants are conflated for hostile purposes. In academic, legal and policy circles, there is now a debate about whether the conditions of the 1951 UN Refugee Convention are too restrictive—limited to a specific fear of persecution—and questions are being asked about whether those fleeing from poverty, material and environmental degradation, and profound social disadvantage should also be considered alongside those with a claim to political refugee status. Is a distinction between voluntary and forced movements still tenable? Richmond's concept of 'reactive migration' (Richmond 1988), linked to those (economic and political migrants) whose life choices and well-being were 'severely constrained' is still of real value. The book will, therefore, expand the concept of 'forced' migration and the terms 'refugees' and 'migrants' will be used interchangeably because the effects of neoliberal regimes of structural adjustment in the developing world deplete biodiversity, create unemployment and conditions of immiseration which force people to migrate 'voluntarily' in search of a better life. Indeed, the "New York Declaration for Refugees and Migrants" at the UN Summit on 19

September 2016 specifically committed to "Protect the human rights of all refugees and migrants, regardless of status".

As is well known, the great majority of all refugees are in the developing world, often adjacent to their countries of flight, for economic and logistical reasons. The refugee 'crisis' in Europe (2015), more of a crisis *of* Europe as many have said, needs to be seen in its wider context of decolonial thinking and what is meant by the coloniality of power. In so doing, we need to situate the mindset which has led to negative European ways of seeing refugees in particular, and migrants in general. Two very different articles have proved useful starting points for this book: Sylvia Wynter's "Unsettling the Coloniality of Being/Power/Truth/Freedom: Towards the Human, After Man, its Overrepresentation" (2003) and Catherine Hall's "The Racist Ideas of Slave Owners Are Still With Us Today" (2016). In order to understand European attitudes to refugees at the level of the State and in popular terms, it is necessary to produce a historical account by going back and discovering the discourses and ideologies which have produced these attitudes and thinking about what Wynter calls the Western bourgeois conception of the human, Man, which *overrepresents* itself as if it were the human itself. The idea of the Western European as overrepresenting itself as human is of value because it helps to see why refugees are seen as disposable and regarded as less than human. Once the idea of dehumanisation takes hold it is accompanied by impunity and indifference at the level of the State and in terms of the popular imaginary. How, otherwise, do we make sense of negative responses to the deaths of thousands of refugees at sea, and elsewhere, in recent years (more than 35,000 since 1990), and policies of exclusion which consist of building walls and fences, in seventy or more countries, to keep out would-be asylum seekers? In Wendy Brown's *Walled States, Waning Sovereignty* she argues that the proliferation of walls in the contemporary world has given rise to a reactionary nationalist populism which acts in support of global neoliberal technologies of governmentality (Brown 2010). My fifth chapter, in particular, will outline some of the characteristics of this far-right nationalist populism.

Any attempt to unsettle this overrepresentation necessitates an understanding of what a number of Latin American theorists (Quijano, Mignolo) have called 'the coloniality of power'. Throughout this book, I shall be using the concept of the 'coloniality of power', in the way developed by Mignolo from the work of Quijano, to "refer to the system that organised the distribution of epistemic, moral, and aesthetic resources in a way that both reflects and reproduces empire" and "as a way to name that set of framing and organising assumptions that justify hierarchies and make it almost impossible to evaluate alternative claims" (Alcoff 2007, 83, 86). It will be seen how time, space, and memory have been colonised, not just by colonialism but by a coloniality which, in Grosfoguel's terms, "allows us to understand the continuity of colonial forms of domination after the end of colonial administrations, produced by colonial cultures and structures in the modern/colonial capitalist world-system" (Grosfoguel 2008, 7). In writing about displacement, generally, we need to ask ourselves (as Europeans) why, and how, we distance ourselves from refugees, and what set of values enables us to do so? One part of the answer is *racialisation*, one of the primary legacies of colonialism, with the idea of race "the most efficient instrument of social domination invented in the last 500 years" (Mignolo 2007). Catherine Hall, from another perspective, speaks of how "in order to make money the [slave] traders had to create a new discourse on 'race'; and the impact of those ideas needs to be remembered too" (Hall 2016). Race as a master code, or narrative *mentalité*, has entered so deeply into common sense and daily discourse as part of the construct of the white Euro-American that the epistemological disregard of the other informs all other forms of 'disregard'. Global inequality is one of the root premises and also effects of this racialisation and a reason why degradation, immiseration, and the violent deaths of refugees are met with indifference. They are, in Judith Butler's words, "the ungrievable", "lives regarded as disposable … are so stripped of value that when they are imperilled, injured or lost, they assume a social ontology that is partially constituted by that regard … their potential loss is no occasion to mourn" (Butler 2014, 35). Whose life *is* a life, Butler asks, and "whose life is effectively transformed into an instrument, a target, or a number, or is effaced with only a trace remaining or none at all" (Butler 2016, ix–x). Systematically representing refugees as figures of lack, without worth or value, those whose lives are not worth living, derives from long-standing ideas about racial difference. As Philip Marfleet argues, "Immigration control, racism and exclusion are inseparable" (Marfleet 2006, 289).

As an imperialising force, Western Europe not only practised slavery and extensive forms of exclusion and dispossession but also developed an accompanying ideological narrative, the distorting vision of coloniality, which persists today. As Walter Mignolo argues, the ethno-racial foundation of modernity was established by "Christianity's victory over the

Moors and the Jews, the colonization of the American Indians, and the establishment of slavery in the New World" (Mignolo 2011). As will be seen in Chapter 5, a few far-right intellectuals argue today for a 're-conquest' by Europe echoing the Spanish term *Reconquista* used in 1492 by the new Spanish crown during the conquest of the Muslims and expulsion of the Jews. This nationalism, the offshoot of imperialism, is one way in which history is still present in all we think and do in Europe. As Mbembe says, when it comes to imagining the inhumanity of foreign peoples, "race has been the ever-present shadow in Western thought and practice" (Mbembe 2003, 4). Quijano seeks to locate this precisely in historical terms: "Although the idea of race was already evolving during the time of the war of reconquest in the Iberian peninsula, it was only with the formation of the world-system in the sixteenth century that it became the epistemic base of colonial power" (quoted in Castro-Gomez 2008, 280). Drawing on Mbembe's work on the postcolony and on necropolitics, Andrés Castro argues that:

> From an understanding of salaries, taxes and adjustment financial programs as disciplinary systems of government, to the orgiastic violence of massacres and extrajudicial killings, the state, the parallel state, and the transnational corporations are able to inflict more death in the Global South through the deliberate destruction of life's infrastructure than through old forms of direct killing. (Castro 2016, 242)

This is a very concise summary of why so many people—the disposable or discardable others—seek to reach the Global North, from Central America, the Middle East and Africa. Apart from the wars, massacres, extrajudicial killings and gang violence, it is the deliberate destruction of life's infrastructure which leads to a sense of abandonment and despair.

In order to offer fresh interpretations of refugee/migration representation, and to account for dehumanisation and indifference to their destitution or death, three main theoretical resources, drawn from the Global South, will be deployed in the analysis of literary, cinematic and testimonial narratives of displacement. The first of these is *decoloniality* which traces the origins, and continuing presence, of the 'colonial matrix of power' and its universals of Western modernity and global capitalism, and the need for delinking from hegemonic Western narratives by means of 'epistemic disobedience'. Related to this is the concept of *abyssal thinking*, developed by Santos. He argues that modern Western thinking operates along abyssal lines that divide the human (Western: above the line) from the sub-human (colonised 'Others': below the line), the former characterised by a dichotomy of regulation and emancipation, the latter by systemic appropriation and violence, marked by colonialism, capitalism and patriarchy. What he terms "post-abyssal thinking" is not simply a theoretical matter but a struggle for global social justice, a decentring effort articulated through global cognitive justice on behalf of "those constructed and constituted through the colonial wound". The final theoretical resource, and linked to both of these, is *border thinking* from the perspective of subalternity; Mignolo says that "by border thinking I mean the moments in which the imaginary of the modern system cracks" and he adds to this that decoloniality means a transformation "of the rigidity of epistemic and territorial *frontiers* established and controlled by the coloniality of power" (Mignolo 2000, 23, 12). I shall be thinking of borders in metaphorical terms at times, but will also be looking at specific borders or quasi-borders (Morocco/EU/Spain; and Israel/Palestine) through a range of narratives which are marked by deportations, segregations and violence carried out by border, or occupying, regimes which oversee all forms of human mobility, but particularly that of the refugee, the migrant, and the 'occupied'. It is at these borders, and in detention centres, where the mobility of refugees is arrested, literally and metaphorically, where they are forced into long periods of waiting, taken out of time and immobilised. This waiting is the focus of my third chapter. It is in such waiting that devaluation and dehumanisation are felt most acutely. Checkpoints, fences, walls and the technologies of exclusion become instruments of forced immobility. These are the material/literal borders, but within all the narratives that will be the subject of analysis are other kinds of border: racial, gendered, sexual, epistemic and ontological, religious and aesthetic, linguistic and national. To justify these borders, a discourse of ethno-nationalist populism has been generated in Europe and the US, with its identitarian narratives and horror stories of Muslim invasion and replacement of the autochthonous. This phenomenon will be explored in Chapter 5, as I have indicated above.

Until recent years, the phrase 'wretched of the earth' (Fanon 1965) would confidently have been applied to those outside the West but neoliberalism, austerity and growing inequality mean that this term also now resonates within the West, with its 'epidemic of disempowerment', hence the growth of populism, the fear of 'invasion' and the political response in the form of intensified bordering—fences, walls, etc. Refugees symbolise precariousness, a liminality, which serves as an unsettling, unwelcome reminder of how many lives in the privileged West are now also potentially remaindered. Refugees occupy the borderland between abandonment and value now shared by many.

Any attempt to unsettle so-called common-sense thinking about refugees confronts ideological forms of nationalism, coloniality and the State. Overcoming prejudice towards refugees is an agonistic process, a struggle on several fronts—generational and demographic. One of the major problems to contend with is the notion of the commonality between always-existing, homogeneous, national subjects, a fundamental aspect of subjectivity at the level of the symbolic: a taken-for-granted European and white ethnicity, what Balibar termed a "fictive ethnicity" (Balibar and Wallerstein 2002). Refugee representations have to somehow interrupt/disrupt this 'continuity' and introduce new levels of diversity and antagonism, expose the contingency and emptiness of nationalist signifiers, and go beyond the nation to formulate other, perhaps global, but not necessarily territorial, allegiances. In other words, the project is designed to locate representations which challenge the hegemonic narratives constructed around the current mobility across the Mediterranean, deserts, and rivers, by the 'less than human' displaced peoples of the Global South.

In order to resist seeing the refugee as a knowing subject, with autonomy and agency, many Europeans essentialise the 'other', reduced to a set of invariable and negative characteristics as racialised subjects, and this enables us to regard their deaths with *indifference*. How this indifference and emotional dis-identification can be challenged is partly by coming to terms with narratives that originate beyond the coloniality of power, or which interrogate this, such as Juan Tomás Ávila Laurel's novel *The Gurugu Pledge* (2017; featured in Chapter 5) or the hybrid text of Behrouz Boochani's *No Friend but the Mountains* (2018; one of the texts examined in Chapter 3).

Apart from the theoretical concepts outlined previously, and connected to them, it is necessary to consider a range of issues related to the representation of refugees in, often reductive, Western discourses, such as the sentimentalised, passive victim, the object of compassion—"often, they are given no story at all, reduced to a shadow that occasionally flits across European vision" (Trilling 2018)—and replace these with the agential subject, the resistant activist ('actors in their own lives') and the newly emergent citizen. How we render the refugee 'knowable' is another challenge, the challenge to the politics of representation. Where there is humanitarian concern and sympathy, the focus tends to be on vulnerability. Of course, the vulnerable must be protected, but to see all refugees as victims, or vulnerable people, is a perspective that needs to be critically examined for its reductiveness and refusal of agency.

This involves a number of methodological challenges. The experience of refugees *is* unrepresentable in a sense, an 'unimaginable existence'—Toni Morrison's *Unspeakable Things Unspoken* (1988)—and representational forms are always inadequate. Acknowledging the limits of representation necessitates the development of other lenses for perception, a greater aesthetic-political reflexivity and sensitivity, a search for new, and radical, rhetorical forms which unsettle and disrupt expectations and preconceptions. From the standpoint of power, the historical narrative is always set in stone. Unsettling this power is the task of provocative narratives, from the perspective of the refugee. So, the forms of representation are crucial, and the central point of radical narratives is to highlight precarity and maintain that *intervention* in the refugee 'crisis' is possible. In *Silencing the Past*, Michel-Rolph Trouillot, in exploring the Haitian revolution, speaks of the lack of conceptual frames of reference for understanding, or even acknowledging, the revolution. In the terms of Western thought, the event was unthinkable: "The unthinkable is that which one cannot conceive within the range of possible alternatives, that which perverts all answers because it defies the terms under which the questions were phrased" (Trouillot 1995, 82). By exploring the limitations of sympathy, the shortcomings of the liberal claim of common humanity, and insisting on the ethical dimensions of representation, my book seeks to discover new frames of reference at the theoretical level (e.g. decoloniality) and interventions in literary and cultural form, a range of possible alternatives, which subvert the presumption of 'knowing the refugee'. The 'unthinkable', the 'unsayable' and the 'unrepresentable' will be examined in several of the chapters.

The book will attempt to show how and why the Third World 'grates' (Anzaldua's word) against the first world, and why 'grate' is an appropriate word to express the violent measures taken to prevent contact. The distinctiveness of this book is the way in which it brings a range of radical and critical theoretical resources to bear on a challenging discussion of contemporary mobilities and displacements linked to a systematic, cultural analysis of migrant/refugee narratives in the form of films, literary fictions, memoirs and graphic narratives. In a sense, the book is designed to address what I term the representational deficit in respect of refugees and migrants.

The book is framed by the issue of forced migration in the context of globalisation and neoliberalism, with its main theoretical emphasis on decolonial thinking which links each chapter. While 'epistemic violence' and the decoloniality of power structure the analysis throughout, different chapters will feature specific instances of displacement, from the subjective construction of the movement of those displaced, to their objectivist 'othering' in racialised and nationalist discourses. Differently inflected processes of 'othering' constitute the main focus of the book.

Textual Methods

The various literary and cultural genres—novel, film, memoir/testimonial and graphic text—have been chosen as a way of producing a complex set of different lenses on displacement, an 'evidence base' of complementary and interdependent texts, with the visual reinforcing the verbal and vice versa. Narrative is seen as a way of text organisation, and each text's schema is actualised in terms specific to the genre. As the focus of the book is on movement and the lack of movement, the way in which time is articulated in different media becomes a crucial issue. Specific encoding and decoding processes structure each text differently, some are synoptic, others more panoramic or pan-optic. Each one textualises temporality, space, mobility and embodiment differently. The tortuous, fragmented and perilous journey of those in flight is shown dramatically in the novel *African Titanics* (2014 [2008]) or in the film *In this World* (2002), for example; whereas, in the film *Those Who Jump* (*Les Sauteurs*) (2016), the technologies of border power are made explicit visually in the form of militarised security and a lengthy and high fence, as is the hunger, cold and immiseration of those in a makeshift camp encircled by the relative privilege of the urban resident and the promise and threat of a border fence. This forms a cinematic complement to the world experienced by the displaced in *The Gurugu Pledge*. The fact that the film was shot by a displaced person himself emphasises the point I make in the book about voice, eye and agency. The visceral effects of trafficking and smuggling are, literally and visually, embodied in films such as *Dirty Pretty Things* (2002) (the trade in body organs) and *Lilya 4-Ever* (2002) (rape and prostitution). All these films show what might be called the endurance of the refugee.

The various narratives of Palestine discussed in Chapter 6, for example, present subjective time in the form of curfews and travel restrictions, checkpoints and the quasi-borders of terminals. Movement as a disciplinary ordering is captured in novels and memoirs which reflect upon and interpret the effects of displacement in time and over time. One final example of textual complementarity and overlap is considered in Chapter 4 through the representations of 'the Jungle' in Calais in the graphic narrative *Threads* (2017) and the film *May They Rest in Revolt* (*Qu'il Reposent en Révolte*) (2010), the former emphasising duration, the various skeins which link the salvaging refugee existence and the reflexive autobiography of a volunteer, with the latter synoptically dramatising a similar experience through the words and actions of characters, focusing on the immersive enactment and embodiment of a global site of displacement. As Alexander Betts shows "Migration control is part of the broader context of North-South relations, in which much of liberal global governance exists to ensure the containment and exclusion from the North of people in the Global South" (Betts 2009, 158).

The Im/Mobilities Paradigm

In terms of movement, John Urry shows that mobility in the form of migration is not peculiar to the contemporary world but as forced mobility (whatever the 'force' which I discuss later) has led to the large-scale movement of people from the Global South to the North (although predominantly within the Global South) limits to this mobility have produced a culture of securitisation and the development of sophisticated technologies to delay, thwart or criminalise this movement. Globalisation is predicated upon mobility (of money, goods, ideas and 'privileged' people) but only that of certain categories of people. The lorry and the boat as modes of travel mean very different things to the person with passport, money or permit than to the forced migrant. Air travel is probably the most popular form of business and leisure mobility but it is never available (legally) to the refugee, only in cases of deportation, another form of forced mobility, or as stowaways in the undercarriages of planes where there are numerous instances of refugees having frozen to death or dropped to the ground when the landing gear retracts. Similarly, mobility on foot is entirely different for the migrant forced to walk miles over inhospitable terrain than for the dog-walker or jogger. Urry locates sedentarism—place making—as the fundamental human experience but not for the refugee whose experience, like that of the nomad, is constituted by erratic lines of flight. Ingold says that "human beings generate lines wherever they go" and that "Everybody has their personal path and is known by it … Paths have their stories just as people do" (Ingold 2016, xvi) but, for the refugee, mobility means tearing up that path and laying down new ones 'involuntarily' and shaping new stories from 'the archaeology of silence' (Spivak) and displacement.

A point which Urry makes and, perhaps, I have not stressed sufficiently is that "migrants mainly originate from 'wild zones' that the globalising world engenders and especially from a 'culture of terror'" (Urry 2007, 36). Actually, this is a feature of almost every chapter of my book (and especially Chapter 5). Urry's chapter "The Mobilities Paradigm" is valuable in the sense that almost every feature of the paradigm (he lists twelve) is absent from the life of the displaced person whose experience totally lacks any vestige of the "durability and stability of mobility" Urry mentions. This lack is a negation of the paradigm to such an extent that it produces an 'immobilities paradigm' with the only mobility available bringing the displaced close to Agamben's 'bare life'. In Urry's terms, the displaced endure the 'burden of mobility' as opposed to motility which is defined as "the way in which an individual appropriates what is possible in the domain of mobility and puts this potential to use for his or her activities" (Kaufmann 2019, 37). In a residual sense, the displaced have traces of motility but, in most cases, lack any agency, or choice, with which to appropriate anything in the realm of mobility, but, as the improvised camps on Mount Gurugu and in Calais indicate, resilience and resourcefulness are not lacking. Martina Tazzioli rightly cautions about confusing movement and mobility, arguing that "politicising mobility means also distinguishing it from movement and bringing to the fore the materiality of the struggles, the racialised policies and the mechanisms of exploitation that sustain and shape different practices of mobility…" (Tazzioli 2020, 102). Peter Adey cites Israeli sociologist Ronen Shamir's assertion that we "are witnessing the emergence of a global mobility regime oriented to closure and to the blocking of access" (Shamir 2005, 199). If this was true fifteen years ago, then it is even more true today, especially since 2015 and the European panic about refugees. As will be shown in Chapter 3, but also elsewhere throughout the book, "the world's mobilities are constituted and patterned by vast amounts of immobility, especially waiting" (Adey 2017, 12).

Refugee Journeys

Going back to what was said earlier about the 'unsayable' and 'unthinkable', it is almost impossible for anyone living comfortably in a European town or city to begin to imagine the horrors of certain refugee journeys, without resorting to clichés. As chair of the Refugee Week festival in Nottingham in 2016, I asked two young male asylum seekers if they would be prepared to speak about their journeys to the UK. The first one came from Syria, mainly by sea in over-crowded boats, in which several people died en route. It was a harrowing story which, eventually, I was to hear several times. The other young man, from Eritrea, while not doubting the Syrian's story, said he felt that the media tended to stress the immense dangers of migrant journeys by sea, and either ignored, or minimised the arduous nature of overland journeys with dehydration, hunger, grossly overloaded transport, and the threat posed by bandits. He then proceeded to show a powerful series of PowerPoint images in which he traced in graphic detail the precise dangers of which he had spoken. Both men presented their experiences in a quite dispassionate way which, I think, added to the impact of their stories on the local audience. They both said that it took some time before they could process their trauma and find a language to describe it.

In the case of the 'territorial displacements' explored in the last two chapters of this book, focusing on the violence of borders, Hagar Kotef's work on regular and irregular movement has been of value in so far as it demonstrates how movement has been placed at the forefront of contemporary security apparatuses in Israel, the US and in Europe, the technologies of power which mark the politics of mobility, what Kotef calls "a regime of movement". As Europe, the US and Israel establish modes of governance predicated upon separation, movement increasingly becomes the target of control with its apparatus of surveillance. If globalisation is a 'government of mobility' in the age of 'surveillance capitalism', then, as Wendy Brown shows, "what we have come to call a globalised world harbours fundamental tensions between opening and barricading, fusion and partition, erasure and reinscription. These tensions show as increasingly liberalized borders … and the devotion of unprecedented funds, energies and technologies to border fortification" (Brown 2010, 19). Barricading, partition and erasure are fundamental components of the narrative of the displaced.

What I shall be tracing in the book is the attempted erasure of the agency, experience, voice and tactics of resistance from the displaced and the search for literary and cultural representations which aim to enable and restore these 'erasures'. The presence of the displaced, at the border or frontier of power, is configured as an *excess* by European countries, something other and beyond.

As Betts, Richmond and others have argued, the 1951 Refugee Convention and the 1967 Protocol are not entirely adequate in terms of the protections offered to forced migrants who may be fleeing for reasons other than those that define refugee status (Richmond's 'reactive migration'), for example, those in flight from hunger, poverty and environmental degradation. Although refugees, in the generally accepted terms of the UN Convention, are the focus of some of my chapters, other aspects of forced human mobility will also be considered, for example in Abu Bakr Khaal's *African Titanics* which traces the stories of 'illegal' immigrants: "the African boat people and their desperate exodus to the merciless shores of the Mediterranean" (book blurb). As claiming asylum has become increasingly difficult, many border-crossers resort to clandestine means, often paying smugglers, to reach a country where asylum can be claimed. The debate around forced and 'unauthorised' migration will be addressed explicitly in Chapter 4 and, while I will observe the conventional distinctions between asylum seeker, refugee and economic migrant, these distinctions will also be questioned. As Castro has demonstrated,

> most unauthorised immigrants were forced to leave their countries of origin because the conditions imposed by neoliberal globalization and neocolonial militarisation made it impossible for them to make a life in their homelands. 'Free Trade' agreements, like NAFTA (1994) for example, have destroyed local economies and small farms in Mexico where farmers are no longer able to sustain their families because they can no longer compete with the subsidised corn from the US .... (Castro 2016, 243)

This is true also for other countries in Central America, with people forced north in order to survive, not only by NAFTA but also, increasingly, by climate change.

I have worked as a volunteer with all categories of migrants mentioned in the last paragraph and am aware of the 'muddied' nature of the field. Under the UK government's Vulnerable Persons Resettlement Scheme (VPRS), for instance, Syrian families (in my area of Scotland) having been granted asylum in Lebanon or Jordan, arrive, quite understandably, with refugee status with 'leave to remain' for five years. Others I knew in Nottingham remained asylum seekers for a decade or more. Sometimes 'overstayers' or the 'undocumented' make a late claim for asylum once apprehended. I stood bail for a woman who claimed asylum on the grounds of domestic violence with a well-documented case, but this claim failed, and she was deported. As I came to understand, asylum legislation is fraught with confusion, contradiction and palpable injustice. I pick up some of these issues in Chapter 3, particularly the demand for a consistent and coherent story and the brutal interrogations which often accompany this demand.

Borders

The situation of the 'refugee' is further complicated in the case of Palestine with its more than thirty camps in the West Bank and Gaza, whose residents have no recourse to asylum. Borders are much more than demarcations of national sovereignty but also occupy the symbolic (and legal) space between categories of belonging, of those 'in place' and those 'out of place', the displaced. They are also, of course, as mentioned earlier, manifestations of power in an increasingly unequal world. Life on the borders—material and symbolic—as recorded in densely textured accounts in visual and verbal form will be the focus of my final two chapters in particular as I consider 'territorial displacements'.

Borders as symbolic, imaginary and performative feature throughout the book and in the final chapters especially. In the case of the EU, for example, one of its borders (Ceuta and Melilla) is on the African continent for historical reasons, and in an increasing number of cases European countries are 'exporting' their borders to African countries secured by the provision of expensive, advanced technologies of surveillance, weaponry, investments and bribes. In Chapters 5 and 6, I shall look closely at specific borders, their role in securitisation, and resistances to them—Ceuta and Melilla, Palestine/Israel. In the latter, there are not borders as such, but the hundreds of checkpoints and roadblocks in the West Bank effectively perform the same function as a border. The symbolic dimensions and the architecture and logistics of the border will be examined in the light of ongoing political challenges and transgressions. Modern political spaces, Mezzadra argues, are born from the "radical geometrical simplification" of the border, increasingly materialised as a fundamental signifier of power and the territorial logic of contemporary geopolitics. 'Border thinking' in decolonial thinking is the analysis of CPM (the colonial matrix of power) from the edge or the border in a metaphorical sense but also linked to Gloria Anzaldua's *Borderlands/La Frontera* (1999) which has extended thinking about borders well beyond its local, material instance, especially in terms of embodiment, a core part of decolonial thinking: the body of the 'other'. This body is, variously, abused, tortured, scarred, shot at, incarcerated and drowned.

As Balibar and Wallerstein (2002) argue, under globalisation borders have become mobile as they figure centrally in a regime that controls migratory movements in Europe; and while, traditionally, borders should be seen as the edge of territory, in the contemporary world they have been transported into the middle of political space. Wherever located, borders have become sites of inclusion and exclusion, contested struggles around 'crossing' and border reinforcement, struggles which have cost thousands of lives in the Mediterranean and elsewhere. Violence, as has been pointed out, frequently shapes lives and relations that are played out across borders worldwide, with more than seventy walls, fences and other fortified structures in place. It is at these borders that the racialisation of mobilities is most accentuated.

These borders are no longer seen simply as lines of demarcation but "symbolic, linguistic, cultural and urban boundaries [that] are no longer articulated in fixed ways by the geopolitical border. Rather, they overlap, connect, and disconnect in often unpredictable ways, contributing to new forms of domination and exploitation" (Mezzadra and Neilson 2013, vii). As Mezzadra and Neilson go on to say, "borders play a key role in the production of heterogeneous time and space of contemporary global and postcolonial capitalism" (ibid., ix). Forced migrants in motion and their challenge to the border are irritants to this order of capitalism unless, and until, converted into sources of cheap labour. While in transit, or seeking asylum, they are surplus, excess. In terms of Europe, Martina Tazzioli summarises the situation concisely: "In fact, nowadays European space is punctuated by mushrooming border zones, spaces of migrant struggles, safe places of temporary refuge and others that have been transformed into hostile environments" (Tazzioli 2020, 1).

Except for Chapter 6, most of this book is concerned with this European space. In a recent book, Ayelet Schachar has identified what she calls a new and striking phenomenon, the *shifting border*: "at times penetrating deeply into the interior, at others extending well beyond the edge of the territory" (Schachar 2020, 4). In this way, it can be seen that the Guatemala/Mexico border is regarded by the US as its border, or Miami becomes a border when pursuing undocumented migrants. The EU border in Morocco—Ceuta and Melilla—is a European example. Schachar proposes a shift in perspective "from the more familiar locus of studying the *movement of people across borders* to critically investigating the *movement of borders to regulate the mobility of people*" (Schachar 2020, 7, emphasis in original). Extraterritorial border control is now a feature of many countries in the West, with 'expedited removal' a key factor in immigration enforcement in the US. On an optimistic note, Schachar speaks of the benefits of breaking the relation between territory and protection which she suggests could "save lives, dry up the market for human smugglers, allow security screening of entrants prior to arrival, permit greater choice and agency for migrants themselves to select their destination country, and help alleviate fear of 'loss of control' among voters in the recipient countries" (Schachar 2020, 85, n. 204). Given the situations I explore in the following chapters this kind of initiative seems very far off.

Another kind of border is the 'abyssal line' which Boaventura de Sousa Santos characterises as the line which divides the human from the sub-human, those discarded in the 'colonial zone', a system of visible and invisible distinctions, the latter being the foundation of the former. His work questions the epistemological presuppositions of Western thought and is concerned with achieving cognitive justice, as well as social justice, by affirming that "the understanding of the world by far exceeds the Western understanding of the world". His work, developing what he calls "epistemologies from the South" is close to decolonial thinking, as is his concept of the "sociology of absences" (Santos 2014, 171). I shall argue that the figure of the refugee constitutes an 'absent presence' in the 'First World/developed world'. Santos's articulation of these absences in terms of what is forced to belong to the *other* side of the 'abyssal line', seen as non-existent, shifts the gaze to an engagement with knowledges from the South, seen from the North as immobile, static, primitive and as irrational, superstitious and incomprehensible. On the contrary, the North/West is modern, always in motion. Santos argues for the need to acknowledge, recognise, and "establish forms of life that are simultaneously the effect and precondition of the continuation of existence of marginalised actors" (Santos 2014, viii) as part of a struggle for a politics of reality, or alter-reality, emergent and, crucially, co-present with Western forms of knowledge. The argument is for 'parity of esteem', the equal recognition of all forms of knowledge, with no superior or inferior claims. This recognition of 'subordinated' epistemologies could also prefigure/accompany the recognition of those from the territory of absences—the poor, the displaced, the othered.

In order to establish this co-presence of value/esteem, Santos points, in the first instance, to the need for a new kind of non-abyssal imagination which has to affirm "the South as if there were no North ... woman as if there were no man ... the slave as if there were no master" (Santos 2014, 171), as if, that is, all the founding binaries of power are set aside as a prelude to a world of horizontal, rather than vertical, belonging. A monumental ideological task, obviously, but one which has already begun, for example, with the World Social Forum and the Zapatistas.[1] Chapter 5, with its emphasis on the complex, colonised mentality of the figures in *The Gurugu Pledge* will make use of Santos, with the novel's narrator who "chose the southern face, that my gaze was turned toward the River Zambezi", opting to turn away from the global North. This lays bare and makes visible the European narrative of power and casts the whole preceding narrative as a committed epistemological resistance against epistemic violence by putting into question the central positioning of the Western gaze. It is as if the novel requires to be read again, from the perspective of the end. Chapter 5 will be framed by Santos's argument that in terms of Western knowledge, "the colonial zone is par excellence, the realm of incomprehensible beliefs and behaviour that in no way can be considered knowledge, whether true or false. The other side of the line harbours only incomprehensible magical or idolatrous practices. The utter strangeness of such practices led to denying the very human natures of the agents of such practices" (Santos 2007, 8). As Trouillot noted, "unmarked humanity is white" (Trouillot 1995, 81). In Toni Morrison's *The Bluest Eye* (1999 [1970]), the main character, Pecola, tragically and understandably as a young, oppressed black girl/woman, yearns for blue eyes and longs to be white, the twin markers of universal beauty and indicators of what it is to be recognised as human.

Decoloniality

As indicated earlier, the historical and theoretical framework of the book will be drawn from concepts of decoloniality which "seeks to interrupt the idea of dislocated, disembodied and disengaged abstraction, and to disobey the universal signifier that is the rhetoric of modernity, the logic of coloniality, and the West's global model … It opens up co-existing temporalities kept hostage by the Western idea of time and the belief that there is one single temporality" (Mignolo and Walsh 2018, 3). This temporality and its hegemonic symbolic order was established, in Trouillot's terms, by the following processes: "The invention of the Americas … the simultaneous invention of Europe, the division of the Mediterranean by an imaginary line going from the south of Cadiz to the north of Constantinople, the westernisation of Christianity and the invention of a Greco-Roman past to Western Europe" (Trouillot 1995, 74–75). In this way and by these processes, Europe *became* the West. By using the theoretical paradigm of *border thinking*, Mignolo proposes a re-reading of the history of the West as modernity, arguing for a displacement of Europe and a rigorous questioning of categories which have reproduced "the marginality of the histories, spaces, and subjects of the colonial frontier of modernity" (Mezzadra and Neilson 2013, 18).

The literary and cultural texts of forced mobility and displacement examined throughout this book will be seen in the contemporary context of what William Robinson calls the "transnational capitalist class", neoliberalism, and what Quinn Slobodian terms the "Globalists". These three terms overlap in many respects and help us to understand the increasing inequality and social polarisation in the world which, on the one hand, is driving people from the Global South to embark upon dangerous and costly journeys while, in response to this movement of peoples north, there is a resurgence of the far-right in Europe and the US which has generated panics around invasion, replacement and white genocide.

Global Context

Inequality, the asymmetries of globalisation and the crisis of global capitalism are at the root of the displacement and movement of people from the Global South throughout this century, particularly in the last decade. As William Robinson has shown, "Capitalist globalisation has resulted in unprecedented social polarisation worldwide. According to the development agency Oxfam, in 2015 just one percent of humanity owned over half of the world's wealth and the top 20% owned 94.5% of that wealth" (Robinson 2019, 158). Deregulation, financial speculation, overaccumulation and the digitalisation of the global economy have deepened social polarisation. With unprecedented global inequalities in recent years has come repression, social control and a growth in militarised securitisation. As Robinson argues, "The TCC [transnational capitalist class] has acquired a vested interest in war, conflict, and repression as a means of accumulation" (ibid., 160). This, in turn, has contributed on a large scale to increases in forced mobility and displacement, with Syria, since 2011, the most egregious instance of this, with millions internally displaced and more than six million refugees. The construction of border walls, fences, global surveillance systems and detention estates to exclude by coercion or detain refugees—the so-called surplus humanity—is a source of considerable profit, as is the reconstruction by Western contractors of towns and cities devastated by Western-backed conflicts (e.g. Iraq and Afghanistan). As Robinson points out, one way of displacing, or diverting, mass fear and anxiety, insecurity and precarity in the Global North is by creating scapegoats. Migration is the most visible evidence of global interconnectedness and the rapid social transformations this generates. Until the early part of this century in the UK, 'bogus asylum seekers' was the generalised target of tabloid abuse but, more recently, this has been replaced by the catch-all term 'immigrant'. Forced, or coerced, migrants face increasing state and media hostility which can be traced to globalising processes. Arguably, as borders close and wars continue, migration will continue to increase. As Roger Zetter claims, "Refugees are perceived as an especially problematic and threatening category ... containment of refugees is the major objective of all the stakeholders, except the refugees" (Zetter 1999, 75).

It is the visibility of non-white immigration which has enabled governments across Europe and the US to deflect the real causes of increasing indebtedness, insecure, 'gig' employment conditions, and unaffordable housing by creating a consensus around the idea that immigration must be controlled. What effects the COVID-19 pandemic will have on this discourse of deflection is yet to be seen. I suspect it will make attitudes towards 'outsiders' even worse. As will be shown in Chapter 5, and elsewhere in the book, part of the drift to the right in political discourse is the way in which immigration is seen to be a violation of the resident population—it is bodily, happening at the level of affect. Already, in this century, entrance points to the UK have been cut from eighty to five, and the virus may well see, in line with Brexit, a clamour for more tightening of borders and the exclusion of asylum seekers. As I write (August 2020), there is a minor panic about a few hundred asylum seekers arriving in Dover by sea; "Racism offers workers from the dominant racial or ethnic group an imaginary solution to real contradictions" (Robinson 2019, 169). Not only workers it must be said. It is at the level of the imaginary and the cultural that current hegemonic practices around migration operate. After ten years of austerity, the fact that the Conservative government in the UK managed to secure a large parliamentary majority in the December 2019 election suggests that these practices work, in accordance with what Benedict Anderson said about the nation: "The nation, argued Benedict Anderson is an 'imagined political community' in which 'the nation is always conceived as a deep horizontal comradeship,' regardless of the actual inequality and exploitation that exists" (Robinson 2019, 169). I am not claiming that this victory was due simply to scaremongering about immigration as there were other 'dark forces' at work, but Brexit was a dominant feature and Brexit had a level of anti-immigration factored into it. For all the rhetoric to the contrary (e.g. 'we want our country back') Brexit will serve the interests of transnational corporate capital, freed from the restraints of EU regulation.

At several points in the book I make reference to neoliberalism as if it were still the dominant ideology and, although I am aware it has come under increasing pressure, I share Quinn Slobodian's reservations that it is yet a spent force: "To diagnose a crisis of neoliberalism is not to suggest that economic inequality has ceased to advance. Nor that the application of market solutions to social problems or the calculation of all human value in monetary terms has ceased, or that we have witnessed a return to a pattern of redistribution or a turn to Keynesian welfare state ideology" (Slobodian 2018, 285). Indeed, all the people (real or imagined) who figure in the narratives which are the subject of this book are part of the calculation of all value in monetary terms and are blamed for the erosion of welfare provision and the growing inequalities in distribution. It has been clear for many years that, as Marfleet puts it, "states have taken a calculated and instrumental approach to people who are vulnerable and often defenceless" (Marfleet 2006, xiii).

The main focus of the book is on attempts by people from the Global South to reach countries in the Global North for safety, protection and a life free from poverty and violence. Both these terms are of fairly recent usage and cover a vast, diverse and heterogeneous number of people, nations and economies. Global South is not a geographical concept and I am using Boaventura de Sousa Santos's definition:

> The South is rather a metaphor for the human suffering caused by capitalism and colonialism on the global level, as well as for the resistance to overcoming or minimising such suffering. It is, therefore, an anti-capitalist, anti-colonialist, anti-patriarchal, and anti-imperialist South. It is a South that also exists in the geographic North (Europe and North America), in the form of excluded, silenced and marginalised populations, such as undocumented immigrants …. (Santos 2016, 18–19)

It might be added there is a North that also exists in the South. The United Nations uses these terms and the UN Development Programme's Human Development Index (HDI) considers that the Global North consists of those sixty-four countries which have a high HDI, with the remaining 133 countries part of the Global South. Santos's definition will inform much of my discussion, even if not always explicitly, and it fits well with my understanding of decoloniality and its historical genealogy of modernity and concept of the West. Human suffering, the excluded, the silenced, the undocumented and marginalised will feature in each chapter but also, without exception, what will figure as well is a range of forms of resistance.

Although the narratives selected for analysis will be drawn from the whole of this century, a lot of attention will be paid to the period from 2015 onwards, the time of the so-called European refugee crisis which, as Bernd Kasparek has argued "is in fact a crisis of the decade-old attempts of European institutions to control, manage and govern migration on the way to and inside of Europe. Under close inspection, the *European refugee crisis* is the crisis of the European border regime—it is a crisis of the Schengen system" (Kasparek 2016, 2).

Chapter Outline

In each chapter, with one exception, at least one narrative has been produced by someone who has been a refugee, an undocumented migrant or a person displaced for other reasons. In the case of Chapter 6, with its focus on the Israeli-occupied West Bank, most of the narratives have been produced by those born, or living, under the Occupation, or in exile. Chapter 2 deals initially with narratives of people smuggling or trafficking from the early part of this century, and latterly with two documentaries developed by, or in collaboration with, Syrian asylum seekers after 2013. Chapter 3 explores issues of detainment and incarceration with an emphasis on disorientation, time and waiting. Two films, one a feature film, the other a documentary, both set in Switzerland prior to the Swiss vote against 'mass immigration' in 2014, are analysed. A written narrative by an Iranian asylum seeker on Manus Island, Papua New Guinea, constitutes the second part of the chapter. The fourth chapter draws mainly on narratives of migration, asylum seeking and encampment in graphic novels, together with a documentary film produced in collaboration with asylum seekers by a radical filmmaker. This is followed by a chapter which examines works by former African refugees, now settled in Europe, two of which focus on the Spanish/Moroccan enclave of Melilla, an EU border in Africa. The other narrative traces the dangerous journey by desert and sea of refugees from sub-Saharan Africa. Chapter 6 centres on the occupied West Bank of Palestine with reference to a number of narratives, fictional, and autobiographical, which, variously, feature the founding origins of the 'encirclement' of Palestine by Israel, and the experience of mobility/immobility produced by the militarised 'security' of checkpoints, roadblocks and curfews.

Note

1. The World Social Forum which first met in 2001 in Porto Alegre, Brazil, is an annual conference of civil society organisations set up to develop an alternative future through advocating counter-hegemonic globalisation. Its motto is: Another World is Possible. The Zapatistas are named after Zapata, the guerrilla leader during the Mexico revolution of 1910. In its current incarnation it was set up after the Zapatista uprising in the Chiapas region of Mexico in 1994, and elsewhere, opposed to neoliberalism and the signing of the NAFTA (North American Free Trade Agreement). The Zapatista Autonomous Municipalities have a measure of de facto autonomy.

References

Adey, Peter. 2017. *Mobilities*. London: Routledge.
Alcoff, Linda Martin. 2007. "Mignolo's Epistemology of Coloniality." *The New Centennial Review* 7 (3): 79–101. https://doi.org/10.1353/ncr.0.0008.
Anzaldua, Gloria. 1999 [1987]. *Borderlands/La Frontera*. San Francisco: Lute Books.
Balibar, Etienne, and Immanuel Wallerstein. 2002. *Race, Nation, Class: Ambiguous Identities*. London and New York: Verso.
Betts, Alexander. 2009. *Forced Migration and Global Politics*. Chichester: Wiley.
Boochani, Behrouz. 2018. *No Friend but the Mountains*. Translated by Omid Tofighian. London: Picador.
Brown, Wendy. 2010. *Walled States, Waning Sovereignty*. Brooklyn, NY: Zone Books.
Butler, Judith. 2014. "Ordinary, Incredulous." In *The Humanities and Public Life*, edited by Peter Brooks and Hilary Jewett, 15–37. New York: Fordham University Press.
Butler, Judith. 2016 [2010]. *Frames of War: When is Life Grievable?* London: Verso Books.
Castro, Andrés Fabian Henao. 2016. "From the 'Bio' to the 'Necro': The Human at the Border." In *Resisting Biopolitics: Philosophical, Political, and Performative Strategies*, edited by S. E. Wilmer and Audronė Žukauskaitė, 237–53. New York: Routledge.
Castro-Gomez, Santiago. 2008. "(Post)Coloniality for Dummies." In *Coloniality at Large: Latin America and the Postcolonial Debate*, edited by Mabel Moraña, Enrique Dussel, and Carlos A. Jàurequi, 259–85. Durham and London: Duke University Press.
Dirty Pretty Things. 2002. Directed by Stephen Frears. London: BBC Films.
Evans, Kate. 2017. *Threads: From the Refugee Crisis*. London: Verso.
Fanon, Frantz. 1965. *The Wretched of the Earth*. London: MacGibbon and Kee.
Grosfoguel, Ramon. 2008. "Transmodernity, Border Thinking and Global Coloniality." *Revista Critica De Ciencas Sociais*, July 4: 1–22. www.humandee.org/spip.php?page=imprimer&id_article=111. Accessed August 12, 2020.
Hall, Catherine. 2016. "The Racist Ideas of Slave Owners Are Still with Us Today." *The Guardian*, September 26. https://www.theguardian.com/commentisfree/2016/sep/26/racist-ideas-slavery-slave-owners-hate-crime-brexit-vote. Accessed May 12, 2018.
Ingold, Tim. 2016 [2007]. *Lines: A Brief History*. London and New York: Routledge.
In This World. 2003. Directed by Michael Winterbottom. London: BBC Films.
Khaal, Abu Bakar. 2014 [2008]. *African Titanics*. Translated by Charles Bredin. London: DARF Publishers.

Kasparek, Bernd. 2016. "Routes, Corridors, and Spaces of Exception: Governing Migration and Europe." *Near Futures Online* 1 (March): "Europe at a Crossroads." Accessed May 20, 2020.

Kaufmann, Vincent. 2019. "Europe Beyond Mobilities." In *Mobilities and Complexities*, edited by Ole B. Jensen, Sven Kesserling, and Mimi Sheller, 155–60. Abingdon: Routledge.

Laurel, Juan Tomás Ávila. 2017. *The Gurugu Pledge*. Translated by Jethro Soutar. Sheffield: And Other Stories.

Lilya 4-Ever. 2002. Directed by Lukas Moodysson. Stockholm: Memfis Film.

Marfleet, Philip. 2006. *Refugees in a Global Era*. Basingstoke: Palgrave Macmillan.

Mayblin, Lucy. 2017. *Asylum After Empire*. London: Rowman & Littlefield.

May They Rest in Revolt (Qu'Ils Reposent En Révolte). 2010. A Noir Prod. Presentation. Directed by Sylvain George. Paris: Independent.

Mbembe, Achille. 2003. "Necropolitics." Translated by Libby Meintjes. *Public Culture* 15 (1): 11–40.

Mezzadra, Sandro, and Brett Neilson. 2013. *Border as Method, Or the Multiplication of Labor*. Durham and London: Duke University Press.

Mignolo, Walter. 2000. *Local Histories/Global Designs: Coloniality, Subaltern Knowledges, and Border Thinking*. Princeton, NJ: Princeton University Press.

Mignolo, Walter. 2007. "Questioning 'Race'." *Socialism and Democracy* 21 (1): 45–53.

Mignolo, Walter. 2011. "Epistemic Disobedience and the Decolonial Option: A Manifesto." *Transmodernity* (Fall): 44–66.

Mignolo, Walter, and Catherine Walsh. 2018. *On Decoloniality: Concepts, Analytics, Praxis*. Durham and London: Duke University Press.

Morrison, Toni. 1999 [1970]. *The Bluest Eye*. New York: Vintage.

Morrison, Toni. 1988. *Unspeakable Things Unspoken: The Afro-American Presence in American Literature*. The Tanner Lectures on Human Values. Delivered at the University of Michigan, October 7.

Richmond, Anthony H. 1988. "Sociological Theories of International Migration: The Case of Refugees." *Current Sociology* 36 (2): 7–26.

Robinson, William. T. 2019. "Global Capitalist Crisis and Twenty-First Century Fascism: Beyond the Trump Hype." *Science and Society* 83 (2): 481–509. Accessed August 2, 2020.

Santos, Boaventura de Sousa. 2007. "Beyond Abyssal Thinking: From Global Lines to Ecologies of Knowledge." http://www.eurozine.com/beyond-abyssal-thinking. Accessed August 24, 2020.

Santos, Boaventura de Sousa. 2014. *Epistemologies of the South: Justice against Epistemicide*. Boulder, CO: Paradigm Publishers.

Santos, Boaventura de Sousa. 2016. "Epistemologies of the South and the Future." *From the European South* 1: 17–29. http://europeansouth.postcolonialitalia.it. Accessed May 15, 2020.

Schachar, Ayelet. 2020. *The Shifting Border: Ayelet Schachar in Dialogue*. Manchester: Manchester University Press.

Shamir, Rouen. 2005. "Without Borders? Notes on Globalization as a Mobility Regime." *Sociological Theory* 23 (2): 197–217.

Slobodian, Quinn. 2018. *Globalists*. Cambridge, MA: Harvard University Press.

Tazzioli, Martina. 2020. *The Making of Migration: The Biopolitics of Mobility at Europe's Borders*. London: Sage.

Those Who Jump (Les Sauteurs). 2016. Directed by Abou Bakar Sidimé, Estephan Wagner, and Moritz Siebert. Denmark: Distributed by Widehouse.

Trilling, Daniel. 2018. "Five Myths about the Refugee Crisis." *The Guardian*, June 6: 9–11.

Trouillot, Michel-Rolph. 1995. *Silencing the Past: Power and the Production of History*. Boston: Beacon Press.

Urry, John. 2007. *Mobilities*. Cambridge: Polity Press.

Wynter, Sylvia. 2003. "Unsettling the Coloniality of Being/Power/Truth/Freedom: Towards the Human, After Man, Its Overrepresentation—An Argument." *The New Centennial Review* 3 (3): 257–337.

Zetter, Roger. 1999. "International Perspectives on Refugee Assistance." In *Refugees: Perspectives on the Effect of Forced Migration*, edited by A. Ager, 46–82. London: Continuum.

CHAPTER 2

People on the Move: Narratives for a Journey of Hope

This chapter is concerned with the ways in which globalisation has impacted upon migration to the EU in this century. In particular, it looks at how the circulation in politics and the media of a set of negative images and vocabularies relating to refugees and asylum seekers has become part of a new exclusionary discourse. However, a number of films are examined which offer a representational challenge to this cultural and political narrative and it is argued that there are signs of an alternative set of discursive currencies emerging as part of a counter-formulation and potentially radical cultural imaginary.

John Berger called migration the quintessential experience of the twentieth century and there is every indication that this will be no less true of this century. The past fifteen years or so have seen renewed flows of refugees and asylum seekers from areas of conflict, violence and human rights abuses. The Brazilian photographer, Sebastião Salgado, referred to those who have taken flight from their countries of origin or have been caught up in the zones of conflict as "globalized people". His book, *Migrations* (2000), contains a vast number of images of people either on the move or trapped in arenas of violence. These images of a new displacement, mainly taking shape in the poorest regions of the world, but also in Europe and the US, help to document, in committed and dramatic

© The Author(s), under exclusive license to Springer Nature Switzerland AG 2021
R. Bromley, *Narratives of Forced Mobility and Displacement in Contemporary Literature and Culture*, Studies in Mobilities, Literature, and Culture, https://doi.org/10.1007/978-3-030-73596-8_2

fashion, labour, human movement and political economy. In a sense, the photographs contribute towards a framework for a newly emergent public imaginary, perhaps even a "global" imaginary. In similar fashion, it will be argued that a number of cinematic fictions, produced in the early part of this century, which deal with "undocumented" migrants, human trafficking and sex slavery, might also be used as resources for a narrative understanding of the new "global civilization" brought about since 1990 by the combination of economic and cultural global capitalism and the mass movement of people across the world. It could be argued that the more the subject remains unimagined (or unnarrated) the more the possibilities of the future cannot be imagined. This chapter is about the un- or under-imagined subject and the denial of the possibilities of an imagined future other than in terms of a form of enslavement to the present and its ideologies of value. These ideologies are underpinned by national, moralistic narratives organised by capital but, in many instances, beginning to show cracks and strains in its signifying chain.

Initially, two films, released in the period from 2000 to 2003, will form the basis of the analysis, while others will also be referred to. In the latter part of the chapter, two very different documentaries relating to the conflict in Syria will be examined, one a brief collaboration between a young female Syrian asylum seeker and a Norwegian journalist and documentarian, the other a feature-length documentary collaboration between three, Italy-based filmmakers and a group of five Syrian/Palestinian asylum seekers. The Syrian conflict was chosen because, as it approaches its tenth year, it has produced the greatest number of internally displaced people and refugees in the second decade of this century. By 2016, more than six million people in Syria were internally displaced, with a further five million having crossed into other countries, mainly Turkey, Lebanon, Jordan and Egypt. Four years later, in 2020, just under one million Syrian refugees are registered in the EU, mainly in Germany.

At the outset of the twenty-first century, Afghans constituted the largest single refugee population with an estimated 3.6 million people. This is the subject of Michael Winterbottom's *In This World* (2002). By 2011, Pakistan, Iran and Syria had the largest refugee populations respectively. In the year of the so-called refugee crisis in Europe, 2015, 13.9 million refugees (86% of the total of 16.1 million externally displaced) were hosted by the Global South, out of a figure of 65.3 million forcibly displaced worldwide (the majority of which were internally displaced). This latter figure represents an increase over twenty years of 75%. In

Europe, more than one million people arrived by sea, four times the number in the previous year.

These approximate figures provide a broad context in which the films analysed in this chapter will be situated. Together, the films form part of a relatively new story that is still in the process of construction, a narrative of profoundly changing spatialities produced by globalisation and territorialised in global cities. The movement of people across borders (the underside of the movement of capital and information) has contributed to the scale of spatial and social-economic inequality found in these European cities. Despised and vilified by the tabloid press, shunned as aliens by many local populations, the flow of refugees and asylum seekers nevertheless constitutes part of a mobilised workforce without which much of the service sector of these global cities could not function. This seems to be one of the principal "pull" factors which draw people to travel thousands of miles, to take inordinate risks and to suffer demeaning and degrading conditions in order to reach the global cities of the Global North. Conflict, violence and rights abuses might drive people out of their countries of origin, but economic deprivation, lack of opportunity and the desire for a better life are also powerful motivating factors.

The challenge facing any counter-hegemonic moment is to bring into accessible narrativity the primary conditions of its alternative practice, those elements that can contribute to meaningful agency and empowerment. Neoliberalism proposes a "global" world outside of which it may sometimes seem impossible to dwell, and it is a proposal which is gradually being sedimented in the contemporary cultural imaginary. It is this symbolic repertoire, and the stories that circulate from it, which sustain global capitalism ideologically, and that the emergent narratives, including stories not yet told or tellable, challenge and resist.

Jerome Bruner and others have written of the power of story to shape everyday experiences through the repetition of normative messages, whether implicit or explicit. Alternative stories have to secure their own modes of repetition, to confront the normative message in subtle and varied ways. As Bruner says, "It is the sense of things often derived from narrative that makes later real-life reference possible" (Bruner 2002, 8), and the analysis of my selected films will demonstrate this. It is this "becoming-referential" that is one of the tasks encountered by the emergent narratives—entering everyday discourse, enabling the transaction between the imaginary and the empirical. As yet, the type of narratives I am concerned with are very much emergent, although two of the later ones did have an immediate impact. Some, like *In this World* (2002) and *Lilya 4-Ever* (2002), succeeded in initiating debates in political forums and reached beyond the arthouse to a wider public domain, even if still very specialised. The same is true of both *Escape from Syria* (2017) and *I'm on the Bride's Side* (2014). They have won numerous awards and gradually acquired high visibility and legibility, as well as having been used as resources to publicise and politicise specific issues.

What is shown in all these films is the encounter between a "comfortable Europe" and an "uncomfortable Europe", whose paths otherwise seldom cross. The films, *Last Resort* (2000), *Dirty Pretty Things* (2002) and *In this World* all, in their very different ways, tell the stories of the "illegal", the undocumented. But each of the figures in these texts is also a carrier of stories, their own interleaved with others; stories which unfold and add layers in the context of the narrative process, to a point where they become "documented", identifiable, subjects of value, rather than subject to value. All are commodified, their bodies traded or raided, at some point, and there are no easy resolutions, but the very fact of their being *storied* is an act of witness in itself. The focus in all the films is on the pressures that drive migration, and on providing an *inline* (as opposed to an outline) of the lives of those who are the cause of "moral panics" in the western media.

Both *Spare Parts* (2003) and *Lilya 4-Ever* deal in people smuggling and, in different ways, sex trafficking. The hallmark of both films is abandonment, desperation and longing. Grey, bleak, under-furnished spaces—road diners, dormitories and hotel rooms—house the dreams of the Russian teenager, Lilya and her young friend Volodya. For Lilya, Sweden might as well be on the moon rather than a short flight away, until she unwittingly trades her body into sex slavery. *Lilya 4-Ever* is a devastating and unrelenting story of neglect, deception and exploitation, in which the only sustaining fantasies of a world other than the one the children and adults inhabit are of American cultural icons—the end of history in post-Soviet Russia. What is interesting about the film is that, despite its clearly fictional structure, Amnesty International, UNICEF, the Confederal Group of the European United Left–Nordic Green Left and the Third Baltic Sea Conference on WoMen and Democracy all took it up as though it were a documentary. This is perhaps not surprising given the compelling direction and the performances but it is rare for a film to be put to such constructive political use. It was screened at the European Parliament in Brussels, following a hearing on the latest developments on EU policy to help victims of trafficking by granting temporary residence, prior to being treated as asylum seekers. By condensing, synthesising and synopsising aspects of the post-1990 fall-out from the collapse of Soviet communism and its worldwide consequences, a film such as *Lilya 4-Ever* could exceed its immediate aesthetic/cultural project and generate oppositional/counter-narratives in new discursive forms. *In this World*, similarly, has been used by refugee organisations and it opened the Human Rights Watch film festival in March 2003.

In this World uses a time-based mode, *duration*, to suggest the circuitous, risk-filled and endlessly protracted nature of the migrant journey, marked by subterfuge, menace and suffering. The director Michael Winterbottom deliberately uses economic migrants as the principal figures in this film as a way of provoking controversy about the specious distinctions made by governments about migration. *Dirty Pretty Things* confines its refugees spatially to the kitchens and service area of a luxury hotel in a global city (London), a refuge and meeting point of migrant stories, of exploiter and exploited, of the buying and selling of the migrant body. The main plot of the film revolves around the sale of their body organs by "illegal" migrants in exchange for new "identities" in the form of false passports and other papers. This is a local instance of the global body trade opened up by neoliberalism and transnational market values. Restricted to the underside, the back passages, the "unclean" areas of the hotel or to the narrow spaces of rented rooms, the migrant workers are bypassed by the sights, sounds and movement of global consumer wealth, their bodies their only "passport" to this world. *Last Resort* imprisons its asylum seekers in the abandoned concrete towers of Stonehaven—a fairly obvious oxymoron—and circles round its blocked and immobilised figures, also reduced to the narrow dimensions of their bodies as they are lured into posing for cyber-porn movies or selling blood for extra cash. They have crossed endless borders only to be fenced in, limited and bounded—on the margins of a "paradise" which they can glimpse but not travel to, or touch. In all of the films, the refugee is seen as a pollutant, a waste product, something less than human—linked, metaphorically, with the "excreta" of western conspicuous consumption; this is a theme that will be referred to briefly throughout.

All the films are concerned with migration to EU countries. In two of the cases, the subjects at the centre of the narrative are "economic migrants", and people smuggling and/or people trafficking is a common feature. In the two texts to be examined later in the chapter, the principal figures are asylum seekers. Although the EU is explicitly committed to addressing the root causes of migration (since the European Council meeting at Tampere in October 1999), what the people in the films experience is the effects of strengthened border controls and the criminalisation of migration. Even though it is widely acknowledged that the distinction between economic and political causes of migration is becoming increasingly blurred, many asylum seekers are forced to have recourse to people smugglers and to enter the EU illegally. Economic conditions have become so bound up with political consequences that the opportunity to escape from deepening inequalities, widespread corruption and devastated economies proves irresistible. Almost all the migrants in the films are "irregular" and journeying in search of a better life.

Not Belonging and Unwanted

There is a moment in Lukas Moodysson's *Lilya 4-Ever* which captures much of the essence of the refugee experience, the experience of those who are outside the images, rhetoric and representations of current geopolitical configurations. Abandoned by her mother, evicted from her apartment, and subject to abuse from her erstwhile friends, Lilya is seated on a bench surrounded by the bleak and desolate landscape of "somewhere in what was once the Soviet Union" (as a caption describes it). Urged by her only remaining friend, the eleven-year-old Volodya, to escape from the taunts and derision of her peers coming from a balcony above, she patiently carves something on the bench and refuses to leave until it is finished. The inscription is symptomatic of the refugee's split condition. She carves her name, Lilya, in Russian script, and then writes "4-ever" in English, the global language, of American "dreamspeak". The abandoned self is bound to her Russian location, without hope, without love, without future. The "4-ever" is the attempt to reinvent an identity, to project herself into a future, a permanent time of expectation and, above all, of possibility. It is this dialectic of a destitute "here" and a "there" full of hope, which motivates so many whose flight is not from overt persecution, conflict or oppression. With the collapse of the Soviet Union, Western capitalism has begun to penetrate many of its former republics, but for the majority of people it has brought no benefits, save the insubstantial images and icons of celebrity with which to fuel their unrealised fantasies.

Although the great majority of the world's refugee population is not in the West, it is the wealth of the EU and the US which is the magnet for those with even the remotest chance of reaching these places. Lilya's mother migrates to the US, while Lilya herself is left behind to fantasise with Volodya about being Britney Spears (they share the same birthday) and when asked later if she knows where Sweden is, simply says, "Somewhere in the EU".

If, as John Agnew argues, "the modern geopolitical imagination is a *system* of visualising the world with deep historic roots in the European encounter with the world as a whole" (Agnew 2003, 6), then migration is one consequence of this encounter. It is partly a reluctance to re-visualise the world produced by globalisation that has led to the recent demonisation of refugees and asylum seekers as a means of shoring up a discourse of national consciousness at a time when the citizen/nation/state continuum is subject to challenge by the massive displacement of people and the shift of power away from the sovereign nation-state (Soguk 1999).

The break-up of the Soviet Union, the end of the bi-polar Cold War world, the fragmentation of, and deep ethnic conflicts in, the former Yugoslavia, and genocide and civil conflict in Africa, have all contributed to the changing geopolitical configuration, to new forms of global governance and to the revision of existing concepts of territoriality. In the paradoxical and ambivalent ideological spaces created by the combination of transnational neoliberalism with renewed state "watchtowers", the presence of the refugee and the asylum seeker adds to the complexity of efforts to script identity from borders and boundaries, territorial spaces. Together the films considered here constitute an emergent, alternative narrative in which the "modern geopolitical imagination" is subject to question. In the process of this narrative, a re-mapping is taking place, with the refugee as the symbolic focus of a shifting in the boundaries of imagined national communities.

The films all try to give space for agency and voice to the complex and multiple "event" of political and economic migration, as part of a counter-hegemonic narrative gradually finding articulation within civil society. My concern is with the ways in which the films challenge "the representations imposed by political and economic elites upon the world and its different peoples, that are deployed to serve their geopolitical interests" (Routledge 2002, 237). The films are part of a conjuncture in which stories are beginning to be told which confront the representational and symbolic repertoire which sustains global capitalism ideologically through its scripting of global spaces. Although the director of each film is Europe based, and the films address quite specific and localised instances of displacement, it is the larger discourse of globalisation which has given them their particular salience and, in some cases, has prompted their wider political and cultural use, as previously indicated. Simon Dalby claims that "the essential moment of geopolitical discourse is the division of space into 'our' place and 'their' place; its political function being to incorporate and regulate 'us' or the 'same' by distinguishing 'us' from 'them', the 'same' from the 'other'" (Dalby 1991, 274). Not only does this process construct a positive, inclusive ideological space but, more importantly for my purposes, it erects a negative, exclusionary, other space, currently occupied by the asylum seeker and, more generally, the refugee. As Michael Shapiro has shown, "the dynamics associated with 'globalization' reconfigure spaces at various levels, provoke cross-boundary flows of people, money, images and ideas, and put pressure on traditional territorial identities, as distinctions between local and global space become increasingly ambiguous" (Shapiro 1999, 85).

What the films attempt to do is to reclaim the refugee and asylum seeker within a universe of obligation, and to render them discursively, spiritually and morally visible, part of a shared, narratable space. 97% of the world's population currently lives in their country of origin, yet it is the 3% who do not which exercise our imagination, both positively and, of course, negatively in political and media vilification. Subordinated, the process of asylum seeking is ideologically inscribed as *insubordination*, a challenge to the settled and territorial ordering of sovereignty. In short, the films represent the first steps in challenging the dominant vocabularies and image resources circulated and referenced by the state, and its mediating agencies, to anchor its, perhaps limited, power in a culture of entitlement and identity. An anxious state is strategically displacing its insecurities onto the "always already" displaced:

> By constituting the people as a fictively ethnic unity against the background of a universalistic representation and which thus divides up the whole of humanity between different ethnic groups corresponding potentially to so many nations, national ideology does much more than justify the strategies employed by the state to control populations. It inscribes their demands in advance in a sense of belonging in the double sense of the term – both what it is that makes one belong to oneself and also what makes one belong

to other fellow human beings. (...) The naturalization of belonging and the sublimation of the ideal nation are two aspects of the same process. (Balibar 2002, 96)

A number of contextual issues have given rise to, and helped shape, the counter-narratives in the films to be examined. These are related to the ways in which refugee images come to circulate in respect of identity, security and rights, how these images are mediated in the discourses and practices of everyday life, and how they come to shape news and stories of asylum seeking. The films seldom address these matters explicitly, of course, but they form the unspoken starting point for their own narrative trajectories. They keep the chance of dialogue open, even if their presence only registers as yet in the arthouse and the broadsheet. They are keeping alive the possibilities of stories that might cut across, interrupt, even deconstruct this representational ascendancy—the map of national/ist certainties. This white European representational regime is increasingly under pressure and coming unstitched, as its seams, its arbitrariness and its contingency are made manifest. Its dominant conceptual and narrative currency is being questioned.

The flow of money, images and ideas—mostly Western-sourced—is welcomed by global capitalism but the circulation of people is something else. The new discourse of security generated by the "war on terrorism" has produced a situation in which Britain and the US are now insisting on transit visas for people, from more than forty named countries, simply changing airports. This regime of regulation is not only designed to identify and exclude the "other", but also to regulate and secure "us" for a raised national/ist discourse in a context of globalisation. These double interpellations are produced by constant repetition and by the successful recruitment of most of the agencies of reproduction to this dominant narrative. This "boundary-producing" narrative is breached and threatened by the mobility of the "globalized peoples", with their awkward and inconvenient visibility—mostly, but not only, their "non-whiteness". The "there", the "then" and the "them" have forced their way into visibility by becoming "here", "now" and almost, but not quite, "us". A lot of legislation and ideological work has gone into preserving the "not quite" by reconstructing real and virtual fences and re-establishing narratives of distance and difference. The new, or renewed, "inhospitality" has been emphasised by Derrida: "In its physical geography, and in what has often been called its *spiritual geography*, Europe has always recognised itself as a cape or headland" (Derrida 1992, 6). This hostility/inhospitality has also shaped the cultural and political narrative of exclusiveness to which the films offer a representational challenge.

In the course of theorising the ways in which refugees have been problematised, Soguk draws upon de Certeau, and others, to formulate what he calls the "statist" imagination. By this, he means that by awarding centrality to the specific category of the state, or the nation or the citizen, a whole signifying and classifying system can be constructed which privileges and normalises those included within these categories, while excluding or marginalising others (gender, race and sexuality hierarchies are comparable classificatory systems). This, in turn, comes to inform everyday discourse, vocabularies and cultural images/representations. Those who are UK, French or US citizens become sites of a specific coherence, or mindset, or classificatory system to which everything is referred for meaning and legitimacy; they are territorialising and naturalising codes, the tropes of common sense. These constitute part of a national, cultural imaginary which becomes the "real" world—seamless and absolute. This refers back to the quotation from Balibar earlier. Beyond these codes, regulations and boundaries are "deficit" figures, the refugee or asylum seeker, characterised as absence or lack, incomplete—a symbol of pollution. With their mobility, they challenge the way in which the West has carved up the world into segments of privilege and deprivation. This segmentation is the coloniality of power, the analysis of which is at the heart of decolonial thinking, and it is the *mobility* described in Chapter 1 which challenges and threatens to de-naturalise European claims to define belonging. Nora Rathzel says that 'unwanted' migrants are seen as a threat because they "make our taken-for-granted identities visible as specific and deprive them of their assumed naturalness, hence, once we start thinking about them, becoming aware, we cannot feel 'at home' any more" (Rathzel 1994, 91). This is at the root of much thinking about 'white genocide' (explored in Chapter 5) and hostility to the "Black Lives Matter" movement because of its presence making whiteness visible as just another ethnicity and no longer the taken-for-granted centre of the world.

The films analysed below also constitute a counter-formulation, a representational confrontation with, and reflection upon, the "bordered" imaginary at the level of the cultural. The people in the films are also, of course, carriers of stories and are given space to become active/voiced subjects/participants in their own narratives, however partial and fragmented—they become hosts, if you like. The migrants are invested with narrative agency and forms which, rather than seeing them as object or image, offer them the possibility of authorship and empowerment. Every identity "is mingled with that of others in such a way as to engender second-order stories which are themselves intersections between numerous stories ... We are literally entangled in stories" (Ricoeur 1995, 6).

In their different ways each film could be linked with ideas developed by Levinas, in particular inauguration into responsibility and what he calls "the very possibility of the beyond" (Levinas 1969, 43). In this process, we are called upon to respond to the vulnerability of the other, to act as the one-for-the-other, the stranger, the widow and the orphan. It is not merely a liberal gesture but a call for an ethical response to an other who cannot be recognised within any shared cultural or political context: "the strangeness of the Other, his [*sic*] irreducibility to the I, to my thoughts and possessions, is precisely accomplished as the calling into question of my spontaneity, as ethics" (ibid., 43). Identity has its source in the engagement with radical otherness resistant to the grasp of appropriation, rather than in the reduction of the other to the same which assimilates everything so that nothing may remain other to it. For Levinas, the *encounter* (and in each film the narrative can be thought of very much as an encounter) is with "the Stranger who disturbs the being at home with oneself", the zone of the "comfortable" referred to earlier. According to Levinas, "The other is always incommensurable with my self, *excessive* to representation". The "I" is put into question by the encounter and the other is "maintained and confirmed in his [*sic*] heterogeneity as soon as one calls upon him" (Levinas 1969, 69).

Somewhere in the EU

Lukas Moodysson dedicated *Lilya 4-Ever* to the millions of children around the world exploited by the sex trade, which could sound like a prescription for a worthy polemic, but the film resists all temptations to preach, instead allowing the narrative and the performances to carry the meanings. The film opens with a heavy metal sound which surrounds images of a teenage girl, alone, running, disorientated, exhausted, bruised and beaten. A series of elliptical images end with a shot of the girl, as yet unidentified, set to leap from a bridge. An abrupt silence follows and a caption announces, "Three months earlier". The film begins again, in a sense, as a girl, Lilya, is shown packing in preparation for emigration to America. Her mother has found a new partner through a dating agency, a Russian living in the US. At this point, sound, light and mood all resonate with expectation, but this is disrupted. Lilya's mother and Sergei plan to go to the US first and call for her later when they are settled, but it is soon apparent that this will never happen. Against the landscape of a bleak and featureless concrete housing estate in the former Soviet Union, the mother and partner drive off leaving the sixteen-year-old Lilya abandoned, desolate and effectively orphaned. The first of a sequence of betrayals is completed.

The film is about betrayal at many levels, and beyond the story of Lilya and her friend, Volodya, is the theme of a larger betrayal in the post-communist world, riddled with images of the West which prove to be illusory and beyond the reach of the teenagers, except at an intolerably heavy price. Betrayed by her mother and her closest friend, Natasha, mocked, reviled and later gang-raped by her former friends, Lilya eventually succumbs to the allure of the nightclubs and trades her body for money. Lilya and her glue-sniffing, drunken friends are—in common with those in the other films—capitalism's dispossessed, the losers in the speculations of globalisation in a world in which, by 2000, the ratio of real income per head in the richest countries to that of the poorest was around 60:1. Trapped within this ratio, tantalised by Western music, Western clothes, Lilya dreams of escape, repelled by the cold, loveless sex she suffers in order to feed herself and pay bills. Her only relationship is with Volodya, a homeless, basketball-loving, eleven-year-old boy, victim of his father's mental instability. Theirs is the only unconditional love in the film and Lilya's departure leads him to kill himself with an overdose. Caught between the violence and neglect of their parents' generation and the exploitative images of the West, the localised situation of the teenagers distils the experience of a much larger political process of globalisation—within the orbit of capitalism, but not of it.

Despite the above description of betrayal and a narrative which sounds as if it is based upon a nineteenth-century melodrama, the film rarely draws upon the stock images of the fallen woman, and the dysfunctional and derelict world takes on a normative quality. All references are emptied of meaning: an image of Lenin, the war medals found in the rundown apartment Lilya is forced to move to, and a 1967 speech by Brezhnev on the 1917 revolution discovered in an abandoned submarine base,

2 PEOPLE ON THE MOVE: NARRATIVES FOR A JOURNEY OF HOPE

mean nothing to Lilya or Volodya. Discontinuity is added to betrayal as another theme in the narrative. Severed from history, rootless and static, Lilya and Volodya are symptomatic of a lost, unwanted generation, their future stolen from them by false promises. This is one of the contexts, reproduced endlessly, which motivate economic migration.

Assuming that all she has left is her body, Lilya's despair is momentarily checked when she meets an attractive young man, apparently interested in a relationship with her, not just sex. Andrei soon suggests that Lilya should join him in Sweden and offers her a job and an apartment. Volodya warns her not to be fooled but she is lured by the prospect of love and the huge disparity between Russian and Swedish incomes. It is at this point that she is gang-raped (a cruel foreshadowing) and her apartment trashed, so she needs no further incentive to leave with Andrei. Little more than a child, Lilya naively accepts Andrei's plausible reason for giving her a false passport and his excuse for not being able to fly with her to Sweden, believing that he will join her in a matter of days. This marks the final, and central, betrayal of the film, as Andrei is a recruiter for a trafficking racket. Lilya is met in Malmö by a trafficker, Witek, taken to an apartment where her papers are confiscated, and she is imprisoned as a sex slave. Trapped by her illegal status, unable to go to the police who will return her to Russia and the mafia, Lilya is subjected to brutal, exploitative sex. These sequences are filmed from her point of view, in a montage-like series that focuses, not on Lilya, but on the faces of the predatory Western males, violating the body of the migrant girl/woman. As in the other films, the migrant is stripped of humanity, converted into a depository for the waste of the consuming male, a marker of pollution. This experience is anchored in the personal and the specific, but it opens out allegorically onto a wider exploitation that produces the trafficking and transportation of over a million children (mainly from Africa) across borders every year for domestic labour and the sex trade.

Like so many children and young women in similar circumstances, the migrant becomes a fugitive and throws herself off the bridge, after a series of shots (as described earlier from the start of the film) in which she runs haphazardly in terror, like a hunted and wounded animal. A repeated image of a bird in flight only serves to mock her. As she lies dying in an ambulance, she briefly reprises a number of earlier scenes and reverses the choices and actions she has taken. This also underscores one of the principal ideological seductions of Western capitalism: the illusion of choice and agency. She tells one of the clients who had taken her back to his luxury home that she is nobody's property and cannot be bought or owned. Ultimately choiceless, bought and sold as so much commodified flesh, her only freedom, like that of Volodya, lies in death. It is always difficult to film convincingly images of the unconscious or dream, and in visualising Lilya being visited by Volodya as an angel with wings, or, later, playing basketball with him on the submarine base in a fantasy image, the director is taking the film into another mode which perhaps clashes with the film's dominant realism. It could be that, trapped in a life of misery she, like slaves earlier in history who coped with their chained lives by imagining that they could fly away to freedom, is using fantasy as means of escape and as a coping mechanism.

As she is classified as an economic migrant, EU states would simply refuse Lilya leave to stay and return her to her country of nationality, so her only freedom of movement is across the border between life and death. This situation has changed for proven victims of sex trafficking since the film was made. The film has exceeded its immediate aesthetic function as cinematic text and has become a resource in generating activist support. Amnesty and UNICEF are using it to promote a greater awareness of international sex trafficking. The DVD version of the film contains a UNICEF appeal to end child exploitation, introduced and narrated by Robbie Williams, and an Amnesty International film about violence and rights abuses in the Russian Federation. One specific point raised is particularly apposite to this film: that in forging alliances with the Federation, the West is prepared to stay silent on rights abuses.

No Longer in This World

The film examined so far has focused upon the prelude to, or the outcome of, the migrant journey. The next film to be considered, *In this World* (2002), takes its narrative shape from the journey itself. The stress is on duration, time passing and survival—living though.

Although a fiction, its use of a digital video camera throughout and its sequential design and mode of filming bring the film close to the structures of the documentary. Captions, voice-overs and other visual devices add to this effect. Many of the actors, all non-professional, play roles "borrowed" from their own lives—fixers, police, border guards, sweatshop workers, and, of course, the two lead refugee figures themselves. If *Journey of Hope* (1990), an earlier film tracing the migrant journey, was a fiction based upon a true story, in a sense *In this World* could be described as a true story based upon a fiction.

Designed as a response to, and intervention in, the asylum debate in the UK, the film is framed implicitly by the Soviet invasion of Afghanistan in 1979 and the US-led bombings of 2001. After these bombings, Michael Winterbottom, the director, and Tony Grisoni, the screenwriter, went to Pakistan on tourist visas, and visited the camp, Shamsatoo, featured in the film. They then made the trip from Peshawar to London as a kind of dry run for the film they were planning. Both Jamal and Enyatullah, the two principal characters, are actual Afghan refugees who were living in the camp. The film tracks their journey from Shamsatoo Refugee Camp in the North West Frontier province of Pakistan through Iran, Turkey, Italy, France (partly filmed at the now-closed Sangatte camp) and, finally for Jamal, London. Using an improvised and minimal script, and understated narrative, one of the effects of the film is the appearance of a record or document of an extraordinary journey by truck, lorry, coach, cargo ship, freight container and the undercarriage of a haulage lorry, through hazardous terrain, border patrols and the demands of fixers and people smugglers. Like *Journey of Hope*, risk is at the centre of their experience. The journey costs $15,000, half paid in advance with the remainder to be handed over by their relatives at the camp when they reach London: one of the magnet cities for the impoverished refugee desperate for a better future. When it is considered that Jamal earns less than a dollar a day, the price is unbelievably high and, if in any way close to the actual costs of such a journey, underlines the scale of commitment and investment by families, "sponsoring" one of their number in the hope that they will flourish and send back income for the rest of the family and/or will trigger a chain of other migrants. Ironically, the journey taken is that of the major ancient trading, smuggling and slavery route of the old Silk Road.

In a voice-over we are told that there are 53,000 Afghan refugees in the camp, and a further million in Peshawar itself; of the 14.5 million refugees in the world at that time (figures vary from 12 million upwards) 5 million were in Asia. Of these, one million each year place their lives in the hands of people smugglers. The information given to the viewer is not simply ballast, but designed to remind Western European audiences in particular of the scale of the refugee and asylum seeker situation, as so many politicians and the popular media speak as if all the world's refugees are massed on the borders of the EU countries. Only the hardiest, most resourceful and enterprising get anywhere near. The film is careful to place its narrative—localised and personalised—in a world context and there are graphics of maps and globes tracing their journey as though it were a military campaign being shown on a newsreel. With conflict as one of the major causes of forced and, indirectly, economic migration, these visual echoes of old black and white war films are not accidental.

The episodic, hazardous journey anchors and shapes the narrative, with the sense of danger heightened at times by the silent, ghost-like night-light filming and the ambient sound. The continuous, but unstated, reference throughout is to the "real" migrant journey, of which the film is but a synopsis and "sampling", an elliptical digest of a brutal and, often, deadly experience. The film encodes and synthesises many styles of migrant travelling, and does not fail to include images of countless children at the camp who cannot move and have no future. People smuggling and trafficking (the former implies an element of volition, the latter deception and coercion) is, apparently, the third most lucrative trade after drugs and arms. The EU spends a lot of time and money to combat "illegal" migration by increasing border controls and criminalisation—the *raison d'être* of smuggling—but, despite rhetoric to the contrary, shows little resolve to fight the causes of migration. Of course, with service economies sustained in part by low-paid, non-unionised, casual and "controlled" illegal workforces, the management of migration is riddled with contradictions. With its calendrical structure, its regulation of precise time and space coordinates, the film's narrative is designed to place the refugee experience in identifiable locations. In fact, location in all senses of the word is very much what the film is about. Although the title of the film is derived from something Jamal says about Enyat ("He's no longer in this world"), the larger meaning is intended to expand the European awareness of refugees as also being in *this* world, not alien or sub-human but of "our" world.

Both Jamal and Enyat experience pain and suffering throughout the journey and are forced to improvise, bribe and "fake" their way through the harsh, physical and human, landscapes, which the European director and writer navigated with ease. In some instances, details of their travel are shown in close-up and at some length, at other times captions summarise the passage of hours or days. The camera is rarely at a distance from them, they are almost always subjects with primacy given to their point of view. It is never a film about "victims" in any detached, liberal sense. The worst journey of all is the most subtly conveyed. We see Jamal, Enyat and a Turkish father, mother and child being secured in a freight container (a space designed to store the non-human), aware of them only through whispers, the cries of the child and the occasional flicker of a lighter. We also see the outcome of this stage of the journey—the death of Enyat and of the child—but the lack of food, airlessness and light deprivation, and the enforced silence is not narrated explicitly or melodramatically, but in a simple caption, "40 hours later". This unendurable experience we are not shown and only barely told about. It is in this way that the viewer is forced to imagine, empathise with and complete the "missing" narrative—what illegal means in human terms, not only in this specific case but in the larger narrative of migration.

This "absent" sequence quotes, in a metaphorical sense, from the event in March 2000 when fifty-eight Chinese men and women were found suffocated to death in the back of a Mercedes truck at Dover. Nothing on this scale happens in the film but, as with so much in *In this World*, and many of the other films referred to, the "40 hours later" sequence is designed to crystallise and synthesise the "illegal" migrant experience.

Jamal finally reaches London and he is seen working in a café, hawking trinkets in bars and hotels, and stealing a handbag. A sense of aloneness, and alienation, rather than paradise is the overwhelming impression, with only the mosque as a space of transnational belonging. In a final move designed to make the viewer reflect on the "truth of cinema", Winterbottom conflates the fiction/documentary dialogic of the film with a screen title which reads: "On 9th August 2002 the Asylum application of Jamal Udin Torabi was refused. He was given exceptional leave to enter and is now living in London and will have to leave the day before his eighteenth birthday". Using unexpired documents, the actor Jamal travelled back from Pakistan to London and claimed asylum. The outcome of this application was that described at the end of the film, so actor and character coincide. Also evoked, indirectly, is the situation of more than six thousand unaccompanied, asylum-seeking children in the UK in similar circumstances at that time.

Although Winterbottom claims that the film is not a documentary but a fiction, it is stage-managed and, one could argue, the characters are manipulated for a polemical purpose, so it is a documentary-style piece of work. Is it, like the two films to be analysed in the next two sections, a work of collaboration? In a sense it is, of course, because the filmmakers secured the consent of the two "actors" but I share David Farrier's reservation that: "In spite of Winterbottom and Grisoni's claims to a reciprocal understanding with their cast, in a fundamental way the voice of the displaced remains beyond the film's capacity to articulate and must therefore be appropriated" (Farrier 2008, 231).

The very precise and insistent timeline in *In this World* is used to construct the conjunctures of the specific and personal journey of Jamal and Enyatullah (what Michael Shapiro calls "now-time"). As well as representing a detailed chronicle of events, the film also condenses and filters the experiences of the two principal characters and links them to a wider contemporary politics of migration in which the possibility of settlement beyond one's country of origin is rapidly diminishing (the three-month period covered by the main narrative in *Lilya 4-Ever* fulfils a similar function). Hence Winterbottom's deliberate emphasis on mobility, on the journey, with arrival—in any but a clandestine fashion—indefinitely postponed/deferred. The new geopolitical order has produced a culture predicated upon speed and mobility but, unlike other, earlier migrations, there is no longer a corresponding obligation of reception, of global hospitality, especially in Western Europe.

In "Cinema and Time", Deleuze speaks of how a purely optical and sound situation does not extend into action as such but "makes us grasp, it is supposed to make us grasp, something intolerable and unbearable" (Deleuze 1993, 180). It is something, he says, which outstrips our "sensory-motor capacities": "something has become too strong in the image". The "40 hours later" moment in *In the World* and the montage of rape scenes in *Lilya 4-Ever* are both instances of this. Empathy is produced, the unbearable is seen "as from a third eye" (181). Something other than confirmation, or recognition, of what we already know is happening; a form of knowledge is generated "forcing us to forget our own logic and national habits" (181). "What happens", the event that is shown, is secondary to the inexhaustible possibility that can be extracted from the "moment".

Although the films derive and distil their narratives from many of the stock tropes of the migrant story, the two referred to above, in particular, manage, in Deleuze's wonderful phrase, to tear "a real image from the *clichés*" (183). Unless the image of the refugee in cinematic narrative is able to break through, to exceed, the *cliché*, then there is the danger of the films becoming part of wider, liberal media saturation and "compassion fatigue". In the films cited above there is a sense of something which implies a "beyond of movement", "an image that never stops growing in dimensions" (Deleuze 1993, 184). These resonate beyond the surfaces of the film's own construction, produce narratives which compel the viewer to trace and extend the meanings into a supplementary story filled with the implications, after-images and incomplete tales of the originating text. The trade in spare body parts (brokered by a migrant) in *Dirty Pretty Things* is an effective metaphor for the ways in which migrants are seen very much as waste, as surplus, as in/human resources in the neoliberal global economy of consumption. The human heart found in one of the hotel toilets early in the film confirms this idea of waste but is also a reminder that the transnational migrant is disposable, devalued currency, once it has been used to service Europe's privileged nationals, those whose identities are validated by an inclusive territoriality predicated upon the exclusion of the "unbelonging". When Okwe, Senay and Juliette (three of capitalism's dispossessed in the film) prepare to hand over a kidney (that of the broker himself), one of the traders says, "How come we have never seen you people before?" Okwe replies, "Because we are the people you do not see. We are the ones who drive your cabs. We clean your rooms. We suck your cocks".

The Longest Journey

In Chapter 1, I spoke of trying to locate representations which challenge the hegemonic narratives around refugees which focus on women and children who are seen as pitiable or young men as potential terrorists. Rania Mustafa Ali, author and subject of *Escape from Syria: Rania's Odyssey* (2017), is certainly pitiable at times but she was determined to tell her story of asylum seeking as she felt that media images of refugees were dominated by men. Twenty years old, a Kurdish student from Raqqa, Syria, but living in Kobane, by chance she met a Norwegian journalist and documentarian, Anders Hammer, and told him that she wanted to make a film of her intended escape from Syria. He taught her the basic skills needed for filmmaking in a period of three weeks and provided her with a Go-Pro camera, small, versatile and light. This was in 2015, a crucial date because, by this time, in the period from 2006 to 2015, forty thousand people had died trying to cross a border. This puts in perspective Rania's challenge, as she would need to cross at least three borders to reach Europe.

Filming begins in Kobane as we see Rania packing her clothes and belongings for the journey, and also watch her walking around the bombed-out city, with ruins everywhere and walls covered in ISIS graffiti. She speaks of having to be fully covered and once being apprehended for offending against the dress code. Thoughts of crossing the sea filled her with fear, she says, but were not as scary as staying in Syria. As she says, to the outside world, Syria is a bombsite but to her it is home. Her first task is to cross the Syrian/Turkish border and, although this is not shown on camera, this crossing took her four attempts and cost her $300 in smugglers' fees. In the process, she had to throw away many of her belongings. Filming from her point of view gives the images a situated effect, an insider's experiential and immersive perspective. Although the many hours of footage are edited by Hammer to a brief twenty-two minutes and nine seconds final cut, all the filming is either done by Rania herself or her friend, Ayman, a Syrian activist friend she meets up with in Turkey. Imprisoned in Syria, he had fled the regime and they had planned to seek asylum together. I hesitate to use the word 'highlights' in this context but the film is edited to show the core features of the asylum journey, specific to Rania's experience but, also, in some respects, common to many refugees. What we see is her range of contrasting moods—light-hearted, nervous, confident, defiant and also petrified with fear.

The media is full of images of shipwrecks and refugees struggling to survive in inadequate and poorly constructed boats, but Rania shows at first hand the effects of such an experience, travelling from Turkey to Greece in a rubber dinghy, designed to accommodate 15 people but overloaded with 50 or more, not even sure if their life-jackets are genuine. The camera shows the faces of terrified children, Rania's obvious distress as the boat rocks, and men moving from stern to bow in an attempt to balance the craft as it tilts dangerously. The filming is not alarmist or melodramatic as all the commentary needed comes from images of the turbulent sea, the sounds of children crying, men and women screaming, and the imminent prospect of drowning. At one point, Rania shuts off the camera as she is overwhelmed. This is not staged or scripted but a way of showing the risks taken daily by people in flight from an unendurable present. Eventually, a ship rescues them and takes them to the island of Lesbos, in Greece. This particular crossing, or its conditions, was nothing unique but the close-ups of people and the movement of the boat made it personal and memorable. It "resists the pull of existing clichéd images and information", as Shohini Chauduri put it in describing ways of representing the Syrian revolution and war (Chauduri 2018, 36).

Another common occurrence takes place in Greece when they discover that the bus tickets sold to them by a smuggler are fraudulent and that they have lost 150 euros which reduces their budget to 600 euros. They learn that two hundred people hoping to board the ferry to Macedonia were taken to a camp and this makes the two of them apprehensive. Eventually, they cross on the ferry and end up in Idomeni refugee camp on Greece's northern border with Macedonia. There are twelve thousand people in tents, with rain pouring down and mud everywhere. People are dying and others in a poor state of health, and there are rumours of women and children being abused. They buy a tent, hoping for a brief stay but in fact spend two and a half months in the camp as the SKYPE system supposedly set up to process asylum applications failed. It is at this point that another very distressing scene occurs as people, fearful of being deported to Turkey, try to breach the fence protecting the Macedonian border. As crowds swarm around the security fence, border guards start firing and many are tear-gassed. Rania and Ayman continue filming while this is happening, but both are blinded by the gas and Rania is tearful and in obvious pain. She is shown in her distraught state and volunteers are on hand offering first aid but, eventually, the camera is switched off. Again, we are immersed in the participant's situation, something outsiders may see in television images but not in this first-hand, close-up fashion. This is an eye-witness account even when the eye is filled with tear gas. Overcome by the cold and the wet, they manage to negotiate a loan of 7,000 euros (how, we are not told). As Rania kept in touch with Anders Hammer throughout the journey, he may have arranged this.

In a complete change of mood, they use their loan to buy fake Bulgarian IDs and are told to act as tourists as they board a plane to Vienna. We are shown their delight as they, like playful teenagers, successfully get through airport security. This is also rare—actual footage of "illegals" shown from the insider's point of view. At Vienna airport, they are arrested by the police and they claim asylum. This is not actually shown but we learn that she is given leave to remain in Austria for three years. It took Rania altogether one and a half years to escape from Syria.

When the film was first shown on the *Guardian* website it went viral and attracted one and a half million viewers. To date, it has received eight million viewers. Rania has said since that she felt that she had the right to tell her story, to put a human face on an asylum seeker's journey. It is, in terms discussed later, an *intervention*, on her terms. The refugee film has, by now, become something of an established genre but it is a genre which has aroused controversy and ethical concerns, with issues of appropriation raised and questions about who tells the refugee's story, how it is presented and interpreted, and for which kind of audiences. As the director of a refugee film festival myself for a number of years, this was something very much to be kept in mind and there were refugees who said critically that they wanted to see films that were not always about the wretchedness of the 'poor' refugee. Bruce Bennett articulated this dilemma effectively: "The ethical responsibility of reportage and film and TV drama lies not so much in the generation or relay of powerful images, but in the curatorial organisation of material—its renarration or insertion into narrative frames that allow viewers to understand its meaningful relation to a variety of historical or generic contexts" (Bennett 2018, 16). The key word here is "curatorial", with its implication of care, and, although a documentary made by refugees themselves does not guarantee quality, it does allow space for the interiority of perspective. The collaboration here between an asylum seeker and a European filmmaker, and the cooperation described in the section below, at least show a shared ethical responsibility and a questioning of the taken-for-granted position of the coloniality of power.

Reversing the Appearance of the Frontier

Borders figure in all the chapters in this book in various guises. For the states of the European Union and the UK, the border is a space of securitisation, of protection, the place where the unwanted are apprehended and delayed. From the perspective of the asylum seeker, it is a barrier, a space of immobility. Seen through a critical lens, borders are where the coloniality of power is inscribed, the signature of the transnational capitalist class which knows no boundaries. For Etienne Balibar: "Europe is the point of the world whence border lines set forth to be drawn throughout the world, because it is the native land of the very representation of the border as this sensible and supersensible 'thing' that should be or not be, be here or there" (Balibar 1998, 216–17). As Balibar says elsewhere, this drawing of borders, markers of inclusion and exclusion, came as a result of Europe arrogating to itself this power as it appointed itself as the centre of the world. It is at the rigidity of borders where the coloniality of power confirms its hierarchy.

Both the films examined in this section are about borders. *Io sto con la Sposa* (*On the Bride's Side* 2014) is a form of advocacy, one of the counter-hegemonic narratives mentioned in Chapter 1, by a coalition of filmmakers, activists and refugees who collaborate to make a film which mocks/subverts the European/colonial narrative of borders. The film is an act of civil disobedience, solidarity and, in the sense discussed previously, part of border thinking. The refugees are not objects of pity or compassion but five people who actively participate in a joint project to reach a place of safety and asylum. All those involved are trespassing on the territory of neoliberal capitalism. The three filmmakers—Antonio Augugliaro (director), Gabriele del Grande (journalist and blogger at *Fortress Europe*) and Khaled Saliman Al Nassiry, a Palestinian-Italian poet and editor (who received notice of his citizenship on the first day of filming)—established a project on behalf of open borders and the freedom of mobility.[1] Del Grande had previously spent time as a journalist reporting from Aleppo, in Syria. When he, and colleagues, came under fire, he tells how a young boy tore off strips of a wedding dress for them to wear as headbands so that the Free Army would know not to shoot. Given the concept of the film, he regarded the 'wedding' headband as a lucky omen.

The film is very much an engaged (*engagé*) project, an ethical commitment. In an interview by Marco Mancuso in *Digicult* with the three filmmakers and a sociologist, the word 'responsibility' occurs repeatedly as part of a code of ethics which shaped the film's production (Mancuso 2014). On the journey, care is taken to protect the refugees from detection by the authorities, not in a patronising way but as a matter of accountability and as a strategic form of care, because in all other respects the refugees share the screen on the basis of equality. One way of describing the whole enterprise is in terms used by Levinas: "Autarchy demands (self-)government and property, that is subjects, enemies and dispossession. Anarchy, by contrast, exiles us from self-possession, subjectification and divisions of friend and foe; it throws us out of ourselves, before others, into a commons of encounters and possibilities" (quoted in Gavroche 2019, 1). The phrase "a commons of encounters and possibilities" neatly sums up what might be called the politics of the film, a product of creative anarchy. It is a repudiation of the border regime and of the regulatory authority of the Global North.

For all the aesthetic qualities of the film, its structure and development, the most remarkable feature is the 'outrageous' conceit upon which it is based. In order to enable the five refugees—Syrian and Palestinian—to reach Sweden from Italy, the filmmakers devised a cover story, based not on clandestinity, but on hiding in plain sight. Consciously or not, this is a tactic derived from Edgar Allan Poe's short story "The Purloined Letter" (1845). The cover was the ultimate in the European heteronormative, bourgeois romance—a wedding party, because, as del Grande said, "You know who the border guards would never stop? A wedding party". The police would never check a bride's documents. By tapping into a staple of European culture focused on the bride's white dress, they insured themselves against discovery. So iconic is the dress that the 'bride' is filmed wearing it for almost the entire film, even stumbling up a steep mountain pass, cigarette in hand.

The concept came about as the result of a chance meeting at Milan train station between two of the filmmakers and a Syrian refugee, Abdallah, who asked them where trains to Sweden left from. On discovering that he was a shipwreck survivor who had made his way from Lampedusa, in Sicily, the two men hit upon the idea of trying to help Abdallah, and others, reach Sweden. Given the Italian law which penalised people smugglers with groups of more than five people with a fifteen years' prison sentence, they sought out four others. The other refugees were Alaa and his son, Manar, and two older Syrian 'Leftists', Mona and Ahmed. Abdullah was selected as the 'groom' and Tasnim, a Palestinian friend of the filmmakers who had a German passport, became the 'bride'.

The whole film is an imitation, mimicry, a repetition of hegemonic codes but from below, including the buying of wedding clothes, visits to the hairdressers, etc. In other words, the simulation was carefully observed in its rehearsal, staging and performance. An actual European wedding is also rehearsed, staged and performed. The mock wedding party represents this world turned upside down, carnivalesque in many respects. By flouting regulation, rule and authority, the whole scenario of carnival is a form of misrule, with its origins in the early Modern period, a reversal of dominant ideologies which, in this case, present the refugee, especially from the Middle East, as a terrorist or invader. Hostility is countered by hospitality: "In the ethical realm, the self is morally obligated to welcome the stranger into the private space of the home" (Levinas in Gauthier 2007, 159). In addition to the filmmakers and the refugees, in order to make it plausible, the wedding party was augmented by fourteen friends, activists, and academics, Italian, Syrian and Palestinian. The irony was that the refugees, who had undergone dangerous journeys to reach Europe, were less at risk than those with papers who could have received prison sentences.

Abdallah, the 'groom', had experienced the most perilous journey and survived a shipwreck in which at least 250 people died. He spent an hour and a half in the water, and his cousin died. This experience becomes an emotional centrepiece of the film when the party pauses on the Grimaldi Superiore mountain pass into France. Each of the refugees had already paid smugglers to be transported across the Mediterranean in dilapidated, makeshift boats. This is an experience which has been repeated thousands of times this century with, often, tragic outcomes. It is the journey to Sweden, orchestrated by *unpaid* people 'smugglers', which forms the core of the film. In a sense, the film takes the by now stock trope of the asylum narrative and *defamiliarises* it. It is one of the central 'claims' of the film that nothing is what it seems.

The plot of the film takes place over four days, November 14–18, 2013, and traces the party's journey from Milan to Stockholm, using four cars and a van, all bedecked in conspicuous, iconic wedding regalia. At each stop on the way—Marseilles, Bochum, Copenhagen and Malmö—they are met by friends from the filmmakers' networks, activists and former refugees from Syria and Palestine, demonstrating unconditional hospitality, one of the premises of the project's ethical commitment. This is contrasted with the conditional hospitality required by law and grudgingly applied by states.

Inevitably, much of the film is in the form of a 'road movie', as many have pointed out, another piece of mimicry, shaped by the US road movie genre, a voyage of self-discovery, an alteration of perspective and a critique of social conventions. Mobility is its core mechanism. It is an opening out from confinement, memorably captured in literature by Huck Finn's "lighting out for the territory ahead", for a future away from attempts to "sivilize him". The "sivilizing" in this case is the European border regime. The film corresponds in some ways to this genre, with its emphasis on a *future* for the five in Sweden, and, more broadly, of a future of open borders, of relationality, cooperation and solidarity, the collective and not the individual. In this way, the film can be seen as a kind of modelling, a prefiguration of another way of seeing, another way of being, a glimpse of another world that is possible. Above all, it is a refutation of the financialisation of all value.

On the road there are numerous shots taken from within the car, giving a sense of proximity, intimacy and interiority, with close-ups of faces. The movement becomes a conversation among equals and not between the privileged citizen and the "other". It is from these conversations that the 'back stories' of the refugees emerge, of hunger, thirst and cold at sea, of families left behind, relatives being killed, of people dying around them at sea, and of neglect by the UN and Red Cross at Lampedusa, as well as tales of forced fingerprinting with, in one case, a man left bleeding on the floor. The fear of fingerprinting arose from the Dublin II Regulation (2003) about seeking asylum in the first country of arrival (though a new Regulation, Dublin III, was adopted in 2013).

Although there is a sense of improvisation and spontaneity, there is an early scene, prior to their leaving Milan, where the filmmakers take out a large map and chart the journey, pointing out likely hazards, reasons for detours and the overall strategy for avoiding detection. The whole trip has been planned with 'military' precision and based upon a well-thought-out plan, even if at short notice, to minimise risk, both to refugees and 'smugglers'. The use of 'military' was deliberate because, in a way, the whole project is a campaign against borders (Fig. 2.1).

Fig. 2.1 *On the Bride's* Side (2014). The bride and groom crossing the border between Italy and France at Grimaldi Superiore (Reproduced by courtesy of Antonio Augugliaro, Khaled A. Nassiry, and Gabriel del Grande. *Photo* Marco Garofalo)

The central scene in the film, the one which in synoptic form embodies so much of the reasoning and commitment behind the film, is when the group pauses at a derelict, windowless villa on the mountain pass into France near Ventimiglia. This steep mountain pass is known by refugees as the path of hope or the path of death. Years ago, as one of the party remarks, the pass was used by Italians "illegally" crossing into France, without papers. This is a reminder that, until some forty years or so ago, Italy, like many countries in the European South, was an outmigration country, with fifteen million Italians leaving in the period between 1880 and 1980.

The walls of the villa are covered in graffiti, in different languages, left by previous immigrant travellers and the floor is littered with discarded clothing and shoes. Mona scratches her name on the wall. There then follows a seminal moment in the film when Abdallah, the 'groom', who survived a shipwreck in the Mediterranean, begins to etch on the wall, in Arabic script, the names of some of those drowned at sea from his boat. He prefaces each name with a comment about them, particularly the lost children. In a sense, at this point the wedding party has changed into a wake. It is a commemoration of, and a memorial to, those whose names he recites in an extended ritual moment. The previously festive group stand solemnly as they listen, the camera slowly moving from face to face capturing their distress. Abdallah says that, of the two hundred and fifty who died, only twenty-six bodies were recovered, and some of them were piled on top of him as he was also assumed to be dead.

This recital of names is an act of recognition, of tribute and recovery, though the naming can only be indicative of the larger tragedy as he obviously knows only a few of the names. This pause in their movement is of symbolic importance because what Abdallah is doing is the act of mourning, an act of restitution. From the perspective of the hierarchy of European value, refugees do not count, the dead especially who are numbers, statistics, without names. In the famous song, "Deportees", Woody Guthrie, many years ago (1948) articulated this precise point when singing of Mexican fruit pickers being deported from California: "all they will call you is deportee". In similar fashion, we in Europe simply call them "refugee". Guthrie goes on to name specific, if also generic, figures—Juan, Rosalita, Jesus and Maria. In the same way, Abdallah's naming is specific but also indicative, projecting a whole generation of refugees "sacrificed" to the coloniality of power. By mourning these lives, they are given back value. It is an act of restoration, a means of making lives "grievable". When he completes his litany, he asks those who know the Koran to join him in prayer. Abdallah has taken on the burden of speaking for others. Speaking of Holocaust survivors, Terence Des Pre said: "Whoever comes through will take with him the burden of speaking for others. Someone will survive and death will not be absolute. This small pledge … is intensely important to people facing extinction … In the survivor's voice the dead's own scream is active" (quoted in Kearney 2002, 167).

As the group moves on up the pass, another action takes place which becomes a metaphor of the relational aesthetics of the film; this is the use of a rope by which members of the party enabled those less agile to manage the last steep section of the pass and reach the fence which is breached through a hole. When the group reaches Marseilles they resume their more cheerful demeanour as they are greeted by locals and share a meal in an Arab restaurant. Manar raps, in animated fashion, on the theme of a refugee camp in Syria, and Tasnim, the "bride", speaks of her relatives in a refugee camp who went a hundred days without bread. Although looking ahead to a future in Europe, each of the refugees never ceases to be aware of what they have lost, have left behind. In a conversation with Gabriele in the car later, Tasnim says that, although she has status and a German passport, she was in Syria until September 2013 and found it hard to leave because others could not. There are inevitable shades of guilt because others were fighting for her. At a later point, she stands alone on the shores of the Mediterranean—the sea of death and also of hope—and sings a plaintive song in Arabic, a reminder that for those displaced, their journey is a form of lamentation.

As the party approaches borders, evidence of the strategic thinking that has informed the planning emerges, as the passport holders drive ahead to reconnoitre the border security. Additionally, the speed of vehicles is determined by the need to leave intervals between the cars and the time taken to arrive at the border. Digital technology was used to calculate possible problems, and seating positions in the cars were allocated in such a way as to deflect any possible suspicion. The last stage of the journey for the asylum seekers, excited but fearful of being repatriated, is by train from Copenhagen to Stockholm as, at that time (2013), there were no border checks or policed borders (these were imposed in 2016). Their arrival in Stockholm is triumphant and joyful as they meet up with people from their network and former refugees. They walk across the station concourse and, in front of the National Theatre, appropriately, sing, dance and perform a celebration. In keeping with the fake wedding façade, a bottle of champagne is broken open. As the credits roll, Manar raps over them and captions relate how, nine months later, Abdallah, Mona and Ahmed were granted asylum in Sweden, whereas Alee and his son, Manar, were sent back to Italy, but gained refugee status there.

The film is dedicated to the children of the filmmakers, "because at some time in their lives, they'll have to choose which side they are on". This encapsulates the project as a whole: *choice*. The filmmakers chose to disrupt border hierarchies and, in the process, "provincialize Europe" (Chakrabarty 2000) by enabling a small number of people, without choice, to fulfil their dream of an alternative future. Through an act of defiance, irreverence and disobedience, an ethical decision converted lives of displacement into ones of replacement. *They were, in fact, on the groom's side...*

Apart from the achievement of the film itself which won several awards and was screened in the European Parliament, its production and post-production generated some landmarks. Crowdfunding raised 100,000 euros from 2,617 donors (all named in the credits) which meant payments could be made retrospectively towards production costs and also made it possible for the film to be exhibited at the Venice film festival in 2014. The whole project is a demonstration, in all senses of the word, including protest, of what could be achieved by shared, collective work and a Global North/Global South partnership which said "No" to Fortress Europe. It is a dismantling of hierarchical opposites, a questioning of the discursive formation of European superiority rearticulated from the perspective of the "othered".

To place this film in the wider theoretical context of this book, apart from "provincializing" Europe, it unsettles/challenges the logic of coloniality by, metaphorically, taking up a place on the border and showing that, "border thinking that leads to decoloniality is of the essence to unveil that the system of knowledge, beliefs, expectations, dreams and fantasies upon which the modern/colonial world was built is showing and will continue to show, its unviability" (Mignolo [2000] 2012, ix). This might seem a lot to place on one eighty-nine minute film, but it captures the spirit of Auden's words when he wrote in 1939, "For poetry makes nothing happen ... it survives, / A way of happening, a mouth" ("In Memory of W. B. Yeats"; Auden 1940). In another poem, Auden adds that poetry does "have a voice / To undo the folded lie" and to "Show an affirming flame" ("September 1, 1939"; Auden 1940). The film *is* such an affirmation. In a memorable phrase, Derek Mahon speaks of "a poet indulging his wretched rage for order— … An eddy of semantic scruples / In an unstructurable sea", and Seamus Heaney thought that poetry functions as "a counterweight to hostile and oppressive forces in the world" and that the poetic imagination offers "a glimpsed alternative, a revelation of potential that is denied or constantly threatened by circumstances" (quoted in Astley 2008). Like *I'm on the Bride's Side*, all these poets were writing in times of conflict, and the film brings the aesthetic into the realm of the political, the sphere of advocacy, not by polemics but by undoing the "folded lie", producing "semantic scruples" and, above all perhaps, offering a "counterweight", "a glimpsed alternative" and a "revelation of potential", of possibility to challenge the border regimes of Europe, of another way of being, civic, mutual and reciprocal. In the text, *Storia Di Un Matrimonio*, which accompanies the DVD of the film, Gabriele del Grande speaks of the film as producing a new aesthetic of the border, of developing a language with the capacity to transform numbers into names, a language both of poetry and sadness and, in a telling phrase, a rhetoric capable of producing "*un 'noi' allargato*", an enlarged or extended "we". This is in keeping with what I said earlier about solidarity. In Gramscian terms, it is an "intervention on the terrain of social and political antagonism", a gesture towards the formation of alternative discourses and narratives in a new "historical bloc" (Sotiris 2018, 105), a work of resistance.

All the films examined in this chapter can be seen both as interventions and, also, whether intended or not, as works of advocacy which challenge the representational norms of European narratives about the "other". They are part of what might be called activist media, acts of witness and testimony which are designed, in the latter two cases in particular, to make space for agency and voice. They are narratives which offer glimpses of hope to those forced to migrate from situations which seem to lack hope. In the next chapter, similar narratives of forced migration are the centre of attention but in circumstances which present frustration, uncertainty and, above all, endless waiting.

Note

1. An excellent discussion of this film which, situates it in its historical background, can be found in Woolley (2020).

References

Agnew, John. 2003. *Geopolitics*. London: Routledge.
Astley, Neil. 2008. *The Guardian*, February 26.
Auden, W. H. 1940. "'In Memory of W. B. Yeats' and 'September 1, 1939'." In Auden, *Another Time*. New York: Random House.
Balibar, Etienne. 1998. "The Borders of Europe." In *Cosmopolitics: Thinking and Feeling Beyond the Nation*, edited by Pheng Cheah and Bruce Robbins, 216–19. Minneapolis: Minnesota University Press.
Balibar, Etienne. 2002. *Politics and the Other Scene*. Translated by Christine Jones, James Swenson, and Chris Turner. London: Verso.
Bennett, Bruce. 2018. "Becoming Refugees: *Exodus* and Contemporary Mediations of the Refugee Crisis." *Transnational Cinemas* 9 (1): 13–30. https://doi.org/10.1080/20403526.2018.1471181. Accessed August 17, 2020.
Bruner, Jerome. 2002. *Making Stories*. Cambridge: Harvard University Press.
Chakrabarty, Dipesh. 2000. *Provincializing Europe: Postcolonial Thought and Historical Difference*. Princeton, NJ: Princeton University Press.
Chaudhuri, Shohini. 2018. "The Alterity of the Image: The Distant Spectator and Films About the Syrian Revolution and War." *Transnational Cinemas* 9 (1): 31–46. https://doi.org/10.1080/20403526.2018.1444929. Accessed August 17, 2020.
Dalby, Simon. 1991. "Critical Geopolitics: Discourse, Difference, and Dissent." *Environment and Planning D: Society and Space* 9: 261–83.
Deleuze, Gilles. 1993. "Cinema and Time." In *The Deleuze Reader*, edited by C. V. Boundas, 180–84. New York: Columbia University Press.
Derrida, Jacques. 1992. *The Other Heading*. Bloomington: Indiana University Press.
Dirty Pretty Things. 2002. Directed by Stephen Frears. London: BBC Films.
Escape from Syria: Rania's Odyssey. 2017. Directed by Anders Hammer. London: The *Guardian*'s YouTube channels.
Farrier, David. 2008. "The Journey Is the Film Is the Journey: Michael Winterbottom's *In This World*." *Research in Drama Education* 13 (2): 223–32. https://doi.org/10.1080/13569780802054927. Accessed July 24, 2020.
Gauthier, David. 2007. "Levinas and the Politics of Hospitality." *Histories of Political Thought* 28 (1): 158–80. https://doi.org/10.2307/2622669. Accessed September 10, 2020.
Gavroche, Julius. 2019. "Anarchy Against Autarchy: Levinas and Anarchy." *Autonomies*: 1–13.
Journey of Hope. 1990. Directed by Xavier Koller. Italy: Antea Cinematografica.
Kearney, Richard. 2002. *On Stories*. London: Routledge.
Last Resort. 2000. Directed by Pawel Pawlowski. London: BBC Films.
Levinas, Emmanuel. 1969. *Totality and Infinity: An Essay on Exteriority*. Pittsburgh: Duquesne University Press.

Lilya 4-Ever. 2002. Directed by Lukas Moodysson. Stockholm: Memfis Film.

Mancuso, Marco. 2014. "On the Bride's Side: Civil Disobedience on Stage at the 71st Venice Film Festival." *Digicult*. https://digicult.it/section/cinema/interviews. Accessed August 21, 2020.

Mignolo, Walter. [2000] 2012. *Local Histories, Global Designs*. Princeton, NJ: Princeton University Press.

On the Bride's Side (Io Sto con La Sposa). 2014. Directed by Antonio Augugliaro. Milan: DocLab.

Rathzel, Nora. 1994. "Harmonious Heimat and Disturbing Auslander." In *Shifting Identities and Shifting Racisms*, edited by K. K. Bhavani and A. Phoenix, 81–98. London: Sage.

Ricoeur, Paul. 1995. "Reflections on a New Ethos for Europe." *Philosophy and Social Criticism* 21 (5/6): 3–13.

Routledge, Paul. 2002. "Anti-Geopolitics." In *A Companion to Political Geography*, edited by J. A. Agnew, Katharyne Mitchell, and Gerard Toal, 236–48. Oxford: Blackwell.

Salgado, Sebastião. 2000. *Migrations*. New York: Aperture.

Shapiro, Michael. 1999. *Cinematic Political Thought*. New York: New York University Press.

Soguk, Nevzat. 1999. *States and Strangers*. Minneapolis: University of Minnesota Press.

Sotiris, Panagiotis. 2018. "Gramsci and the Challenges for the Left: The Historical Bloc as a Strategic Concept." *Science and Society* 82 (1): 94–119. Accessed August 25, 2020.

Spare Parts. 2003. Directed by Daman Kozole. Slovenia: E-Motion Film.

Woolley, Agnes. 2020. "Docu/Fiction and the Aesthetics of the Border." In *Refugee Imaginaries*, edited by Emma Cox, Sam Durrant, David Farrier, Lyndsey Stonebridge and Agnes Woolley, 146–64. Edinburgh: Edinburgh University Press.

CHAPTER 3

Policing Displacement and Asylum: Giving Voice to Refugees

The focus of the last two sections of the previous chapter was on people who had been successful in achieving asylum status in European countries and in so doing managed to circumvent what is, effectively, a war on immigration. It is a war fuelled by the territorial imagination and carried out by extremely vulnerable sovereign nations. Thousands have lost their lives over the past twenty years in attempting to reach Europe. In 2000, fifty-eight Chinese men and women were found suffocated to death in a container lorry on arrival at Dover and there was a similar incident in Essex in 2019 when thirty-nine people were found dead in the back of a lorry; in 2004, twenty-three Chinese men and women were drowned in Morecambe Bay, Lancashire, while searching for cockles at night. In the first four months of 2011, 1,500 migrants from North Africa, in the wake of the 'Arab Spring', drowned trying to reach European coasts. In October 2013, more than 360 men, women and children drowned in the Mediterranean off the coast of Lampedusa. Many hundreds of other instances could be added to these, but the point that I am making is that each one was killed by the territorial imagination. In this chapter, unlike the previous one, attention will be paid to people *seeking* asylum and an analysis will, initially, be made of two films—*Escape to Paradise* (2001) and *La Forteresse* (2008). In the second half of the chapter, the focus will

© The Author(s), under exclusive license
to Springer Nature Switzerland AG 2021
R. Bromley, *Narratives of Forced Mobility
and Displacement in Contemporary Literature and Culture*,
Studies in Mobilities, Literature, and Culture,
https://doi.org/10.1007/978-3-030-73596-8_3

be on a written text—*No Friend but the Mountains* (Boochani 2019), a work which combines memoir with cultural and political analysis.

The territorial imagination is produced by ideologies of nation or, more precisely, the quartet of birth, territoriality, nation and state upon which concepts of national sovereignty and citizenship are constructed, with territory—'our country'—seen as a signifier of identity.

From 'the territorial imagination' was born the concept of an authentic national identity with the outsider as 'inauthentic'. Authenticity is a crucial part of border rhetoric and imagery. In the formulation 'the British people', for example, the 'people' are not explained or defined because it is taken for granted that they are a given. National belonging—'our way of life'—simply reflects this, rather than being seen as the construction that it is. It is a powerful fantasy or fiction—a fiction of power—which impacts upon the asylum seeker, always conscious of being out of place, displaced from his or her territory but also seeking an alternative. The asylum seeker not only exposes the fiction of sovereignty but also the fiction—the fixed, but arbitrary, notion—of belonging. The asylum seeker is a figure of time and movement, but not of place until granted refugee status. The texts examined in this chapter also show the asylum seeker as contained, or detained, immobile and subject to endless waiting, in some cases even criminalised.

On this basis, citizenship and identity become categories of and for inclusion/belonging. For example, British politicians frequently refer to 'our island story'. The island is only notionally territorial in this usage, more a cultural and ideological narrative: it is a code for heritage and a 'white' heritage at that.

Crisis at the Border

In Günter Grass's wonderful formulation, refugees become "irritants to the rigid orders of the self" (in Soguk 1999, 15), and, as Soguk claims: "In this way, refugees help remake the conventional language in which the narratives of the so-called citizenry, national community, and territorial state are told" (ibid.). They help to sublimate internal anxiety, fragmentation and precarity at a time when governments lack the prescriptive power to inscribe what is an increasingly empty and obsolescent national imaginary, as the social state has yielded to the globalised, market-state. This has led to the current preoccupation with borders and security. There is no longer a national narrative or symbolic vocabulary available that can produce discursive solidarity, hence the growth of far-right nationalism and populism across Europe. Is national identity only now possible in a continuous state of emergency (levels of alert) where a threat has to be constantly imagined by its citizens so that a form of self-enclosure can be validated? A real emergency in the form of the continuing global pandemic, which started in January 2020, has not yet lent itself to nationalist responses except in the posturings of Donald Trump or in the terms of conspiracy theorists who declare COVID-19 as 'fake', refuse to wear masks or observe laws about assembly or other forms of socialising.

Until the pandemic, for the past ten years or so we have been witnessing a renewing of the cultural script of nationalisms (core values): a restoring/a restorying which is also an act of narrative foreclosure as far as the unbelonging are concerned. Hence the frequent reference to borders and border security. Borders here mean literally the limits of a nation's sovereignty but they also refer to those borders which help to construct the cultural, social and national imaginary. Immigration control has come to occupy a central position in discourse about the identity of the country, as well as other issues relating to security and citizenship.

What the asylum seeker challenges is the dominant vocabularies and image resources circulated and referenced by the nation-state, and its mediating agencies, to anchor its (perhaps limited) power in a culture of entitlement and identity. An anxious state is strategically displacing its insecurities onto the 'always already' displaced and seeking to renew and replenish the weakened territorial imagination of its increasingly alienated citizens. Value, meaning, worth and dignity (distinction) are all distributed within the field of sovereignty whereas the asylum seeker is subject to humiliation, abuse and detention (in some cases) in a 'zone of indistinction', forms of social displacement and unbelonging. (S)he is included only by means of exclusion, the withdrawal of the law. The coloniality of power uses both time (waiting) and space (containment) against asylum seekers.

European governments talk up the nation and the national through a rhetoric of 'core values' but also, and more importantly, use the concept of sovereignty to re-seal and control their borders while, at the same time, exercising the prerogative of determining who to exempt and who to include in their territory.

As Dalal has shown, "Differences between groups of people turn into ethnic boundaries only when heated into significance by the identity investment of the other side" (Dalal 2002, 24). Identity investment, I shall argue, is at the root of the need to exclude and the politics of securitisation and is made even more urgent by the loss of meaningful symbols. As Mirzhoeff argues, "the current moment of globalization is … based upon a reactionary redefinition of identity that, from the point of view of government, requires new modes of surveillance and internment" (Mirzhoeff 2004, 137).

Dalal goes on to define the issue in this fashion:

> The fact that there is the constant danger of the imaginary 'us' dissolving into the 'them' resulting in another kind of 'us' and 'them' sets off two interlinked anxieties. The first is a profound existential anxiety that comes about as one starts to feel the sense of self dissolving, and so is resisted. The second anxiety is evoked by the potential loss, dilution or disruption of access to the vortices of power and status. (Dalal 2002, 24)

THE LIBERAL DILEMMA

Switzerland, the location of the films under discussion, has long been regarded as a haven for refugees, the site of the Geneva Convention of 1951, the base of the International Red Cross, a space of peace. Until recently, it embodied the essence of a liberal democracy, outlined by Benhabib: "Not only politically, theoretically as well, the incorporation and acceptance of immigrants, aliens and foreigners into liberal democracies touch upon fundamental normative and philosophical problems concerning the modern nation-state system" (Benhabib 2002, 160). For some time now, it has been clear that closing borders has assumed primacy over the claims of those who seek asylum in Europe, mainly because to continue to behave in accordance with the precepts of liberalism leaves governments in danger of losing their constituencies of power. For example, following a referendum in 2009, the Swiss government, under pressure from the right, has not only banned the building of any further minarets (seen by the Swiss People's Party as symbolic of Islamic power) but has also introduced a stringent set of immigration rules which are distinctly illiberal. On 9 February 2014, Swiss voters narrowly approved (by 50.3 percent) a right-wing proposal to curb immigration by imposing limits on foreigners coming into the country. As Vincent Kaufmann suggests, "The February 2014 vote was merely the local expression of a series of more structural upheavals currently affecting the European continent" (Kaufmann 2019, 157). The 'crisis' of 2015 accentuated these upheavals and, as will be seen from the experience of Behrouz Boochani, later in this chapter, it is not something confined to Europe, but applies also to Australia.

The liberal dilemma referred to is at the core of much current political discourse: "Defining the identity of the sovereign national is itself a process of fluid, open, and contentious public debate: the lines separating 'we' and 'you', us and them, more often than not rest on unexamined prejudices, ancient battles, historical injustices, and sheer administrative fiat" (Benhabib 2002, 177). By allowing asylum seekers to be used as a means of reinforcing unexamined prejudices, the lines of separation referred to by Benhabib are very firmly reinscribed with the result that public debate ceases to be fluid and open but is subject to authoritarian closure. She argues that the rights of refugees and asylum seekers mark the threshold and boundary "at the site of which the identity of 'we, the people' is defined and renegotiated ..." (Benhabib 2002, 177).

To sum up thus far, in Soguk's words, "Regime practices, while purportedly concentrating on the problem of the refugee/asylum seeker, thus work not so much to 'solve' the 'refugee problem' as to utilize those bodies marked as refugees in order to stabilize various territorialized relations, institutions, and identities that afford the state its reason for being" (Soguk 1999, 52). The asylum seeker is a challenge to the boundedness of territory.

Displacement helps us to think about place and belonging, to complexify these concepts in order to articulate the conditions of new possibilities, lived spaces of mutuality and reciprocity, hospitality which overcomes borders. Arguably, the displaced offer the greatest challenge today to traditional concepts of sovereignty.

Mapping Separation

Maps inscribe and demarcate borders because, as de Certeau argues, "the map wants to remain alone on the stage, central to modern imagination", whereas the displaced interrupt the performance of the map and claim space on the stage—what the map cuts up, "stories cut across" (de Certeau 1984, 129). The displaced person embodies the movement of exile away from symbolic structure, the national fiction (Canning 2000, 351), which is why the national(ist) narrative is designed to stop the 'native' from meeting the displaced, literally and metaphorically speaking:

"When we meet another being, we begin to experiment with our relations and create possibilities together. This creation of possibility is an aesthetic act, an experiment in vibration, resonance, composition of affects ..." (Canning 2000, 352). Hence sovereignty puts in place a range of symbolic/cultural barriers to prevent that encounter so that the displaced is represented as danger and chaos because he/she seeks, demands, claims opportunity, the advantageousness of site or position at the expense, it is argued, of the indigenous. Detention camps and centres, of course, situated at a distance from urban populations, are the physical embodiment of this separation. As Shapiro argues, "the selves that nationalists seek to separate are all ambiguously mixed rather than ethnically pure selves. The drive to partition constitutes a denial of a history of intermingling and acculturation" (Shapiro 2004, 68). It is this denial, materialised in the barbed wire, surveillance cameras and security guards in the 2008 film, *La Forteresse*, directed by Fernand Melgar, which shores up asymmetry and inequality, the sovereign conditions of 'Fortress Europe'.

The refugee, juxtaposed with the name of the national subject, is signified as the figure of lack, indicating an absence and an aberration, an incompleteness and limit vis-à-vis the citizen subject. By excluding the refugee, the national asserts its own boundedness, plenitude, completeness: it is foundational. In order to be reconstituted as a whole, as a subject of value and meaning (like 'us'), of ontological security, the refugee must return to their nation/home/community (the circumstances of their flight are overlooked in this ideological, and contradictory, narrative). As Soguk argues, "the refugee is incorporated into [the discourse of] the national life only to be distanced from the possibilities in it—they are both legally and popularly marginalized" (Soguk 1999, 53). So, however insecure, limited and arbitrary the possibilities in the national life are for the subject, it becomes a privileged site of identity, and the ideological narrative achieves closure.

The governance of refugees is a surrogate for the governance and circumscription of the 'nation-people'. As Cynthia Weber says, the modern state must control how its people are 'written' and how their meaning is fixed—a forever incomplete project but one which has to be tackled if the state is to retain its claim to legitimacy and representative agency (Weber 1995). The policing of immigration helps to restore hierarchies of identities and meanings, and the refugee is used as a means of restoring an axiomatic centrality to the state and its sovereignty. My argument throughout has been that 'immigration control' is a displacement activity, a fabulation, which incites protest by an oblique or subliminal racism, and transfers attention from real doubts by a repetition of manufactured anxieties, ambiguities and indeterminacies. It is a generative project that is activated by the repeated circulation of links between asylum seekers and crime, disease, prostitution, gang masters, terrorism and welfare dependency.

Displacement, in all senses of the word, dominates the experience of asylum seekers as they journey from country to country, crossing borders in search of refuge. Although they are moving in time, in a sense they are out of time as well as out of place, in a state of arrested development, being temporarily arrested in time in the waiting zone, whether it be airport, accommodation centre or detention centre. When the journeying stops and they find themselves in the waiting zone, they will be infantilised, rendered static and inert, subject to curfews and a behavioural regime of containment that strips them of agency, voice and adulthood: sleeping in bunk beds, barred from alcohol, regulated and reduced to passive dependency and submission. They are perceived as a threat to be controlled. In the film *La Forteresse*, the guards are employed by a firm called Securitas, a term which points to the role of asylum seekers in what Nira Yuval-Davis calls 'the securitization of migration' (Yuval-Davis 2005, 41). The detention, or containment, centres are spaces for the victim, the vulnerable and the powerless (definitions which fit with the decision-making regime) where signs of agency, autonomy and independence are treated with suspicion.

The experience of displacement is that of interruption and discontinuity, the loss of the power to impose a shape upon oneself and the attempt to construct continuity and shape against 'arrest', literal or metaphorical. The asylum seeker is not only a figure in transition but a figure of transitional identity, changed profoundly by dislocation, with the need to compose a story in order to move beyond im/mobilisation imposed by the 'claim'—a claim which is simultaneously a demand for something which is due (protection) and a bid for recognition at a time when Europe has created structures to minimise access to asylum and also criminalised those seeking it. As Arthur Helton has shown (Helton 2002), in the Cold War period asylum seekers had an ideological value, a trophy-like status, whereas today this currency is devalued and each asylum claimant has to negotiate the nationalist scripts of insecure and hostile countries within what Balibar calls a "European apartheid", marked by the socially discriminating function of borders (Balibar 2004, 113). In Rancière's terms:

> The new racism of advanced societies thus owes its singularity to being the point of intersection for all forms of the community's identity with itself that go to define the consensus model ... So it is only normal that the law should now round off this coherence ... turns its unity into the mode of reflection of a community separating itself from its other. (Rancière 1999, 174)

The extensive asylum legislation in the EU since the early 1990s testifies to the role of law in attempting to formulate a coherence and unity predicated upon separation from its 'others' and materialised in *"detention zones and filtering systems"* (Balibar 2004, 111, italics in original).

Storying the Stranger

Governments resort to ideological manipulation in attempts to establish 'legitimacy' through appeals to 'core values', 'shared identity' and 'our way of life', and it is this ideological work, and its impact upon public attitudes, which I wish to address now with reference to particular asylum narratives. This ideology manifests itself in what Michel Agier calls "frozen otherness" which, he argues, "is the basis of all rejection—racial, cultural and xenophobic" (Agier 2008, viii). The films under discussion demonstrate this 'frozen otherness' but also reveal the complexity of lives and, rather than pointing to irreducible differences, reduce their alterity. To a certain extent, they reduce the alterity of the asylum seekers by making them the focal point of the narrative, by bringing the 'stranger' in from the margins of silence and invisibility, breaking down the representative category of 'refugee', and making them the subjects of vision and speech: "Those who have escaped and survived the threats facing them find a meaning in their experience from the moment that their story is recognized as a voice ... and not only as suffering" (Agier 2008, 110); the films help to produce a narrative anchorage, forms of subjectification and recognition, however circumscribed by their conditions; the end of 'liminal drift' and denial.

Escape to Paradise (2001) and *La Forteresse* (2008) were both produced in Switzerland and are also located there. They have been chosen specifically because one was made prior to the September 2006 national referendum on the new asylum and foreigners' laws, endorsed by 68 percent of the vote and all twenty-six cantons, which made Swiss legislation on asylum the most restrictive in Europe, and the other was made after the implementation of the law. An initiative of the right-wing People's Party, the law signalled a major shift in the country's humanitarian tradition, although some have claimed that this is a veil that has covered a xenophobic heritage. Under this law, asylum seekers who do not produce an identification document within forty-eight hours of arrival in Switzerland will be excluded from the asylum procedure. For many of those fleeing persecution or war this is an impossible requirement and can only be seen as a cynical move to severely limit asylum claims. The Swiss Federal Office for Migration (FOM) in outlining its 'Basic Principles of asylum legislation' spends quite a lot of time justifying the restrictions on the grounds that asylum proceedings are routinely abused, many asylum seekers are simply in search of a better place to live, and "many of them invent a dramatic story of persecution for the hearing by the authorities. With such tactics they hope to be granted refugee status" (FOM 17 June, 2010). It is undoubtedly true that a few asylum seekers fit this description but what needs to be acknowledged is that increasing barriers to legitimate points of entry into Europe have helped to bring this situation about. Unsubstantiated claims about many people making up stories to say they are asylum seekers are common and, repeated enough times, become a popular 'truth', part of 'what everybody knows'. It is a theme which links with both films in some respects, but with the first in particular it is part of the core narrative.

On the contrary, it is what Hans Lucht, in his compelling study of migrants in southern Italy, *Darkness Before Daybreak*, calls the "global disconnect" which makes the dangerous journey to Europe almost the only strategy left to those in Africa, and elsewhere, in search of improving their life chances (Lucht 2012, xi). In other words, globalisation has brought about the free movement of goods, capital, services and the privileged elite, but has left people in the global South, upon whom this movement has impacted most, profoundly disconnected from this mobility unless they are prepared to imperil their lives.

Isin and Rygiel refer to what they term "abject spaces" as places where "those who are constituted through them are rendered as neither subjects nor objects but inexistent insofar as they become inaudible and invisible" (Isin and Rygiel 2006, 183). They speak of frontiers, zones and camps as such abject spaces and, in the context of the films, the asylum seekers are contained in zones, present but without presence—dehumanised and depoliticised, separated from the resident community—unseen and unheard. These zones are "spaces nestled within state and city territories" where the asylum claimants are under "conditional freedom and surveillance" (Isin and Rygiel 2006, 193), with military style security guards, CCTV cameras and curfews. In *La Forteresse* there are frequent shots of the zone in its picturesque, Swiss setting but rarely any sign of any claimant presence beyond its perimeter fences. The zones are processing spaces for screening and filtering the 'abjects'.

In *Escape to Paradise*,[1] a Kurdish man (Sehmuz) and woman (Delal), with their three children, flee from Turkey to Switzerland and are housed in an asylum holding centre, waiting for their claim to be heard. Alongside them are asylum seekers from Pakistan, Iraq, Cuba, Bosnia, Africa and Russia—all of whom refer to each other by their country of origin. Many of those involved in the production are themselves refugees, including Duzgun Ayhan who plays the lead role of Sehmuz. Unlike the waiting zone in *La Forteresse*, the claimants in this film are given considerable scope for moving outside the centre and freely visit the local town, shot in the high density colour of 'paradise'. Despite this, the reception centre (Camp 50) has all the characteristics of the camp *dispositif* with its perimeter fencing, the military-style uniformed guards and the apparatus of containment and security—fingerprinting, photographing and injections. The youngest child in the family asks, 'Daddy, are we in prison?' Before the family arrives at the camp, one of their friends who has been granted asylum says 'they [the border security] are interested in the border' which sums up so much of what the asylum seeker has to encounter. The wife of that friend had referred to Switzerland as 'paradise' and the film works initially with a number of contrasts between the dark of the Kurdish background experience and the light of the Swiss location— the repeated flashback scenes of the violent raid on the family home, Sehmuz's imprisonment and torture, and his abandonment, hooded, in the countryside are all shot in half-light and silhouette, juxtaposed with the sharp colours of the hostel.

It is stressed to Sehmuz by Aziz, a fellow asylum seeker, that the authorities will want to know details of their journey and see documentary evidence of imprisonment and torture. The emphasis is on *proof* (the catalyst for the central narrative theme) yet Sehmuz has nothing which testifies to his, or his family's, experience. After 2006, this would have immediately disqualified him from the asylum process, but the family is allowed to stay in the country pending their asylum procedure and are moved to an accommodation hostel in another canton. They are repeatedly told by officials that they will be obliged to cooperate and to prove, or make plausible, their case for asylum. This is the crux of the film as Aziz gradually persuades Sehmuz that his story is not plausible since he does not know which prison he was in because he was blindfolded, nor can he offer proof of his torture. When Delal says that he has scars, Aziz replies that everyone has scars and there is a humorous scene in which a number of the claimants parade their scars to underline the point Aziz is making.

Even in the more enlightened times of 2001 (from 1985 to 2000, Switzerland received the largest percentage of asylum applications in Europe) there is still a culture of suspicion and refusal in the asylum process and the trauma of the negative decision is shared by all the claimants. When Sehmuz sees an African man's head being bandaged after he has harmed himself following a negative verdict, he decides to take Aziz's advice and seek to purchase a plausible story for which he has to sell all the family's jewellery. As Aziz says, nine out of ten claimants are sent back and 'that's nine bad stories that no one believes and all are true'. True maybe, but not plausible.

Credibility—a convincing narrative—begins to dominate Sehmuz, hence his recourse to the *storyseller* recommended by Aziz. As Robert Thomas argues, "In some cases, but by no means all, the issue of credibility may be the fulcrum of the decision as to whether the claim succeeds or fails" (Thomas 2006, 79). Credibility, and the model of the 'plausible' client, is based upon a Eurocentric concept of the individual and society, not necessarily appropriate for many refugees, hence the need shown in the film for the asylum seeker to produce a narrative to fit the likely preconceptions of the asylum procedure.

In both films, the procedure seems to be predicated upon a negative presumption based upon suspicion and the likelihood of deceit and abuse, in line with the FOM comments referred to earlier. Knowing this, a Swiss citizen in *Escape to Paradise* has set up a storyselling enterprise in which he exploits the anxieties and fears of claimants and the negative disposition of decision-making, by producing coherent and plausible narratives, derived from an outline of the claimant's situation, together with a set of 'authentic' documents based upon skilful counterfeits. These false—and realist—narratives are sold for an extortionate sum of money.

Evidence is commodified, with credibility a script which has to be learned and performed. In the film, we see Sehmuz working painfully day and night, like a child desperately doing homework, to make himself word perfect from the script. The key to 'truth' lies in the performative competence of the self. The older daughter says that "tomorrow you will buy your story and we'll all get positive … and if we don't then you will tell your true story—your own story". So distressed is Sehmuz by the whole process that he wonders, "who the hell am I?" The flashbacks, the inserts and excerpts from their experience in Turkey, shown over and over again, but each time with an expanded perspective, tell the true story for us as viewers but it is not available to Sehmuz because it is another model of narrative, derived from the refugee as a figure of time and movement—fragmented, silent at times, interrupted, indistinct and not always coherent—one based upon trauma and profoundly disturbed memory patterns.

Michel Agier's comments on testimony are applicable to the structure of the film and its double narrative:

> The context, issues and shaping of testimony create an event—an act of speech, writing, even theatre—that is distinct from what it refers to. Furthermore, the relationship between the testimony given in the camp and the events experienced in war and exodus may be inverted. For these past events continue to exist in the long run—and in memory—as soon as they take a narrative form, thanks to the words … of the author of the testimony. (Agier 2011, 172)

The function of the flashbacks, therefore, is not simply to provide a background and context of trauma but to create an event in itself, distinct from what it refers to—torture, the raid on the family—which takes gradual narrative form throughout the film and produces a common space for the presentation of the asylum seekers' experience, revalued and reclaimed from the institutional discourse.

In her article "Displacement in Asylum Seekers' Narratives", Katrijn Maryns focuses on "entextualization" by which she means the ways in which particular discourses are de- and re-contextualised "in the direction of standard criteria that are often not accessible to the people concerned" (Maryns 2005, 177). It is this asymmetry which is at the heart of this film. Dislocated, displaced, Sehmuz's experiential narrative is similarly dislocated whereas the storyseller has produced a *text*—rich in data but without context, independent of the actual situation itself, deterritorialised, that is, a re-entextualised version tailored to the official procedure.

Storyselling exists because "credible witnesses are presented as products of our own witnessing regimes which demand that refugees and asylum seekers represent themselves with *authentically intact* ethnic histories, clearly enunciated accounts of violence and trauma, and precise legal documentation" (Matthews and Kwangsook 2008, 2, my italics). It is these 'witnessing regimes' with their Western-eyed stereotypes and class-based ideologies of the 'authentically intact' which help to determine refugee status. When Sehmuz's daughter (Zelal) is asked if she was maltreated, she wordlessly lowers her eyes—a combination of trauma, guilt and shame producing her own silent body narrative.

Robert Thomas's summary of the main conditions of Article 4 (5) of the EU Qualifications Directive shows how close the balance of probability (the level of credibility required in the asylum determination process) and proof is to the trajectory of a realist narrative with its basis in positivism: "the applicant must have made a *genuine* effort; provided a *satisfactory* explanation; their statements must be *coherent* and *plausible*; and have established their *general credibility*" (Thomas 2006, 91). In other words, the model of credibility needs to be a *knowing* narrative (itself culturally specific), and 'genuine', 'satisfactory', 'coherent and plausible' and 'general credibility' are all taken as self-evident, as if they have some basis in objectivity. The storyseller's profit is built upon knowledge of "an organizational 'culture of disbelief' towards claimants" (ibid., 84) and the vulnerability of the asylum seeker who, to correspond to the passive refugee model, needs to be presented as a convincing victim, one who has suffered, in order to fit in with prevailing relations of power. In *Escape to Paradise*, the storyseller's assistant even measures Sehmuz's scars to add to the 'realism'. Storyselling works within a horizon of expectation and consistency. Objectivity—or its successful dissimulation—is supplied by the verification of the (fake) documentation. Everything hinges on the asylum interview in which proof literally becomes a burden for the claimant.

Although the storyselling business in the film is fictional (based on true events, we are told), Thomas's argument that recent changes in UK Immigration rules have led to "the elevation of negative criteria from the realm of administrative rules to primary legislation" (Thomas 2006, 92) may well mean that such unscrupulous practices come to exist for 'real' as asylum becomes more and more difficult to achieve. The stories sold in the film anticipate the likely evidential presumptions of the determination process. They are articulate, literate and coherent, whereas the traumatised asylum seeker may be none of these things, especially as they depend upon interpreters. The storyseller is also a kind of interpreter, representing the claimant as what he/she *is* although, in truth, it may be what the claimant is *not*. From a negative a positive (fiction) is generated. This presents a challenge to the whole presumption of the credible witness.

In the event, Aziz's narrative, bought from the storyseller, is rejected and, upon learning this, Delal interrupts Sehmuz's interview at the point where, word perfect until then, he has got the weather wrong at the time of his arrest and his story is falling apart. She urges him to "tell the truth" and this (which we are not shown but only another flashback to prison and torture), combined with her own narrative, which stresses how much she has left behind and has had to give up, secures the family a positive verdict. Their children run outside in a hail of blinding light but, as they are driven to their new home, the green countryside of picture postcard Switzerland yields to the colourless stone and concrete of a tower block, with no lift and with narrow, dark corridors. The family are shot in shadow, almost featureless, as they look out of the window with a view of the facing tower block and, as the credits roll to the accompaniment of a thunderstorm, the same child who had earlier asked, "are we in prison?" says, "do we have to live here now?" So, although prior to 2006, there was still scope in Switzerland for undocumented 'truth' and, although the film, perhaps sentimentally, shows the fact that the fragmentary narrative trumped the coherent one, the predicted future is one of isolation and far from paradise. As the film's strapline says: "Being here doesn't mean being home".

In using films to discuss displacement, I am seeing the filmmaker as someone analogous to what Ricoeur calls the "critical historian", whose role is to reinforce the 'truth-claim' of memory against falsifiability and to reverse, or refute, dominant history. By memory, in this sense, I am thinking of the myth of a unitary national identity, of hierarchical and exclusionary subjectivities. For Ricoeur, the critical historian initiates a critique of power and this, I consider, is similar to the function of the 'critical' filmmaker:

In admitting what was originally excluded from the archive the historian initiates the critique of power. He gives expression to the voices of those who have been abused, the victims of intentional exclusion. The historian opposes the manipulation of narratives by telling the story differently and by providing a space for the confrontation between opposing testimonies. (Ricoeur 1999, 16)

The 'voices of those who have been abused' I refer to later as 'the always already narrated' and it is the task of the critical filmmaker to 'tell the story differently', to produce an alternative legibility.

TELLING THE STORY DIFFERENTLY

It took the director of *La Forteresse*, Fernand Melgar, six months of negotiations to secure access to film in the Centre for Registration and Procedure in Vallorbe (one of five such centres), on the Swiss-French border, the first director to be granted such permission. He filmed over three months from December 2007 to February 2008 and produced over 150 hours of footage, edited down to 100 minutes for the final version which won the Leopard D'Or at the Locarno Film Festival in 2008 and several other nominations. Although doubtless motivated by the September 2006 and 2009 referendum outcomes, the film is studiously impartial and non-polemical. Its basic technique is observational and avoids voice-overs or captions to direct the viewer's responses. Working with multiple points of view, both individual and ensemble, it produces a series of complex perspectives by using certain 'focalisers' to present information, so much so that, lacking any extraneous detail, the viewer occupies a kind of interior frame, metaphorically shared with claimants, the officials, the interviewers and the chaplains. No one point of view is privileged except that we are constantly reminded—by the frequent shots of doors being locked and unlocked—of the overall relations of power. The approach is immersive and mediative, with the camera an absent presence. The editing gives a semblance of detachment and there is no sense of 'fly on the wall' intrusiveness or of voyeurism. For instance, during interviews to establish their claim to asylum, people often are overcome with emotion and the interview is momentarily suspended but the camera does not close up on the face of the distressed person nor linger on their tears; nor are there any manipulative face-to-face interviews. The objective of the film is compassionate understanding not sentimental pity (Fig. 3.1).

Fig. 3.1 Refugee excluded and waiting in La Forteresse, Switzerland (Reproduced by courtesy of Fernand Melgar [director])

The film constructs an interesting aesthetic contradiction because, on the one hand, there is never any doubt that the location is a prison-like space with impersonal guards but, on the other, the claimants are rendered visible and audible, with no presumption on behalf of the filmic narrative of their credibility or otherwise. Nor do we ever know who is or is not successful in gaining asylum but are left at the end with information that, out of 10,387 requests filed in Switzerland in 2007, 1,561 were offered asylum and 2,749 given provisional admission (for twelve months).

In the course of the film we become aware of incidences of insomnia, depression and a sense of separation and loss. Almost half of the Centre personnel agreed to be filmed and they are shown in a mostly positive light, with the Centre Manager emerging as enlightened and compassionate, although from the body language at a staff meeting not all his colleagues perhaps shared his position. However benign the regime (it has to be remembered that the staff were fully conscious of being on camera), the perimeter fencing, the curfews, surveillance cameras, the body searches each time someone arrives, or returns, from the outside and the omnipresent locked door remind us of the criminalisation of the asylum seeker who is seen "as a threat, a trouble maker and a profiteer that one should be wary of" (Melgar 2008, DVD notes, 9). After just two interviews, carried out by civil servants, the asylum process is determined; for some, registration is not even sanctioned and they are given twenty-four hours to leave the territory.

The 2006 vote was most probably not really about asylum seekers as such, but any non-European foreigners, Muslims in particular. The 'fortress'—a converted luxury hotel but with no residual traces of luxury—becomes a metaphor of Switzerland as a whole—headquarters of the UNHCR—and ultimately, of course, 'Fortress Europe' itself, cheering on democracy in other people's backyards while hastily barring all entrances to its own, particularly in the past ten years or so.

Heard and seen the claimants may be, but they are also infantilised by the regime of curfew (gates close at 5.30 p.m.), the dormitory existence, the fact that Securitas (the company employing the guards) had confiscated musical instruments, and the prohibition on alcohol. They also need permission to leave each day and have to register on return. The asylum interviewers betray no sense of irony when they speak of the need to form a 'contract of trust' against lies and deception. Although it is not overstressed, there is an unspoken context of, not so much seeking out probability, but detecting fabrication and deceit, as though these are part of a common presumption.

Credibility—a convincing narrative—is at the core of the asylum application process which is still dominated by a culture of suspicion and refusal.

In discussing the play *The Bogus Woman*, Agnes Woolley speaks of the way in which narratives of traumatic experience, such as those of asylum seekers, are marked by fracture and incoherence and thus render virtually impossible "a verifiable and historically accurate version of events leading to an asylum claim" (Woolley 2012, 32). She cites the work of Roger Luckhurst who describes trauma as "'anti-narrative' and 'a challenge to the capacities of narrative knowledge'" (Luckhurst 2008, 79). The following case of the young Somali man exemplifies this contradiction between trauma and the 'convincing narrative'.

One particular segment (the film is composed of twenty) highlights the previous point and marks the contrast between the chaplain and the civil-servant interviewer. The claimant in question is a young Somalian who tells the chaplain about his escape from Somalia across the desert over a journey of thirty days, terminating in a boat trip with fifty people crammed in an eight-metre-long craft. Without food, they were forced to eat the body of a young child who had died en route. The chaplain is horrified by the story and deeply moved by, and convinced of, the man's experience. This moment is immediately juxtaposed with a conversation between two interviewers, one of whom has granted a 'negative provisional admission' indicating that she doubts the man's claims. This takes us back to the credible witness issue discussed earlier, as the interviewer feels that the story is too stereotypical and second-hand, a borrowed narrative from a stock of possible scenarios that he had heard from others. It is the credibility of the journey itself that is in question but she makes no comments on the bullet wounds and scars which we have observed in the previous scene which, details of the journey notwithstanding, indicate that a return to Somalia might be life threatening. Her colleague, Olivier (seen earlier talking to claimants about the 'contract of trust' and the need to co-operate) is convinced by the story but it is her negative determination which prevails, although she does acknowledge that his poor physical condition will mean that if the provisional admission is lifted, he will need a health check.

The Iraqi claimant, Fahad Khamas, seen in interview speaking of how, as a translator for the US forces in Baghdad, he was targeted by the militias as a traitor, became a *cause célèbre* in 2009, as he was deported twice to Sweden from where he was likely to be sent back to Iraq. His presence in the film helped to generate extensive public support for his case.

This film only presents a handful of claimants—from Armenia, Iraq, Kurdistan, Columbia, Bosnia, Somalia, Nigeria and Togo—some in official interviews, others in informal conversations with one of the four assigned chaplains. It is in the latter that some of the more horrific experiences are relayed. In spite of the fact that many of the claimants are Muslim, only Christian chaplains are available, something which is not commented upon but which, like so much of the film, the viewer is left to deduce. Similarly, the celebration of Christmas seems a little incongruous, although the children of all faiths (who give the film much of its animation and energy) are happy to receive gifts, not surprisingly. Given the adaptability, playfulness and mobility of the children it is easy to forget momentarily that they are effectively criminalised in this 'waiting zone'. It is against this momentary 'forgetfulness' that a number of exterior shots of the 'camp' are designed to act as a reminder—the shots of an isolated guard, torch in hand, patrolling the inner perimeter, checking locks and lights, the aerial view of the segregated spaces of the centre, and the Hopperesque, underlit frames—the latter accentuated when the dawn transfer of claimants is produced on 'deteriorated' film stock, as if shot on CCTV, sharpening the sense of prison and the ghost-like quality of the inmates. The latter scene is characterised by an extraordinary moment when the Bosnian Roma family, seen in an earlier interview, is part of the transfer cohort and is chased by a security guard who confiscates the wheelchair used by the paralysed teenage daughter, forcing her older brother to carry her up a steep hill. One of the last shots of the film, this reinforces the power/powerless undercurrent throughout the narrative. The final shots are of graffiti on the walls and pillars of the camp—names, dates, signatures, a poem: residual inscriptions of presence, legibility in the face of absence, seen in many examples from elsewhere in this book.

The film tells stories of the 'displaced'. But each of the figures in this text—undesirable and placeless—is also a carrier of stories, their own interleaved with others; stories which unfold and add layers in the context of the narrative process, to a point where they become identifiable, subjects of value, rather than subject to market price. All experience the loss of identity, memory and relationship, but the very fact of their being storied is an act of witness itself. The film is, in all senses, about finding a language other than that which already forms the basis of pre-existing representations: the always already narrated.

By now the term 'Fortress Europe' is already overused but the post-2008 recession and the subsequent politics of austerity have given it renewed salience. An increasingly anti-immigrant discourse has emerged which conflates refugees with economic migrants, advocates an exclusionist and ethnocratic politics and devalues the lives of 'others' as subhuman. Far-right parties, including the Swiss People's Party, the explicitly violent Golden Dawn in Greece and the populist, libertarian UKIP and Brexit parties in the UK, have emerged from years of relative anonymity to electoral and media prominence in the past few years. In varying degrees, these parties share deep opposition to the EU, espouse forms of cultural and biological nationalism, are based upon inward-looking and non-reflexive identities and claim ethnic homogeneity and belonging. A fear of loss of sovereignty, a feeling of being unrepresented by an untrustworthy political class (many of whom are taking up negative positions on immigration) and the depredations of neoliberalism and globalisation have produced a sense of abandonment and loss. This sense of abandonment and powerlessness has given rise to a xenophobic polemical space, heated into significance by popular media amplification, in which the immigrant (especially the Muslim immigrant) has become the scapegoat for what are undoubtedly real anxieties and the disappearance of an imagined, unified, national space and time.

Myths of national belonging are part of a defensive territorial self-fashioning and develop in relation to concepts of not belonging—the foreigner, the other, the stranger. These others are configured through a set of fixed stereotypes which form the basis of wished-for political, social and cultural exclusions. The asylum seeker is often used to consolidate the ideology of shared identity and national sovereignty. What the films do is break into these stereotypes and fragment them by introducing a range of complex and contradictory figures, a multiplicity of voices, whose presence *in*, but not *of*, the national space constitutes a *claim* or entitlement to inclusion which goes against long-standing constructions of the alien and points up the provisional and arbitrary nature of identity.

INTO THE ABYSS

In this final section, I want to turn to a very different set of administrative procedures for asylum seekers and a humiliating form of reception as detention which diminishes the humanity of its residents and renders them as less than human. It is a spectacular example of the ways in which the coloniality of power manifests itself as a continuation of historic colonialism. In "Less than Human Geographies", Chris Philo speaks of an approach to the study of worldly geographies which confronts "not what enhances the human … but what diminishes the human, cribs and confines it, curtails or destroys its capacities, silencing its affective grip, banishing its involvements: not what renders it lively, but what cuts away at that life, to the point of, including and maybe beyond death" (Philo 2016, 256).

This is a very precise description of how life was experienced in the Regional Processing Centre on Manus Island, Papua New Guinea, in the period 2013–2017. Life was endured as something *subtractive*, "what takes away, chips away, physically and psychologically, to leave the rags and bones … of bare life" (ibid.). There were several instances of murder, suicide and self-harm during the period in question, as well as many examples of mental health deterioration.

The establishment of the Processing Centre was the result of Australia's 'offshoring' of refugees arriving by boat, mainly from Indonesia. Two specific incidents lie behind Australian asylum policy this century. The first was in August 2001 when an Indonesian fishing boat, with 438 asylum seekers on board, was headed for Christmas Island (an Australian external territory). Its engines failed and the boat was stranded in international waters for a few days. A Norwegian cargo ship—*MV Tampa*—en route to Singapore from Fremantle, rescued the boat's passengers and crew. *Tampa*'s captain, in response to a delegation of asylum seekers, prepared to take the passengers to Christmas Island. The incumbent Australian Prime Minister, John Howard, took the decision to ban the ship from entering Australia or its territories. Six weeks after the ban, the boat's survivors were forcibly removed to Naura (asylum processing centre, part-funded by Australia). During this period, ten more 'unauthorised' boats tried to make the same journey to Christmas Island. These boats were labelled under the acronym of SIEV (suspected illegal entry vehicles) and numbered. One of these boats, SIEV-10, sank with the loss of the lives of 350 of its 400 passengers.

Two years later, the fishing vessel *Minasa Bone* made an 'unauthorised' landing on Melville Island, an Australian territory off Darwin. The boat was escorted back to Indonesia. This action was made possible by an amendment to the Migration Act of 1958, the Migration Amendment (Excision from Migration Zone) Bill 2001. This was a crucial amendment as it allowed "for the excision of territory from Australia for the purposes of the Migration Act, 1958, and was the piece of legislation enacted as a response to the entry of *Minasa Bone* and its passengers into Australian territory. The excision amendment allows for chunks of Australia to be removed from the migration zone" (Rajaram 2007, 264). Melville Island was, accordingly, excised from the migration zone retrospectively, rendering *Minasa Bone*'s presence illegal. So, what was expropriated under colonialism has been excised under coloniality.

I cite the above incidents and responses as a way of framing a discussion of Manus Island and the exclusionary practices of Australia through "the performative acts of sovereignty" (ibid.). The treatment of refugees on Manus Island exemplifies the suggestion by Vin D'Cruz and William Steele that "the Australian political imagination is run through with a fear of the 'world's most dispossessed people (invariably people of colour) whether refugees or Aborigines'" (quoted in Rajaram 2007, 265). In terms similar to those used elsewhere in this chapter, Ian Duncanson speaks of racialised migrants and asylum seekers in this way: "The refugees, fragmented, dislocated, 'out there' confirm my being as unified, placed, 'in here', at the same time as they threaten my identity with their implied numbers and sheer otherness" (Duncanson 2003,

268). Altogether, Australia excised almost 4,000 islands, the scale emphasising an ongoing fear and anxiety about otherness. This approximates to Foucault's concept of biopolitics, the right 'to make live and let die'. In Foucault's terms, Australia is a 'society of normalisation': "Racism is tied to the functioning of a state that is compelled to use race, the elimination of races and the purification of the race to exercise its sovereign power" (Stoler 1995, 86, 84). Racist discourse, in Ann Stoler's terms, "fragments the biological field, it establishes a break inside the biological continuum of human beings by defining a hierarchy of races, a set of sub-divisions in which certain races are classified as 'good', fit and superior" (ibid., 84). Historically, as we have seen, these 'races' are invariably white, and the hierarchy Stoler describes is a characteristic of settler-colonial states, like Australia, and will be discussed later in the chapter on Palestine.

The focus of this section is the Manus Island Regional Processing Centre (RPC), situated on the Papua New Guinea (PNG) naval base, Lombrum. It was opened in 2001 as part of the Pacific Solution policy of the Howard government (discussed in Perera 2007, 201–27), closed in 2008, and then reopened in 2012 as part of the PNG solution. This solution meant that those sent to Manus Island would never be resettled in Australia, a policy designed to deter 'unauthorised' boat arrivals. This was extended into the Operation Sovereign Borders policy, part of the 'theatre of sovereignty' mentioned earlier, aimed at stopping maritime arrivals of asylum seekers to Australia. This policy was implemented on September 18, 2013, four days before the arrival of a boat from Indonesia which included on board a Kurdish Iranian asylum seeker—Behrouz Boochani—whose creative activities—memoir, film, exhibition—would bring Manus Island to the attention of a worldwide audience. His book about the detention centre on the island was awarded the prestigious $100,000 Victorian Prize for Literature as well as numerous other awards. Apart from the book, and many other pieces of journalism, he is also co-director (with Arash Kamali Sarvestani) of the 2017 feature film, *Chauka, Please Tell us the Time*[2] and collaborator on Nazanin Sahamizadeh's play, *Manus* which was performed in Iran and elsewhere.

WRITING THE MIGRANT INTO THE NARRATIVE

Boochani is a Political Science graduate and Kurdish-Iranian radical journalist, member of the Kurdish Democratic Party (outlawed in Iran) and co-founder and former editor of the Kurdish language magazine,

Werya. When other writers on the magazine were arrested, he felt his life threatened and fled Iran, eventually arriving by plane in Indonesia. His auto-ethnography/memoir, *No Friend but the Mountains: The True Story of an Illegally Imprisoned Refugee* (2019 [2018]) is a literary work as well as being a social, cultural and political analysis of the time he spent in Manus *prison* (a description he insists upon) from 2013 to 2017. An epic story of displacement and of a repressive asylum regime, it is a remarkable work which can be compared with Ngugi wa Thiong'o's *Detained* or Bobby Sands's *Prison Diary*, works of subversion and resistance, of refusal. Almost as extraordinary as the book itself is the manner of its production and the nature of the collaboration which brought it about.

The way in which the book was produced is described in the Translator's *Reflections* which are included as an appendix to the main text, and I am drawing upon these in my comments. Prior to writing the book, which was completed in late 2017, Boochani had already published numerous pieces of journalism in a range of newspapers and magazines, including the UK *Guardian* newspaper. These pieces were created in ways which were similar to those used for the book. Anxious not to leave any traces of his work on paper, which might be seized by the guards, his writing was conveyed by mobile phone messaging—text or voice message—to various collaborators. His translator, Omid Tofighian, was the main recipient of these messages but he also communicated with him by sending his writing directly by Whatsapp text. More commonly, he sent long passages of text to Moones Mansoubi, another collaborator, who arranged the messages into PDFs. Having done this, Mansoubi would mail the PDFs of full chapters to the translator. The texts were written in Farsi and the translation process began in December 2016, with many interruptions. The challenge for Tofighian was to develop a style and structure in English which would do justice to a very different, original and poetic language, a language which issued a challenge to the hegemonic language of power. The later chapters were being written at the time of a three-week siege which followed the closure of the camp in October 2017. Its existence had been declared unconstitutional by the PNG Supreme Court but Boochani, along with a number of other detainees, refused to leave until their asylum claims had been registered. Eventually, they were violently removed to another holding centre, until finally being released and granted asylum by the PNG government in 2018, when he was free to move around the island but not leave it. After travelling to New Zealand, on a visitor visa, to attend a literary festival, he stayed on and was granted asylum on 24 July 2020.

Apart from its literary qualities, the book is a chronicle of deprivation, torture (physical and mental), brutality and humiliation carried out, by proxy in a 'client state', by a government whose overriding legacy was a 'white Australia' policy (only abandoned in 1973) and a history of settler-colonialism. Informed by a range of theoretical and philosophical perspectives, the work is, in Tofighian's words, "a decolonial text, representing a decolonial way of thinking and doing" (Tofighian in Boochani 2019, 389). It is the answer to a hypothetical question, 'Can the subaltern think?'[3]—a claim to be the knower and not only the known. It is a story from below, so to speak, a refusal to accept the category of 'the other' and an insistence on finding a space in the hegemonic narrative for the migrant, the asylum seeker: "The refugees have been able to refashion the image of themselves as the 'other'. We have reshaped the understanding of us as politically inept and have been successful in projecting an image of who we are. We now present the real face of refugees for Australia to discern" (Boochani 2018, 18). Like many of the other texts in this book, it is a work of advocacy and of collaborative resistance, a decolonial intervention. Known only by their numbers, in Boochani's case MEG45, the book invents a whole litany of nicknames and pseudonyms which are designed to subvert the border-industrial regime of the institution. This is part of a larger refusal of the ascriptions of governance. Another example of this is the reference throughout all his writings to 'Manus Prison', which is the sign of a refusal to acknowledge the euphemism of management-speak—Regional Processing Centre. It is a gesture of reclamation and, in Tofighian's words, "Conceptually, he owns the prison" (Boochani 2019, 391) which denotes a small, but important, shift in power.

I am not competent to comment on the translation but Tofighian goes into considerable detail about the process and the difficulties of finding equivalents for some of the myth and folklore usages, and the ways in which Boochani expressed his critical and political analysis in theatrical forms, with performance seen as part of philosophy and advocacy (Boochani 2019, 396). Boochani corresponded with three Iranian friends—Najem, Farhad and Toomas—who contributed to intellectual conversations which helped shape the book. One interesting decision which Tofighian took was to render certain passages of Farsi prose into poetic form as he felt this conveyed the original meaning more accurately than prose. The consequence of this, and similar decisions, makes the book a collage of genres, although I think the overarching term of 'autoethnography' effectively captures the spirit of self-reflection, combined with the analysis of power and colonialism.

Before looking in closer detail at certain features of the book, it is necessary to refer to the disclaimer which precedes the main text, in which the author speaks about his aim of giving a 'truthful' account of his experience of being detained on the island. It is worth quoting his words about the composition of the text in full as they convey an important message about his methodology which is comparable with others used elsewhere in this book:

> No detainee or refugee in this book is based on a specific individual, however detailed their stories. They are not individuals who are disguised…Their identities are entirely manufactured. They are composite characters: a collage drawn from various events, multiple anecdotes, and they are often inspired by the logic of allegory, not reportage. The details around the two men who died on Manus, Reza Barati and Hamid Khazaei, are in the public domain and so they are each identified by name as a mark of respect. (Boochani 2019, [xv])

The fact that this disclaimer resembles those often used in works of fiction or feature film raises further questions about how to classify the book. This is perhaps not that crucial unless the book were to be challenged in a court of law and, as far as I am aware, it has not so far. It is a multi-perspectival synthesis of experience and observation, confirmed by many others who either experienced, or observed as journalists or legal representatives, the conditions of the detention centre. As Rancière says, in the Preface to the new English edition of his book, *Proletarian Nights*, "A narrative is not a simple relating of facts. It is way of constructing—or of deconstructing—a world of experience" (Rancière 2012, x). Rancière's book is a reinterpretation of the 1830 Revolution in France and may seem a long way from Australia, or PNG, in the second decade of the twenty-first century, but some of the same principles obtain. Boochani's work is an overturning of a given order, a defiance of the predetermination of the lives of the imprisoned refugees, a counter-myth and counter-narrative. In Rancière's words: "In this world, the question is always to subvert the order of time prescribed by domination, to interrupt its continuities and transform the pauses it imposes into regained freedom. It is to unite what separates and to divide what it ties together by asserting, against the rationality imposed by its managers ... a capacity for thought and action that is common to all" (2012, xi). By finding time and space to think and write, Boochani enacts this subversion but there are also other ways, performed by refugees in the prison, of upturning the order of the regime and its predeterminations which I shall refer to below. The writing is a form of rupture in the carapace of domination, a bid to force recognition from those in power, the very act of writing itself a form of heresy.

The phrase "to unite what separates and to divide what it ties together" echoes an analytical category used by the author in the book: "the Kyriarchal System". This system, identified by a North American feminist, Elisabeth Schussler Fiorenza, explains how ethnicity, class, economics and education, as well as gender, intersect to oppress everyone, men and women alike. Boochani uses this term as a framing narrative for his analysis of the conditions of oppression in the prison and its techniques designed to set refugees off against each other. Certain appropriations by the detainees produce the creation of a 'stage' on which refusal, or defiance, could be enacted.

The opening four chapters detail his journey from Indonesia by sea, with smugglers, in 'a tiny boat'—a site of a struggle for space as it is overcrowded. This is preceded by three months of wandering, displaced, hungry in the country, and is followed by a lengthy, uncomfortable, cramped truck journey marked by fear and anxiety.

Starting in the third person, the narrative almost immediately turns into 'we', something which will happen throughout the text. The poetic inserts act as a kind of chorus or complement. Already at this stage of writing, a characteristic usage is introduced—"The Blue Eyed boy", the "toothless fool", the "cadaver" and many others—composite types, figures out of a medieval Morality play, or, in a term used earlier, shaped by the 'logic of allegory'. A series of distorted and broken images convey the fear and terror of the voyage, although there are also signs of solidarity and a common cause among passengers.

As in so many cases discussed throughout this book, what the author is doing at this early stage is trying to find a way to write the unthinkable disaster, the sinking, the drowning bodies: "I see shoes drifting away" (Boochani 2019, 40). When the boat splits, lives are lost and many battle with the waves to survive. Boochani's survival is prefigurative—his body is capable of withstanding the sea—an anticipation of the struggle to survive the prison later. To convey the fear and danger of this experience,

Boochani deploys a range of verbs of action, a kinaesthetic, immersive prose which simulates the scale and dynamic power of the oceanic waves and the body's attempt to resist their power, all written in the historic, or dramatic, present to give a sense of immediacy. This style will be used at several points in the text, with the poems a way of reconfiguring the more mundane reflections, giving them a different quality. This journey is Boochani's second attempt to reach Australia, and this voyage is looking similarly doomed until they are picked up by a British cargo ship, a rescue which releases refugees from the earlier paranoia, suspicion and masculine competition, as the fragmented scenes assume a coherent shape. Then, on the brink of being transferred to an Australian military vessel, Boochani introduces another key trope, one that is at the centre of this whole chapter, and is not just of his own situation but the experience of all refugees: "I have always despised waiting. Waiting is a mechanism of torture used in the dungeon of time. I am a captive in the clutches of some overbearing power" (Boochani 2019, 62).

Assuming that he is on the edge of arrival in the 'land of freedom', he meditates on courage and on the need for non-violence against the language of Kurdish armed resistance. He turns away from the lure of the mountains and the gun, commits to the power of the pen and cultural expression as resistance. However, he is also honest enough to wonder if, for him, this is a matter of principle or cowardice. The ocean experience has compelled him to go beyond theories and abstractions, to a point where he has come to internalise and *embody* his beliefs. These reflections occur throughout, intermixed with quotidian descriptions of prison life, and passages of poetry in a quite different register. The incarceration of the body is a recurring theme, acted upon, and weakened, by hunger, lack of sleep, beatings and waiting.

Boochani arrived in Australia exactly four days after the new law, mentioned earlier, whereby no unauthorised boat arrivals will ever be allowed to settle in Australia. The warship takes the refugees to Christmas Island and Boochani pictures himself arriving as: "A skeletal man with light-coloured eyes / Holding a soaking book of, poetry / His feet held tightly in a pair of flip-flops / This is all there is" (80). Seen from the outside now as an object, this is the onset of another stage in his loss of subjectivity. The remaining eight chapters document this as well as his efforts to recover the loss.

The next stage of the journey is a month on Christmas Island, another phase of *waiting*. Writing in the 're-created' present tense gives a sense of immediacy. This is a prelude to 'exile' on Manus Island and the image of the place created by Australian officials (full humans) is of savages and cannibals, so the refugees (not quite humans) are to be located with a local population that consists of non-humans, in terms of the racialisation hierarchy (Weheliye 2014). By providing him with clothing twice his size, Boochani's body is diminished and transformed, and this is one among many such instances where "they utterly degrade us"—the subjects of their securitised gaze. They are held in cages as they wait, like exhibits in a zoo. Before they board the plane, nurses outline the health dangers of malaria, as if this is the worst of the hazards that await them.

Boochani is critical of the journalists and camera people gathering round: "The airport on Christmas Island has become a studio for a photo shoot", emphasising his powerlessness and lack of subjectivity: "They are waiting to make me a *subject* of their enquiry. They want to strike fear into people with the movement of my possessed corpse" (Boochani 2019, 93). At one point, some Lebanese refugees objected to the conditions in which they were held; in response, they were beaten into submission, a foretaste of the brutal treatment to come. One of the proclaimed motives for the use of Manus Island was to deter other potential boat people. The bus containing the refugees is parked some distance from the plane, deliberately, so that the men can be 'frog-marched' as a display, performing their captive status as a way of staging their debasement and degradation—their lack of *value*. Value, worth, dignity are all denied to the men by the regime. All the men are reduced to a code according to their boat—Boochani's is MEG45—and known as UNCs (unlawful non-citizens) he, and others, are transformed into someone else, an identity he will hold, and challenge, throughout his time on the island. He repeatedly refers to his own degradation as a crushed person: "I take a few deep breaths, trying to breathe some dignity back into my spirit" (99). Eventually, his writing becomes this 'breathing', a means of recovering value.

From the plane, he says, "Manus is beautiful". This beauty recurs throughout as a profound contradiction of the ugliness of incarceration. In the video of the island he made, *Chauka* (see Note 2), the natural beauty of the island, green and tropical, punctuates the misery of the narratives emerging from the interviews with fellow detainees. In the island prison itself, comedy, song and poetry mask the terror they experience, and the writing itself reflects this complexity of suffering and endurance. He is billeted in a dilapidated structure, in an extremely small room with few beds, situated in a suffocating space with the tropical heat and large metal fans which barely function.

The prison is a place of sharp contrasts—coconut trees, the sea "that lies beyond our reach", yellow and red flowers, combined with fences which cordon off everything and the ubiquitous stench of human excrement. Despite this, Boochani's room is full of memories, of previous inmates, 'monumental memories', inscriptions of an Iranian family with names and dates which enable him to construct an imagined family: mother, father, two daughters. Also inscribed are fragments of Persian poetry "which everyone uses to interpret their destiny, to interpret their future, to interpret their lives". The poems in the text have this interpretive, reflective role—they introduce another rhythm, another way of seeing, a means of raising the writing above the quotidian routine of degradation, dehydration, hunger, abuse and torture. There are also children's drawings on the walls and Boochani empathises with the father, emasculated, humiliated and disempowered, unable to protect his family. This causes him to think back to an actual family which travelled on the boat from Indonesia, with Firouz, the father, unable to assist his children in the face of the storm. A family now incarcerated miles away on Nauru: "Where in the world do they take children captive and throw them inside a cage?" (Boochani 2019, 117). As we have seen, the answer is Australia and the USA. In a nightmare, Boochani dreams of the children—one from the imagined family, one from the actual one, on an island which sinks into the abyss of the ocean.

Boochani analyses the demographics of the prison—the bonds forged by a shared boat which shift towards other identifiers such as language and nationality which produce the basis of an internal migration, the shape of a brotherhood but also a space of division and enmity, historical feuds. He adopts the theory of the Kyriarchal System which, with its roots in feminism, describes a process of interconnected social systems established for the purposes of domination, oppression and submission. It is a feature of the Australian detention regime to turn the prisoners against each other and generate hatred between people. In this way, power is exercised over time (the men waiting endlessly, queuing for food, toilets, medical supplies) and space—the fences, the locks, the bounded confinement. Agency is denied the men and reposes in the regime, as the men are fragmented and disrupted. The control over space is physical and visible, that over time is mental and debilitating as "there is nothing to occupy our time" (126). They exist in a never-ending and repetitious present in humiliating and demeaning conditions designed to break the spirit.

Boochani feels himself as a stranger, the community as alien, as he longs to create that which is poetic and visionary. He retreats into creativity, his writing the only means of tracing the outlines of hope. The past is there as a memory and a set of images, the present is sempiternel, the future can only be *projected* through writing/texting; how otherwise, he wonders, is he to give shape to his conflicting, multiple personalities?

Writing a Name in the Sky

Boochani has his writing as his retreat, and he describes how one form of survival and resistance is the staging of a dance orchestrated by Maysam the whore, so named because of his performances of farce and bodily displays. It is an illusion of festival but also a demonstration to the contemptuous Australian guards of a form of power, the power of the humiliated, a spirit of community to spite the Kyriarchal System of divisiveness. Caricature, the surreal, becomes a form of critique; it is the hierarchy of the weakened. In this carnival, the world is turned upside down momentarily, Maysam is the Lord of Misrule. Later, however, beaten down by the system, he is deflated, his energy and enthusiasm dissipated. This is true of many of the other young men, their spirits crushed.

In sharp contrast to this carnivaleseque sequence, Boochani develops an analysis of the G4S security guards, whose *gaze* dominates the prison, and whose presence heightens the feelings of the men as captive. They are characterised by their propensity for violence, some are ex-servicemen who fought in Afghanistan, others are Manus Island locals or from Port Moresby, who are less absorbed by the Australian culture of systemic violence. The local people are low in the security hierarchy—almost but not quite of the hierarchy, separated from the white guards by uniform and pay, one notch above the prisoners whom some bond with, but under the eye of the complex regulatory structures the locals "have to rein in their ways of engaging" (Boochani 2019, 169). The rule-bound, white Australians embody the power of the fences and the locks.

Boochani is located in the Fox Prison where the architecture of the spaces, the layout and the diminutive scale of the rooms structurally incarnates the physical and mental constraints of prisons, heightens the heat, fear and suffocation of those condemned to a monotonous routine of killing time, the metaphor all too literal as they wait on lengthy queues for medication. One of the very few acts connected to sabotaging the prison's designation of space is that of urinating on the plants which surround the prison, a defiance of the men's abjection. More frequent is the self-harm which is a regular occurrence:

> The place [toilets] can be a sanctuary where people banish the daily psychological struggles and turmoil of all the other places in the prison. But in the end, at sunset or during the darkness of midnight, someone takes hold of one of those razors with the blue handles, chooses the most appropriate toilet, and over there, in the moments that follow, warm blood flows on the cement floor. (Boochani 2019, 171)

As so often in the text, it is not just what is described but *how* it is described. With the effect of slow motion, the pace here, its deliberate style, the sense of choice and the attention to detail—"one of those razors with the blue handles"—and the use of historical present tense all register the indescribable: "the clash between terror, hopelessness and outbursts of deep anguish". Another feature of the mental torture which is part of the regime's power of domination is the queuing: "Young men stand in the sun for hours, queuing for dirty, poor-quality food. The meat is like pieces of car-tyre" (190). The process of waiting for food is emblematic of the Manus Prison logic of control:

> Domination: five people need to leave the dining area so five people can take their place. The community has to wait until five people leave, and then the officer can control the next five with his finger, giving permission to enter. We are like puppets on a string, put in motion with the flick of a finger. Every mind is caught up in a process, a process that has become normalised. A domesticating process. (Boochani 2019, 190)

It is easy to visualise this scenario, this display of power and subjugation, with its undertow of contempt and sadism. The word 'domestication' suggests the breaking in, or taming, of animals. Nor is it hard to imagine a bureaucrat, miles away in Australia, devising this logic of five to maximise the time spent waiting. The prison regulates the quantities of things and limits the time: "The queue is a replica of a factory production line" (Boochani 2019, 191) but also that of a prison camp, a symbol of command. It is against this logic of command, the 'rational' (rationing) allocation of time and space, that Boochani uses the language of the imagination, of poetry and of affect throughout the text, although the punitive situation just described—the logic of five—is characterised by an unsensational style of writing, its understatement emphasising the futility and horror.

For a man known as the 'Prime Minister', widely respected for his knowledge and intellect, blocked toilets contribute to his humiliation as, unable to find an empty cubicle, he is forced to defecate in a corner. This becomes a source of gossip, played up theatrically by Maysam, and the man is subjected to ridicule, with perhaps an element of *schadenfreude*. It is difficult to determine the tone of this section as I am not sure whether terms such as "esteemed", "eminent", "our noble figurehead" or "our distinguished fellow" are meant to be taken 'straight' or are they quotations, metaphorically speaking, taken from those who find his presence intolerable because his principles and demeanour are a reproach to them. He allows himself to be deported rather than continue so demeaned. Boochani offers a clue to reading this sequence of events by again invoking the Kyriarchal System which required the men to see themselves, through the eyes of domination, as wretched and contemptible, the 'broken' Prime Minister brought down to their level.

The refugees are subject to routine humiliations and the smell of starvation. The whole food area is a theatre of the absurd—at one point, chefs are seen standing in a row for an hour, with no food left. Everything is geared towards dependency and control: "In sum, a twisted system governs the prison, a deranged logic that confines the mind of the prisoner, an extremely oppressive form of governance that the prisoner internalises, a system that leaves the prisoner simply trying to cope" (Boochani 2019, 208). New rules and regulations are devised every week for the cigarette queue, for example. Every part of the regime is designed to unsettle the rhythm of the prisoner, to interrupt any developments of habit or routine.

Leveraging the Queue as a Technology

Cigarettes, food and telephones are the core essentials of the prison, so manipulation of these needs produces a 'cultural stratum of beggary in the prison' giving rise to new social chasms and social divisions. Scarcity is a primary mechanism of control; rules change regularly and arbitrarily:

"The system fragments and disorientates the prisoner to such an extent that he is alienated from his sense of self":

> A grandfather, a father, a month-old child
> A day for fathers, a day for all fathers
> It's always Father's Day here
> That's why there are no fathers here
> Fathers don't exist within the Kyriarchal System. (Boochani 2019, 224)

In other words, the men are stripped of all roles and relationships, other than the bare life of the prisoner. Physically or mentally, all are forced into submission. The fractious are moved to the solitary confinement cell—the Chauka. This was the fate of a young man, "the Father of the month-old child", and Boochani inserts a lengthy poem structured around the word "Imagine" in which a different scenario is postulated to the situation in which the man is denied the chance to call his father, one where the young father is not refused the right to telephone his dying father.

Boochani is both inside and outside the prison—he has the power to distance and detach himself through analysis and reflection, by immersing himself in the landscape and allowing his senses space in which to be fulfilled, or when he dreams of Jezhwan (285–87) on another level of consciousness. He also transports himself to Kurdistan and reflects on war and the mountains, pinioned between Iraq and Iran. Determined not to lose his past, his history, his writing is an attempt to re-politicise the world which he inhabits as the purpose of the regime is to depoliticise the refugee. In the terms used by Aletta Norval, Boochani is "The figure of 'writing a name in the sky'—projecting and inscribing new and unheard-of ways of being and acting onto existing political imaginaries—captures and condenses what is at stake here" (Norval 2012, 813). In the face of oppression, he insists on his presence as a speaking being, someone of account. Adopting a phrase from Stanley Cavell, I see Boochani as an *exemplar*, of the possibility of being and acting differently, he puts "the social order as such on notice" (Cavell 1990, 109). All of the texts in this chapter, in their different ways, challenge and put on notice existing asylum regimes, staging the relationship between creativity and resistance.

Observer-like, and interpreter, Boochani detaches himself from the conflict, but in fact, "I am disintegrated and dismembered, my decrepit past fragments and scattered, no longer integral, unable to become whole once again" (Boochani 2019, 265).

One lengthy episode extends into a metaphor of the power relationships in the camp. It is like a scene out of the theatre of cruelty where our senses are assaulted. It is also surreal in the way it is played out. A prisoner has escaped solitary confinement and is being chased by officers. Naked except for underwear, he moves in ways which seem to disorient the officers who appear to panic. Declaring himself a prophet, he booms a message of humanity and care to an uncomprehending array of regular officers supplemented by the Strike Force wearing black gloves with metal spikes. Boochani, as onlooker, scripts the encounter as between rhinos and a single leopard, like something in a colosseum. The role of the Strike Force is to beat the man down and the scene which follows shows him being knocked to the ground, with knees in his back, his body crushed into the earth, head and neck twisted, his attempt to speak cut off, "his words are extinguished" (Boochani 2019, 278).

To complete what Boochani is describing dispassionately as a ritual, a team of medics in white enter the scene and administer treatment. Finally, "The Prophet is incapacitated. The Prophet is passive, he has been disgraced. The Prophet has been forced into submission" (281). The rhythm of the syntax and the repetitions enact the man's final capitulation and subordination.

This violence is symptomatic, in condensed form, of the purpose of the camp. It is designed to annihilate any claim to individuality or articulateness, any hint of entitlement to power: "The principle being force must be met with force". The following sentence is absolutely central to understanding the dynamics of incarceration: "In reality, the extent of the violence administered on the body of the Prophet is equivalent to the power that he took from them" (278). It was the presumption to speak of a future (the prophet's role) other than that predetermined by the nation-state or its agents, itself a form of violence or violation, which is why his face (signifier of distinctiveness, of identity) has to be crushed into the ground, his body disempowered and his power of language destroyed. The man's crime was the temporary theft of power, insubordination, his exemplary punishment was the restoration of subordination, rendered as object, without capacity, agency or status: submissive. At the time of writing, it is hard not to think of the images of the killing of George Floyd in Minneapolis in May 2020, the knee in the back, the face smothered: another country but the same racialisation and coloniality of power.[4]

Violence is the currency of the prison, evidenced by the murders and suicides. Dehumanisation is a two-way street: not only are the prisoners treated as less than human but the security officers behave in ways which challenge their humanity and is possibly why the beating of the prophet was so vicious because he dared to speak about "humans caring for humans. And not humans antagonizing humans" (Boochani 2019, 276). Boochani is able to present this all through the lens of a theatrical metaphor: "By doing this, I detach myself from the stage with its characters of the Prophet and the Rhinos" (283). The style of the analysis is almost a parody of power, comedic in some respects with its staging of figures in a morality play, stylised types, choreographed into a performance of power and failed resistance.

Power is not only exercised by physical violence but also in ways which are designed to undermine the well-being of the refugees. The Health and Medical Services (IHMS) seems to be an outlet for the staff's power complexes: "A prisoner is reduced to a useless piece of meat to be destroyed ... thrown away, back to the country or homeland from which the refugee fled" (Boochani 2019, 303). This is part of the overall waiting and dependence system of degradation: "Day by day the long queues for paracetamol become longer and rowdier. They become an integral part of prisoners' everyday lives":

> This is what life has become after all
> This is one model constructed for human life
> Killing time by leveraging the queue as a technology
> Killing time through manipulating and exploiting the body. (Boochani 2019, 307)

In the penultimate chapter (11), Boochani combines the role of anthropologist and spectator, standing back and commenting on the prison system and the culture it engenders: "Self-harm has become established for some in the prison as a kind of cultural practice". Boochani describes how, when it happens, there is a simultaneous feeling of terror and fascination; "a performance stained in blood, a theatre in which they all have a role" (317). This chapter builds on the theatrical metaphor used earlier to describe the system. The chapter is constructed primarily around the figure of a young man—dubbed "The Smiling Youth"—who is in poor physical and mental health. The scene unfolds like a medieval festival—steeped in blood. Death is reported on at a tangent:

> The smiling youth is dead
> Just as the smile in the corner of his mouth begins
> to fade into an arid emptiness
> Hamid, the smiling youth, dies. (Boochani 2019, 326)

Hamid Khazaei is the first prisoner with his own name in the text, a man with a serious psychiatric condition who hanged himself in the local forest.

In the last phases of the book—the final chapter, "In Twilight/The Colours of War"—the focal point of the riot is Mike Prison, where a disturbance had been raging for three days. Two weeks of peaceful protest had culminated in a bloody war, with the refugees mutinying against being reduced to mere numbers in a system. The conflict became "a performance of power"—traces of the hierarchy met the sound of resistance which reached the other three prisons: "the sound of power".

As the riot finally encompassed all four prisons, the locals formed an alliance with the Australian guards, "arming themselves for war", evidencing the hegemony of white power. Prisoners bonded, they felt free as they stomped on the power of the prison. This is presented in the form of kinetic prose which gives a sense of energy and movement to the conflict. The men sought to erase the system of oppression, rules and regulation, to riot against the Kyriarchal System in a show of solidarity. The riot squad is characterised in terms of iron men, and as robotic:

> They took some steps forward / then they stopped
> They stood there for a few minutes /
> Then they moved forward a few steps again. (Boochani 2019, 344)

The style reproduces their movement, their relentless approach—two steps every ten minutes. The generator is switched off and plunges the whole area in darkness and disorder, followed by gunshots: "He's been shot. Move aside. They've put a bullet in him" (348). Defeated, the men become submissive and obedient but, instead of being allowed to re-enter the prison peacefully, the men are subjected to brutal violence: "The ground covered in blood / Men all over the place with crushed bodies / Men all over the place with smashed bones / Men all over the place with cracked faces / Men all over the place with broken legs / Men all over the place with fractured arms / Faces mashed / Lips split" (Boochani 2019, 353).

The repetitions enact the comprehensive nature of the violence. The recurring 'adjectival verbs', almost synonyms, underline the abjection of the men. Reprising his role as witness, Boochani comments: "We are to witness a scene that will ensure that no-one will ever again risk even contemplating the possibility of challenging the *Kyriarchal* System" (353). The frequent use of theatre metaphors gives the sense of the whole book as a staging of evidence, bearing witness to an outside audience of readers, of potential activists, of the barbarity of the Manus system.

Throughout the book, various prominent 'actors' are allocated sobriquets which give them an allegorical role akin to a figure in a morality play, with examples such as "the comedian", "the hero", "the prophet" and "the cow", ascriptions which locate a specific aspect of their self-presentation or are conferred upon them by their peers. One of the most prominent of these is the man who is the second, and final, one to be named, in the last line of the book: Reza Barati: "They had killed Reza. They had killed the Gentle Giant" (Boochani 2019, 356).

No Friend but the Mountains is a complex narrative, a composite of many forms—memoir, testimony, chronicle and auto-ethnography—and it does not only add to the stock of prison literature, but also develops new methods for understanding the experience of 'political' incarceration. Although Boochani does give an immersive sense of the daily experience, its routine humiliations and indignities, he also does more than just document or detail the quotidian life as he stands back, detaches himself and sees the detention centre in terms of its ritual processes and symbolic actions, its metaphors and paradigms. Without in any way reducing the impact of the oppressive apparatus, he sees the rituals and exchanges in terms of cultural performance, hence the assignment of roles to many of his fellow detainees as they seek to negotiate the hostility of their environment in, at times, almost playful terms. Boochani frequently deploys metaphors from theatre—scene, performance, stage—as anchorage for his analysis of the social drama of detention. In saying this, I am drawing on the work of the anthropologist Victor Turner whose understanding of the power dynamics in societies in terms of structure and anti-structure fits Boochani's approach: "Turner contrasted … social structure (e.g. status, power, top-down authority) with 'anti-structure' (bottom-up creative responses and pressures to change). Anti-structure is the liminal arena; the greater the powerlessness, the greater the need for positive anti-structural activities, which he styled communitas (positive community activities)" (Bigger 2009, 209). Although power ultimately resides with the asylum regime, and their agents and clients, Boochani cites many examples of positive anti-structural activities despite the powerlessness of those in the liminal area.

This chapter has featured a range of asylum systems, all of which have been characterised by *waiting*, the control over movement and of time and space. To a greater or lesser extent, the different systems have manifested forms of violence, psychological or physical, and, in the last example, both. In each case, refugees have been infantilised, subjected to hierarchies of power, and reduced to anonymity, treated as being of no value, less than human. Technically speaking, each text, fictional or documentary, has featured refugees who are in asylum processing institutions, although, in the last instance, in real terms it was a process of offshore 'warehousing'. Displacement is the condition which links them all together.

In the following chapter, displacement is also the key experience featured in each of the four texts but with different inflections and deriving from contrasting situations. Colonialism was a system of displacement—evicting people, seizing land, and marking out arbitrary borders—and coloniality has continued this legacy in the form of corporate neo-extractivism, leading to "the dilemma of many Africans: a 'maddened flight' to go away at any cost and escape the 'terrible alternative' of staying behind" (Palladino and Woolley 2018, 131). Three of the texts are written in the form of graphic narratives, the other is a documentary film. In one case, the focus is on the estrangement and adaptations of an economic migrant, in the second it is on a refugee who has been granted an asylum application and is faced with a labyrinthine set of bureaucratic procedures; the remaining two texts represent people who are not in any formal, or institutional, system of asylum but are outside the legal processes and living in informal, makeshift camps.

Notes

1. This is an Insert Film production directed by Nino Jacusso, who works with techniques of new realism based upon the concept of Real Acting, in which non-actors perform a dramatised story based upon actual events and developed with the cooperation of the people involved.
2. *Chauka, Please Tell us the Time* (2017). Chauka is a native bird and the symbol of Manus Island, but also the name of the solitary confinement

unit in the island's regional processing centre. The film was shot clandestinely over six months on Boochani's smart phone and images were sent for editing to his co-director in the Netherlands, Arash Kamali Sarvestani. The film attempts to convey a sense of the beauty of the island set against the deprivation, suffering and pain suffered by those detainees who are interviewed. Local people tell the time from the Chauka's regular singing, and time, of course, is a major preoccupation of the men detained in the 'prison'.
3. This is my fairly obvious variation on the title of Spivak's famous essay title, "Can the Subaltern Speak?" (1988).
4. George Floyd, a 46-year-old black man, was arrested by Minneapolis police officers on 25 May 2020 on suspicion of fraud. Shortly after his arrest, he became unconscious after being forcibly held on the ground by three police officers. One officer knelt on his neck for eight minutes and forty-six seconds while he cried out "I can't breathe". He subsequently died. All the officers involved were dismissed, one was charged with murder and the others with aiding and abetting. The time during which he was pinioned to the ground has been disputed but 'eight minutes and forty-six seconds', together with the cry 'I can't breathe' became symbols for the Black Lives Matter protests which erupted all over the US and in many other countries.

References

Agier, Michel. 2008. *On the Margins of the World: The Refugee Experience Today*. Cambridge: Polity Press.

Agier, Michel. 2011. *Managing the Undesirables: Refugee Camps and Humanitarian Government*. Cambridge: Polity Press.

Balibar, Etienne. 2004. *We, the People of Europe: Reflections on Transnational Citizenship*. Princeton, NJ: Princeton University Press.

Benhabib, Seyla. 2002. *The Claims of Culture: Equality and Diversity in the Global Era*. Princeton, NJ: Princeton University Press.

Bigger, Stephen. 2009. "Victor Turner, Liminality, and Cultural Performance." *Journal of Beliefs and Values* 30 (1): 1–5. Accessed October 6, 2020.

Boochani, Behrouz. 2018. *A Letter from Manus Island*. Adamstown, NSW: Borderstream Books.

Boochani, Behrouz. 2019 [2018]. *No Friend but the Mountains*. London: Picador.

Canning, Peter. 2000. "The Imagination of Immanence." In *The Brain Is the Screen: Deleuze and the Philosophy of Cinema*, edited by Gregory Flaxman, 327–62. Minneapolis: University of Minnesota Press.

Cavell, Stanley. 1990. *Conditions Handsome and Unhandsome: The Constitution of Emersonian Perfectionism*. Chicago: Chicago University Press.

Dalal, F. 2002. *Race, Colour and the Process of Racialization: New Perspectives from Group Analysis, Psychoanalysis and Sociology.* London: Brunner-Routledge.

de Certeau, Michel. 1984. *The Practice of Everyday Life.* Translated by Steven F. Rendall. Berkeley and Los Angeles: University of California Press.

Duncanson, Ian. 2003. "Telling the Refugee Story: The 'Ordinary Australian,' the State of Australia." *Law and Critique* 14 (1): 29–43.

Escape to Paradise. 2001. Directed by Nini Jacusso. Switzerland: Insert Films.

Helton, Arthur. 2002. "Terrorism's New Victims and Possible Recruits; Refugees Suffer as the West Focuses on Its War Efforts." *Los Angeles Times*, July 12.

Isin, Engin F., and Kim Rygiel. 2006. "Abject Spaces: Frontiers, Zones, Camps." In *Logics of Biopower and the War on Terror*, edited by E. Dauphinee and C. Masters, 181–203. Basingstoke: Palgrave Macmillan.

Kaufmann, Vincent. 2019. "Europe beyond Mobilities." In *Mobilities and Complexities*, edited by Ole. B. Jensen, Sven Kesselring, and Mimi Sheller, 155–60. London: Routledge.

La Forteresse. 2008. Directed by Fernand Melgar. Switzerland: Climage.

Lucht, Hans. 2012. *Darkness Before Daybreak: African Migrants Living on the Margins in Southern Italy Today.* Berkeley: University of California Press.

Luckhurst, Roger. 2008. *The Trauma Question.* Abingdon: Routledge.

Maryns, Katrijn. 2005. "Displacement in Asylum Seekers' Narratives." In *Dislocations/Relocations: Narratives of Displacement*, edited by Mike Baynham and Anna de Fina. Manchester: St. Jerome.

Matthews, Julie, and Kwangsook Chung. 2008. "Credible Witness: Identity, Refuge and Hospitality." *Borderlands* 7 (3): 1–15.

Melgar, Fernand. 2008. *La Forteresse.* DVD notes.

Mirzhoeff, Nicholas. 2004. *Watching Babylon: The War in Iraq and Global Visual Culture.* New York: Routledge.

Norval, Aletta. 2012. "'Writing a Name in the Sky': Rancière, Cavell and the Possibility of Egalitarian Inscription." *American Political Science Review* 106 (4) (November). https://doi.org/10.1017/S0003055412000445.

Palladino, Mariangela, and Agnes Woolley. 2018. "Migration, Humanitarianism, and the Politics of Salvation." *Lit: Literature, Interpretation, Theory* 29 (2): 129–44. https://doi.org/10.1080/10436928.2018.1463591.

Perera, Suvendrini. 2007. "A Pacific Zone? (In)Security, Sovereignty, and Stories of the Pacific Borderscape." In *Borderscapes: Hidden Geographies and Politics at Territory's Edge*, edited by Prem Kumar Rajaram and Carl Grundy-Warr, 201–27. Minneapolis: University of Minnesota Press.

Philo, Chris. 2016. "Less Than Human Geographies." *Political Geography* 60: 256–58. https://doi.org/10.1016/j.polgeo.2016.11.014.

Rajaram, Prem Kumar. 2007. "Locating Political Space Through Time: Asylum and Excision in Australia." In *Borderscapes: Hidden Geographies and Politics* at *Territory's Edge*, edited by Prem Kumar Rajaram and Carl Grundy-Warr, 263–82. Minneapolis: University of Minnesota Press.

Rancière, Jacques. 1999. *Disagreement: Politics and Philosophy*. Minneapolis: University of Minnesota Press.

Rancière, Jacques 2012 [1981, 1989]. *Proletarian Nights: The Workers' Dream in Nineteenth-Century France*. London: Verso.

Ricoeur, Paul. 1999. "Memory and Forgetting." In *Questioning Ethics: Contemporary Debates*, edited by M. Dooley and R. Kearney, 5–11. London: Routledge.

Shapiro, Michael. 2004. *Methods and Nations: Cultural Governance and the Indigenous Subject*. London: Taylor and Francis.

Soguk, Nevzat. 1999. *States and Strangers: Refugees and Displacements of Statecraft*. Minneapolis: University of Minnesota Press.

Spivak, Gayatri Chakravorty. 1988. "Can the Subaltern Speak?" In *Marxism and the Interpretation of Culture*, edited by Cary Nelson and Lawrence Grossberg, 217–313. Basingstoke: Macmillan.

Stoler, Ann Laura. 1995. *Race and the Education of Desire: Foucault's History of Sexuality and the Colonial Order of Things*. Durham, NC: Duke University Press.

Swiss Federal Office for Migration (FOM). Latest modification, June 17, 2010.

Thomas, Robert. 2006. "Assessing the Credibility of Asylum Claims: EU and UK Approaches Examined." *European Journal of Migration and Law* 8: 79–96.

Weber, Cynthia. 1995. *Simulating Sovereignty: Intervention, the State, and Symbolic Exchange*. Cambridge: Cambridge University Press.

Weheliye, Alexander. 2014. *Habeas Viscus: Racializing Assemblages, Biopolitics, and Black Feminist Theories of the Human*. Durham and London: Duke University Press.

Woolley, Agnes. 2012. "Questioning Narrative Authenticity in Kay Adshead's *The Bogus Woman*." *Moving Worlds* 12 (2): 30–41.

World Socialist Website. 2013. "Lampedusa Migrant Deaths: The Real Face of the European Union." http://www.wsws.org/en/articles/2013/10/17pers-o17.html. Accessed January 21, 2018.

Yuval-Davis, Nira. 2005. "Human Security and Asylum-Seeking." *Mediactive* 4: 38–55.

CHAPTER 4

Out of Focus and Out of Place: The Migrant Journey

This chapter briefly touches upon the debate about whether the conditions of the 1951 Geneva Convention are too restrictive in so far as they limit the definition of the refugee to a specific fear of persecution. It asks questions about whether those fleeing from poverty, material and environmental degradation, and profound social disadvantage should also be considered alongside those with a claim to political refugee status. Richmond's typology of "reactive migration" (Richmond 1993) demonstrated the inadequacy of existing criteria which surround the refugee situation and, with this in mind, the chapter examines four different cultural texts—three graphic narratives[1] with very different styles, and a documentary film—all of which feature migrants with varying statuses, including an 'economic' migrant, an asylum seeker who fled from 'a genuine fear of persecution' and was permitted to make an application, and two 'illegal' migrants living in camps, hoping to seek asylum. Although the protagonists in each text face quite different challenges, they all suffer from a profound ontological insecurity.

As Europe four years ago was, apparently in the midst of a humanitarian crisis, with thirty times more refugees entering the continent in January and February of that year (2016) than in the same two months in the previous year, it is timely to ask what kind of lives these people have

© The Author(s), under exclusive license to Springer Nature Switzerland AG 2021
R. Bromley, *Narratives of Forced Mobility and Displacement in Contemporary Literature and Culture*, Studies in Mobilities, Literature, and Culture, https://doi.org/10.1007/978-3-030-73596-8_4

been able to live in spaces of asylum, presuming that these were granted. In far too many cases, migrants will still be waiting for asylum, are living in camps or have been deported. Given that the majority of refugees will have already suffered trauma, exclusion, conflict and personal loss well before they reach the borders of Europe, then what is the likely impact of these experiences on their well-being, their emotional or mental capital? The fact that so many have got so far, across deserts and seas, suggests a certain amount of resilience and cognitive resource, an ability to meet and overcome challenges. How might they enhance their 'wellness' in the face of the complexities of different asylum processes, assuming that they have managed to surmount the obstacles placed in their way by fences, border patrols and local hostilities? How can they develop and flourish in their new environment? Apart from the physical depredations of the migrant journey, account also has to be taken of the effects on mental health. Will this generation of refugees be able to progress from a condition of passive victim to flourish as an active citizen with choices? Inner resources are likely to be severely depleted and each family, or individual, will need assistance in acquiring the various dimensions of well-being and of accessing new living spaces, physical and mental health care, and social networks.

All of this has to be done in the context of what Foucault called *biopolitics*, the preoccupation of the state with the health and well-being of its populations, a preoccupation which does not necessarily extend to, and in many cases is actively opposed to, those not entitled to national health programmes. At one point, a British government minister discouraged the rescue of those drowning in the Mediterranean on the basis that it only led others to make the same journey. Biopolitics often implies a 'reciprocal exclusivity'—a policy of live and let die—which minimises, where it does not totally deny, the rights of 'others' to welfare. This leads to policies and legislation designed to deter the migrant, except for certain privileged categories. The vast majority of displaced people never get anywhere near to Europe. The influx of refugees into Europe in the past four years or so—mainly, but by no means only, from Syria—has been seen by some states as leading to a crisis of the sovereignty of the border which, in turn, has produced a militarisation of border controls. Far-right political parties have grown in strength in many parts of Europe, demonising and 'othering' the migrant, who has been relegated to the status of the 'sub-human', with Muslims being targeted in particular. The so-called war on terror, a term dropped from political discourse for a while but now returned, has been used to generate a culture of fear and ethno-nationalism in Europe and the US.

So far, my explicit focus has been on the refugee but, in the popular imagination, distinctions between asylum seekers, EU migrants and 'irregular' economic migrants are conflated. In academic, legal and policy circles, there is now a debate about whether the conditions of the 1951 Refugee Convention are too restrictive and whether a range of other factors which cause people to migrate should be taken into consideration as well as those with claims which meet the Convention's criteria. Does material destitution, threats to well-being and 'involuntary economic migration' constitute a deterioration in mental capital and ontological security which should merit consideration together with those currently with a right to claim asylum? Anthony Richmond (1993) emphasises the point that:

> [T]he complex interaction between political, economic, environmental, social and bio-psychological factors [determines] the propensity to migrate. Thus it demonstrates the inadequacy of any definition of a "refugee" which singles out one element in the causal chain, such as having "a genuine fear of persecution", because such fear is often only one factor in a much more complicated relation between predisposing factors, structural constraints, precipitating events and enabling circumstances. (23)

In addition to this, Michelle Foster argues that "a range of emerging refugee claims challenge traditional distinctions between economic migrants and political refugees" (Foster 2012) and this situation is not likely to improve, at a time of ever-widening global inequality and risks to well-being, as environmental disasters are added to already existing levels of economic deprivation, hunger and resource depletion. Writing in the early 1990s, Richmond anticipated much of this contemporary debate by claiming that "a distinction between voluntary and involuntary movements ... is untenable". He constructed a set of twenty-five categories of what he called "reactive migration", linked to those whose life choices and well-being were "severely constrained", such that "decisions made by both 'economic' and 'political' migrants are a response to diffuse anxiety generated by a failure of the social system to provide for the fundamental needs of the individual, biological, economic, and social"

(Richmond 1993, 17). With all the media emphasis on Syria, it is important to remember that what Richmond says applies to many countries today, including Eritrea, Somalia, South Sudan, Afghanistan and Iraq.

Richmond's typology of "reactive migration" demonstrated the inadequacy of existing definitions which surround the refugee situation. Initially, I shall examine two cultural texts—both graphic narratives—which feature migrants, one, on the surface an 'economic migrant', the other an asylum seeker who fled from a 'genuine fear of persecution' in terms of the 1951 Refugee Convention. Although the protagonists in both texts face very different challenges, they both suffer from a profound ontological insecurity, or *dépaysement*, that insecurity and disorientation felt in a foreign country or culture. In the one case, the man in Shaun Tan's *The Arrival* (2006), this fear and anxiety is produced by the migrant journey of displacement and 'unsettlement', and in the other, the case of the figure of M in Mana Neyestani's *Petit Manuel du Parfait Réfugié Politique* (2015), it is the asylum process itself which destabilises and unsettles. In both instances, this experience has a significant impact on their mental capacity and ability to function at the level of well-being, as their senses are atrophied and, although aware of the objects and forms around them, they are not capable of understanding their functions or meanings.

Each protagonist in the texts under discussion undergoes a process of transformation in which they are rendered temporarily superfluous and those skills, resources, understanding and knowledge which they had developed prior to migration are almost totally undermined as they become figures of 'expulsion' almost, and dispossession: disposable people. Their previous well-being might be described as a form of possession, empowerment and self-ownership, part of their belonging. The migrant journey, in the first instance, is a journey of 'unbelonging', of defamiliarisation, in which all habits of recognition, language, time, space and relationships become precarious. Mobility on one level produces a measure of immobility at the level of cognition and navigation, a feeling of maplessness is undergone. If, as Thomas Nail argues, "the migrant is the political figure of our time", then the figures in these texts are both specific and individuated, as well as being, in some ways, archetypal in so far as they represent people within "regimes of circulation" (Nail 2005), who are in flux, moving from a sedentary, territorially defined *heimat* (homeland) to being in motion and in spaces of unpredictability, the unknown. The whole process is one of re-cognition, explored through what Bidisha Banerjee (2016) calls "the lens of difference". This leads to the restoration of a sense of territory and habituation, and of temporal and spatial predictability as a precondition of a renewal and of mental and physical capital, that movement from the status of the "expelled other" (Nail), metaphorically if not always literally, to a position of resettlement, arrival.

While accepting that well-being is a dynamic process, in many instances it is related to what has been called mental maps or 'mental capital'; that is, having the resources and command of life skills which enable a person to navigate the circumstances of everyday life. It could be argued that such mental capital stems from an ability to be at home with one's self. Not always, of course, but often this means literally being in a place surrounded by family and the familiar, forms of attachment— people, objects, images, sites, routines, language, spaces; perhaps, above all, proximity. Together, this matrix of perceptions and actions form a prism through which later experiences are filtered. For the migrant, forced or otherwise, who travels across the world in search of a better, or at least different, life, the moment of departure marks the beginning of a rupture, the first of a series of interruptions to the known and the customary, the initial stages of a loss of well-being in which a sense of lack and abandonment sets in. As the journey progresses and each new obstacle is encountered, and each new experience is seen as strange, all the ready-made sources and resources of meaning and belonging break up; above all, language and customary codes and modes of understanding. Habitual reflexes no longer function effectively and identity has to be totally re-thought and newly configured, like beginning to walk again—finding a place in a realm of placelessness.

TELLING A STORY WITH A VOICELESS PENCIL[2]

These ideas will be explored initially through an analysis of Shaun Tan's *The Arrival* (2006), a graphic narrative which traces the long and tortuous journey of a father and husband from an unspecified location through a range of alienating, nameless spaces and surreal events to a point of eventual arrival and family reunion, the resumption of shared mental capital; the last gesture of the book is that of his daughter pointing towards the future. Technically very sophisticated in its design, the displacement at the centre of the journey is charted wordlessly, the silence carrying the absence of meaning at the core of much of the narrative, suggesting the painful struggle to decode new and challenging signifiers.

The design of the book is integral to its narrative of displacement, a narrative which is eclectic in its sense of both time and place. The book has the physical appearance of a well-worn, partly 'distressed' photo album, a familiar register of the private and the familial. Its cover, title page and publication details bear the stains of time and usage as well as, in their sepia colouring, carrying the traces of inspection, certification and registration (date-stamped documents, etc.), signifiers of immigration, of mobility. The album framework and the signs of passage denote the personal and the individual—on the title page there is a small photo insert of the protagonist, the hat and tie recognisably male but with an undefined face. The narrative trajectory which follows supplies the definition. Countering, and accompanying/framing, the individual marks of journeying are the sixty images on both end papers, each individuated and drawn from a range of, mainly, non-European ethnicities, predominantly male, and presumably forerunners of migration and displacement, those expelled and 'othered' on a global scale, mainly by colonialism, and over a considerable period of time, going back to the nineteenth century and earlier. These expressionless faces are part of a generative archive designed to historicise and generalise the specific migrant journey to follow but also to suggest that the migrant experience is ongoing, one repeated story in a continuum.

The narrative starts at a point of departure with a grid of nine panels of images and objects of domesticity, symbols of belonging and belongings, resources of value—a clock, a hat and coat on a peg, a cracked teapot, a chipped cup, a child's drawing of a family, a family portrait, travel tickets, an origami crane and an open suitcase with clothing inside. The bird, the travel tickets and the suitcase are indices of flight/travel and suggest a fracture in the domestic, a rift in belonging. The furnishings, the damaged crockery and the battered suitcase secured by a belt give an overall impression of relative deprivation and insecurity which hints at a motive for the husband's decision to leave. Man and wife clasp hands over the suitcase, a time of parting and sorrow. It is a familiar migration scenario, the man leaving in the hope of a better life for his wife and child. The time is indeterminate, some point in the early to mid twentieth century. There is a sense in which the book is designed as a document of post-memory, a narrative to be read at some time in the future by the daughter perhaps or her descendants.

There are several images of the daughter which indicate the future, the need for a legacy of security. The family travel together in a darkened street, shadowed by a monstrous dragon-like tail, a possible index of oppression, and pass by shabby, asymmetrical and identical tenement buildings which almost dwarf the family who are diminished and obscured. The fact that the man has travel tickets and departs from a train station suggests that he is an 'economic migrant'. A number of other, indistinguishable passengers wait in the smoke-filled station, presumably on a similar journey. The father tries to distract the child with the origami bird—a motif which will recur throughout as a bond between them. The wife weeps and the child, husband and wife join hands. Child and mother return home alone, the tail of the dragon still looming.

The book is very much about *scale* and *perspective*—ways of seeing and being seen, and, as the man is viewed in transit on a ship, placing the family portrait—itself a recurring point of anchorage—on the cabin chest of drawers, an image of him seen through a porthole gradually diminishes as his specificity is lost among numerous portholes. The ship, in turn, is diminished and displaced in a vast, darkening sky and seascape as sixty panels of differing cloud formations signify the sea crossing, and the passage of time and increasing distance. The passengers are grouped on deck as 'huddled masses', already figures at a loss, lacking any eye contact as they watch huge dragonfly-like, origami figures flying above them. Apart from the earlier dragon tail, these figures are the first break with the 'photorealist' drawings, the initial signs of the non-real, the surreal, indicating the migrant's entry into a de-familiarised, discontinuous world—zones of indistinction—where images are no longer anchored in a knowable context. As 'knowability' is a condition of well-being, this marks the first stage in the gradual depletion of mental capital. Although the images of estrangement are given a strong visual presence, they could also be seen as projections of a sense of internal loss and anxiety, of cultural/mental incapacity. The husband, trying to recover a thread of continuity, writes in his journal/diary and tears out a page to shape into an origami bird. The attempt to sculpt and fold meaning in the form of this bird is a moment of anamnesis, a link with his child.

The arrival at an unspecified port is shown in contradictory, full-page panels from different realms—on one page a realistic cityscape with 'bleeds' into the facing page showing a mythical space in which a giant-sized 'oriental' traveller is greeted by a similar-sized host, their identities indicated by their headgear, their presence a symbol of 'welcome', analogous to the Statue of Liberty in New York harbour. The disembarkation scene is drawn, Tan says, from iconic Ellis Island imagery which suggests a generational and archetypal moment, but the immigration hall has a large banner in a non-Western language, an *ersatz*, Cyrillic-styled alphabet positioned to signify the strange: unfamiliar, unknown codes which are part of the estrangement of migration, the language deficit. Migrants, seated in long rows, are processed—medically examined, labelled, and tagged—as yet another stage in their transformation, their re-inscription. The man is shown in numerous poses indicating bewilderment, failure to understand, at a cultural and cognitive loss, part of the diminution in well-being. Characterised by passivity, he is infantilised as his coat is covered in tags and stickers, his signed and stamped papers issued. These are all new forms of recognition, of certification, of emergence into migrant space, the first of many thresholds encountered.

The man leaves the hall—an atemporal, liminal space—and enters a new temporality, an 'Eastern' cityscape, a surreal, fantasy scene with dream-like qualities, perhaps an analogue of the migrant hope but also a space of alienation and category confusion. He is transported in a Pegasus-like, Tardis structure and deposited in a bizarre, part-realistic, part-fantastic space with mythical birds. This is the most dramatic stage of his disorientation, at a loss and unable to decipher, the lowest point of his loss of well-being, virtually resourceless. He wanders the city trying to read the signs, attempting to wrest meaning from the new environment, his ontological status suspended. The whole book is wordless, emblematic of conceptual and cognitive ruptures, the migrant 'lack', and the man uses graphic means to communicate with someone who takes him to a lodging where a 'real' landlady is mixed with surreal creatures, and his room is full of tubular structures which puzzle and confuse because they are outside his framework of understanding. He now has a place but is still dis-located and struggles to make sense of any of the household implements, objects of an alien domesticity which he will have to learn. In the process, he comes across a small, alien creature—described as a "walking tadpole" by Tan (www.shauntan.net)—who will figure throughout the narrative as a kind of 'familiar', a magical companion. If the man is an Everyman type of figure, then the "tadpole" could be compared with Knowledge in the medieval play *Everyman*, who says "Everyman, I will go with thee, and be thy guide, in thy most need to go by thy side". As a bearer of Knowledge—a key component of well-being—the guide is there to help the man navigate the new world of migrant experience and to find ontological security. Migration, apart from all the features already mentioned, is also a form of disenchantment—almost akin to depression or trauma—and the creature is a guide back to a world of enchantment. Slowly settling, the man opens his suitcase and re-acquaints himself with his knowable past, aspects of his mental capital, by imaging and imagining his wife and daughter by hanging the family portrait. A series of familiarising images follow which are seeds of agency but these are intruded upon, punctured, by the still, as yet, alien creature. That this is a period of relative well-being is indicated by an outside view of the hotel whose windows look like picture frames and the city resembles something from a magical fairy tale, a space of potential enchantment.

Although his sleep is troubled and he is still uncertain about his 'familiar', the man does manage a series of normative actions—showering, shaving, dressing—which are tokens of an incipient agency, the beginning of a new mobility, despite the unreadable map with which he sets off for the surreal city of conical structures, flying boats, and spaces and images which resist meaning. He has the confidence to approach a woman who shows him how to get a ticket for one of the flying boats. By introducing himself to the woman by means of his ID card he takes a step towards sociality and, as she shows her ID, the onset of reciprocal mutuality, itself a condition of well-being. What we become aware of is that this is a city of migrants, newcomers who exist on a graduated scale of acculturation and in/security. In twenty-four dark-toned panels, the woman tells a story of abjection and the trauma of her abduction, confinement and forced labour cleaning industrial chimneys. This very different backstory from the man's indicates that she is a refugee, trafficked and treated as less than human. She eventually escaped her captors and sought refuge in this cosmopolitan space. The man parts from her and continues his journey through the fantasy spaces in continuing bewilderment but meets a man with Western features and draws pictures of food in order to make his hunger understood. This man and his son provide food and guide him to the port. The father relates his story of terror and flight from unspecified persecution. He and his wife are shown in a number of darkened panels and enclosed in a vast Cubist structure, from which they finally escape with the help of a friendly figure who guides them to a harbour where they find a small boat to take them to where they are now. The presence of their son, absent from the dark story, indicates that their refugee journey has lasted about eight years. The family offer hospitality, sharing their now relative comfort, another example of empathy and the kindness of strangers. The man makes an origami figure of a fox for the son, metaphorically substituting him for his daughter. This family story, like that of the enslaved woman, is specific and also generic, exemplary parables of the migrant situation, securing for the man evidence of the fact that integration and adaptation, a process of continuous adjustment, can take place even if 'arrival' is a long drawn-out process. The origami is linked to "the production of spatiality [which] results in folded spaces" (Ek 2006, 383), as the man gradually unfolds the spaces around him.

As the man makes his way through the city in search of employment—another condition of well-being—the range of people he encounters all indicate, through their differing clothes and headgear, a city of displacement but also the positive difference of a postmigration situation. He seeks work at four sites but to no avail. Finally, he is taken on as a bill poster but hangs them upside down as he does not understand the signs. Literacy/legibility is a symptom of well-being, missing at this stage. A delivery job enables him to make some sense of the city until he is chased by a giant alien creature. Eventually he settles into a factory assembly line, standing alongside vast numbers of workers in the shadow of huge machinery. Twenty panels of limited motion show people monotonously placing objects in a tube, the images evocative of Chaplin's film *Modern Times* (1936). This is another generic stage in the migrant journey, the availability of low-level, unskilled and repetitive labour, jobs vacated perhaps by earlier migrants who have moved on. A fellow worker, in a conical hat, shares a drink with him on the assembly line, another phase in his 'welcome', another mark of sociality. The factory images are grey/black and, in a series of flashbacks, his fellow worker is shown as a younger man, part of a returning army parading through a city to a ticker tape welcome. We see the images deteriorate from hard, cobble-stoned paving to feet wading through mud and slime, and soldiers retreating under an overwhelmingly dark cloud. The skulls and corpses on the battlefield, which show the other side of the victory parade, give way to twelve images of an individual amputee, finally seen alone in a ruined city. The fellow worker is another generic and particular exemplary figure, the migrant in flight from conflict, finding refuge in this cosmopolitan space. The conflation of refugee and 'economic migrant' offers a challenge to the rhetorical use of these distinctions in both popular discourse and legal procedures. The motivations for flight are demonstrably complex and infinitely variable.

Clocking off together, and collecting their wages, the two men walk into a huge surreal sunset, augury of a new level of consciousness, and the man is invited to a game of skittles with his fellow worker's ethnically diverse friends. Gradually, the new culture becomes part of his nature, through a series of appropriations of the strange objects and environment, and he is moving to the centre of his own being after displacement. Having established a measure of security and social integration, the man writes a letter home, folding the paper into an origami bird and adding some money. The bird, as has been said, is an emblem of his bond with his daughter and the letter a sign of confidence that he has achieved the necessary stage in his path to 'arrival' which will enable family reunion. The shared hospitality, the drink at the factory, the game of skittles, the wages and the letter are all features of a renewed well-being, the restoration of mental capital, a feeling of being at home with himself. These are all stages of internalisation of the strange, of familiarisation, beginning again. Yet another 'guide' shows him where the postbox is.

This moment of confidence is followed by a series of images depicting the changing of the seasons and the passing of time. The man's room is no longer bare but furnished with objects of his new belonging which are now endowed with meaning and usefulness. A letter in the form of an origami bird arrives. The man rushes through stormy, wet streets towards a Pegasus-like structure. Images, of his wife dismayed and his child uncertain, emerge from the vehicle and echo his earlier bewilderment in the face of the strange and incomprehensible. Now, he runs with ease towards them, hailing wife and child. The daughter's face is transfigured. The man, woman, child merge into one—father/husband/wife/mother/daughter/child—in the dwarfing, surreal landscape, as their footsteps are traced away from the vehicle moving inwards, mirroring the perennial migrant journey. Images of a new domesticity mirror the original home—the same, nine-grid structure of panels is used—but almost every panel now has a new inflection; only the hat on the peg and the family portrait are the same, and the latter has taken the place of the earlier suitcase. The man's hat is a recurring, and important, signifier, as Banerjee has shown, an image of continuity as well as being a signifier of a generational belonging, part of the homing instinct. The cup is now intact and the teapot complete but they are also now of a different design, auguries of the new. The changed images are metaphors of adaptation, negotiation, and compromise, signs of transformation, markers of arrival; the structures are familiar but they are converted into new forms, different belonging/s. They are not the objects the family has kept but are part of a recognisable continuity. The family meal is now in a comfortable room and the daughter's drawings, which proliferate all over the room, depict her new world, readily absorbing the different shapes and perspectives. Independent and competent, a figure of well-being, she has acclimatised rapidly and has the confidence to find her own way round the streets, accompanied by the pet 'familiar'. In a recall of her father's original experience, she meets a woman, with a similar—iconic—suitcase, trying to make sense of a map, and the child, arm outstretched, points her with certainty in the right direction for her migrant journey, enacting the guidance her father received earlier. This 'relay' effect is a key part of the migrant experience. The final page of the book—Artist's Note—has no traces of the earlier signs of transit, of temporariness, but instead carries a child's drawing of a substantial house/home with smoke coming from a bold, red chimney, emblem of habitation, a secure future, of well-being.

In all the texts in this chapter, each of the primary figures experiences a range of the objective and subjective factors which confront the migrant. Stories of migration are, as Shaun Tan has commented: "a constellation of intimate, human-sized aspirations and dilemmas; how to learn a phrase, where to catch a train, where to buy an item, whom to ask for help and, perhaps more importantly, how to *feel* about everything" (Tan 2010, emphasis in original). Problems of language, finding accommodation, seeking employment, and negotiating officialdom are common to almost all migration stories but it is the *affective* level which is often experienced as the most unsettling as the migrant shifts from her/his position of a relatively privileged gaze and familiar visual and verbal codes of the place of origin to being the object of scrutiny, lost in a regime of unknowable symbols.

In the Labyrinth

Where *The Arrival* draws upon an extensive use of sepia panels with dense backgrounds, and deploys varying degrees of timbre, tone and colour, *Petit Manuel* relies almost exclusively upon relatively simple pen and ink, line drawings, a fair amount of hatching and cross hatching, and sketchy backgrounds. Both protagonists undergo considerable discomfort but this is represented in very different genres of suffering—the epic journey and the picaresque satire.

As Linda Kinstler shows (2015), *Petit Manuel* draws upon George Mikes' 1946 classic novel *How To Be an Alien* in its parody of the tyranny of the asylum procedure in France (equally applicable to the United Kingdom) with its grotesque, two-dimensional, mechanical and puppet-like bureaucrats, simplistic and stereotypical, pitted against the *naif* asylum seeker, M, optimistically assuming that, having fled the vicious Iranian regime, his entry into civilised France would be easy. Mana Neyestani's graphic memoir, *An Iranian Metamorphosis*, which details his experiences in an Iranian jail, has been widely described as 'Kafka-esque' and this is no less true of his *Petit Manuel* which is a quasi-autobiographical account, in comic form, of the everyday experience of an asylum seeker in the French administration system.[3] Originally an editorial cartoonist for a number of reformist and oppositional publications in Iran, and subsequently a children's comic book writer, Neyestani was imprisoned by the Iranian regime for an allegedly offensive cartoon and eventually fled into exile. A combination of autofiction, reportage and newspaper cartoon, the book draws upon traditions of classical satire and features of the Theatre of the Absurd. The *Petit Manuel* comes with a replica of the author's "Titre de Sejour" (residence permit) issued in 2012 (and due to expire in 10 years) which underlines the quasi-autobiographical nature of the work. An illustration of a maze on the front cover anticipates the asylum journey to follow. In the foreword, Neyestani points out that the story of each refugee is unique and that his experience of the procedure was a lot simpler than the majority of cases, as his situation was documented and known, and he entered France at the invitation of the city of Paris. He had accommodation, regular work with dissident Iranian websites, and much less red tape to contend with than most asylum seekers, like the hapless M in this graphic novel. The French word for red tape is *paperasserie* which is much more expressive than the English equivalent—paperwork.

Although the book is only *quasi* autobiographical, Neyestani was aware of the many obstacles faced by asylum seekers who are ontologically devalued by long queues, humiliating situations in waiting areas, strict and arrogant attitudes, delayed decisions as a result of negligence, and erratic office opening hours. His protagonist is, therefore, specific and generic, both the author and an archetype based upon a number of interviews with his associates. This being the case, I have designated the protagonist as M. Portrayed as the little man, a Chaplinesque or Woody Allen figure, M is, with his small stature and oversized spectacles, shown as anxious, nervous and oppressed, the innocent abroad, without language or resources, trapped in an irrational and illogical system, the coils of a serpent. Condemned to navigate an absurd, dystopian procedure, he is forced into a series of repetitive actions in the face of circumstances described by the author in his Foreword. Like a character from vaudeville, M is both comic and almost tragic at times. Above all, he lacks any of the resources or skills necessary for well-being, his mental capital is severely depleted, as he journeys through an undecipherable system, bewildered and frustrated, subjected to the arbitrariness of the bureaucracy, a plaything of power, of semiotic instability. France, like other western powers, reproduces in its asylum system the discourses and forms of its former colonial authority—a narrative designed to enlist and license the 'other' on its own, incontestable terms. The satirical account of this system constitutes a decolonial critique, a questioning of the "coloniality of being": "This is in great part achieved through the idea of race, which suggests not only inferiority but also dispensability" (Maldonado-Torres 2007, 259).

Although, unlike *The Arrival*, *Petit Manuel* uses words and captions, the strength of the work lies in what I would describe as its graphic, visual theatre, the drawings expressing what language is not capable of putting into words. Each panel is an articulate metaphor of both an external situation (delay, obstruction) and an internal affect (frustration, depression). Were it not for the fact that what is represented in comic form is the very real experiences of countless asylum seekers, the work could be seen as akin to Edward Lear's nonsense verse, a ridiculous dystopia which makes its points through the graphic medium of 'extremity'.

This absurdity is located right at the start of the story as the diminutive M is contrasted with a number of militant, placard carrying protesters and bomb-throwers who are ignored by the regime while he is seen as more dangerous and is arrested simply for wielding a pen for "scribbling" (*griffoner*). This contrastive method highlighting incongruity is used frequently, for example when two facing pages (14 and 15) show, on the one hand, the open, smiling faces of the Paris of romance and myth, of tourist attractions and cafes (shown in montage) and, on the other, the Paris of shabby back streets where the Refugees office is based and where faceless men and women gather, a prostitute lingers, and a man urinates against a wall. Here, the only colour on the tourist page is the yellow of the sun which is contrasted with the yellow liquid trickling from the wall. The next page contrasts a physically upright figure, with a tourist visa or an invitation to a cultural event, with M bent over double entering the country illegally concealed by a bunch of sheep. These postural and gestural contrasts recur throughout and the visual caricature is far more expressive than the accompanying words. This use of an extreme visual example extrapolates from the general tendency of the asylum process nowadays to require convoluted deceptions, something discussed in the previous chapter.

M becomes an asylum seeker and is shown approaching a group of aimless refugees still queuing late at night. Half the full-page panel is taken up by a banner in colour signalling the office of the association "France Terre d'Asile" (FTA). The lateness of the hour is indicated by the bizarre image of a cockerel fast asleep on a pillow in the street, the absurdity of which would be impossible to convey verbally compared with the simple visual of a snoring cockerel (at the same time, this animal being the national symbol, it may be seen as hinting at the simple fact that 'citizens' are supposed to be asleep). M is also portrayed as a pawn in a game on a large chess board played by the over-sized, iconic faces of party-political opponents, the electoral success of one of which will determine his fate—either as a gentle kick up the backside (shown as red footprint) or a massive kick to his whole body (portrayed as a blue footmark). Caught in the large and confusing spider's web of the FTA, M seeks advice from refugees gathered in a local park. This place and its inhabitants, dispensers of street wisdom, act as a chorus throughout, a space of sanctuary and refuge from the nightmare of the asylum process. Here, he receives more guidance and direction than from official sources. Once inside the offices, M is diminished even more in scale—a giant hand is seen flicking him away to search for an address, a lodging place, before he can start the asylum application. As M makes a phone call, he dreams of an ideal house (shown in a bubble as a childlike drawing) but makes no progress. The list of charitable and philanthropic organisations he is given has been photocopied so often that it is falling to pieces. Again, a contrast is shown between the refugee taken on by 'do-gooders', almost as a trophy or pet (M is visually 'paired' with a small dog), and the person sent to accommodation miles from the city centre on the outskirts, the *banlieues*. The absurdity of this spatial remoteness, a commonplace of migrant experience is shown temporally when he encounters Asterix and Obelisk, comic figures from another timescale and era, with cult status as well-known cartoon characters in France. This exaggeration is one of the characteristics of satire used frequently in the text. Later, finding himself in a claustrophobic, prison-like lodging house (indicated by a resident who chalks up his 100 days waiting for his application to be processed), M, ironically, tells another resident how happy he is now that he is no longer in an Iranian prison. The verbal/visual incongruity carries the satire.

An alternative scenario is developed in which, as a journalist, M is welcomed with open arms at the House of Journalists (La Maison des Journalistes), given access to a library, a place to work and to live, but is thrown out after the maximum six-month period has expired. Moving to a large city, he visits the Préfecture where, in normal times, he takes a few seconds to reach the entrance but on days when it is open to refugees, the waiting time is up to three hours. Instead of space-time compression, the asylum seeker experiences space-time expansion. Once inside the office, the scale of the drawings emphasise the power relations, as large, bureaucratic figures bark orders at 'shrunken', intimidated refugees. Like many others, M does not speak French and his documents are incomplete. In an aside, one of the most absurd moments in the whole satire depicts, in flashback, a mother telling M as a small child defacing a picture of the Ayatollah, that if he is to become a refugee he should start learning French now—all good refugees should in their infancy anticipate that they will seek asylum and, as a consequence, learn French.

Once the asylum procedure starts, each refugee is shown with their identity number having replaced their face and M goes through the process of being photographed, contorting himself into various poses for the photo booth, only to be told that spectacles are prohibited. This is one of many false steps on the route of a nightmarish sequence during which his dossier is placed on hold for five months while his fingerprinting is completed, and he is immobilised in a zone of total indifference. His increasing anger and frustration are shown through exaggeration as eighteen fingerprints are reproduced. The park sages advise committing a minor infraction so that he can be fingerprinted by the more efficient police system and speed up his delay. His lack of identity is graphically indicated by an image of his severed head hovering over his body. To obtain the necessary papers, he has to start all over again, filling forms, being photographed and waiting endlessly. This waiting is represented hyperbolically by a skeleton in clothing holding a number. In a later panel, M's headstone is shown, suggesting that he has died before exhausting the asylum process. This, along with distortion (e.g. the inflated lawyer who is literally shown being pumped up), exaggeration and magnification of scale, is all part of the technique of incongruity and extremity to reveal dysfunction, designed to arouse indignation at the inhumane treatment of both the Candide-like figure of M in particular and asylum seekers in general, in order to inspire a re-modelling of the system.

The hardest part of the asylum process in many ways, apart from all the delays, is the demand placed on the applicant to produce a convincing narrative of dissidence and persecution, the interview feared by most asylum seekers. Again, advice is given by the park sages about body language—the caricatures of possible poses are reduced to absurdity—evidence of scars, and the problems with interpreters. Attention to minutiae and trivia is advised, irrespective of political militancy, but he is told to construct a narrative of continuing protest in France against the Iranian regime. Accordingly, M shows that he can 'out activist' any of his peers, on the streets and online. In other words, the asylum process is reduced to a *performance*, a series of gestures, timing, and poses which the graphic form is able to capture very effectively. Framing all of this is the experience of waiting—both duration and endurance—missing train stops, going to the wrong place, misreading acronyms, all aspects of insider decipherability, the kind of skills and knowledge characteristic of well-being, resources of mental capital. Duration is linked, again through hyperbole, to M's period of imprisonment in Iran, an ideal preparation for seeking asylum, especially the refusal and appeal process which is time-bound. Even when asylum is granted, another set of procedures follows, related to accommodation, employment, language learning, social security, health insurance and transport passes. Again, there is constant queuing and delays as he is bounced back and forth between different sectors of the bureaucracy—graphically enacted in the form of a table tennis match between two large, iconic figures with M as the ball. He has progressed from pawn in a chess game to a celluloid object. The relentless bureaucracy extends to every aspect of his life, including attempts to join the societies for artists or writers, neither of which accepts him as his designs have too many words for the one and he has no publications in French for the other. He is enmeshed in a latter-day Catch-22 situation as he tries to set up a bank account, claim benefits or secure permits to travel beyond France.

The penultimate page of the book is a sequence of nine different body positions and expressions as M fills in a visa form which requires him to indicate his nationality. He fills in "Iranian", then erases it and then "French" and erases that, until on the final page M is shown at a desk, asking where he belongs ("Où suis-je à ma place?") with his legs morphing into rootless trees. Erasure has been the potential condition of the asylum seeker throughout, forced to adapt to, and adopt, the style, norms and performative gestures of the host society that sees him as the dangerous 'other' it seeks to limit and control. Success, or otherwise, depends upon how far he can become a mimic man.

In the best traditions of satire, *Petit Manuel* works against its professed function as a short guide. A guide presupposes a set of procedures, is logically set out, with step-by-step instructions, coherently laid out and leading to clear outcomes. Its format would be sequential, proceeding from A to B, linear and progressive. Its purpose is, presumably, positive and enabling, a 'how to' manual. The book does outline the asylum process in France but through a series of Orwellian negations and disruptions, incoherent and inconsequential, designed to obfuscate rather than illuminate. Rather than proceeding from A to B, the applicant metaphorically zigzags through every letter of the alphabet to finally arrive at his destination—residence, though even this is conditional and provisional. So, the book is a mock Guide (as in mock-heroic), a 'how not to' rather than a 'how to' manual, step by mis-step, more akin to a game of snakes and ladders than an ordered procedure. Each stage of M's process carries the risk of being sent back to square one, a state of conditional probability or a sequence of random variables in a continuous, time-absorbing Markov chain. In this ironic sense, the structure of the book accurately reproduces its ostensible subject.

The book is organised principally around *time* in the form of waiting, delay, duration, repetition. Sequential in some respects but also reversible, it is a continuum confined and determined by spaces and spatial forms—queues, interiors, reception areas—staffed by iconic, monumentalised officials bearing the prevailing relations of power over the asylum applicant. The marks of time are also carried by hourglass timers, headstones, skeletons and scratches on a wall. There is an illusion of forward movement but this is countered by a sense of people marching on the spot, marking time in the military sense. The supplicant outsider is subject to measurement, quantification, categorisation and objectification as his subjectivity is exposed to random erasures by the hierarchy of authority. In an irregular labyrinth of time and space, the person is evacuated and the appearance of order gives way to its opposite. In *Petit Manuel*, the forces which inhibit and limit the migrant and his well-being are active, explicit and categorical, and time is inimical, convoluted and negative. In

The Arrival the forces which constrain are more the consequence of fears projected upon his circumstances and environment by the man himself, anxieties and doubts brought about by being a stranger, a figure lacking the decoding vocabulary needed to 'read' the new and the different. In a sense, his progress through the alien terrain is almost a learning partnership or a process of recognition, a gradual unfolding in which time could almost be seen as benign.

The European Middle Ages

The preceding section focused on M, a composite figure, and his struggles with the bureaucracy of the French asylum system. This section deals, on an entirely different scale, with thousands of refugees 'contained' in an area of Calais on what is, effectively, the United Kingdom/France border even though it is on French territory. These are people living in what came to be known as 'The Jungle', hoping to reach the UK and claim asylum. The inhuman conditions in the Jungle have been extensively documented (Godin et al. 2017; Agier 2008; Hicks and Mallet 2019; Refugee Rights Europe 2016; Refugee Info Bus 2018; Ticktin 2016). Muhammed, a refugee from Syria, summed up the 'camp' very aptly: "I was surprised that I saw no houses, no electricity, there were just shelters. I arrived knowing no-one, with no connections, to see a place that belonged to the European Middle Ages" (Godin et al. 2017, 113).

It is not the purpose of this section to add to the numerous accounts of the physical conditions of the Jungle or the extensive police violence, except in so far as these arise from the two texts I wish to examine as representations of the Calais experience: a graphic narrative, *Threads from the Refugee Crisis*, by Kate Evans (2017), and *Qu'ils Reposent en Révolte/Des Figures De Guerre* (May They Rest in Revolt/Figures of War) (2010), a documentary film by Sylvain George, which was the result of the three years he spent filming the life of 'illegal' migrants in Calais. Both texts confirm Michel Agier's description of the Calais experience, "The lives of the refugees in the camps are lives of waiting" (Agier 2011, 274).

CALAIS CONTEXT

Towards the end of the last century, particularly since the end of the Cold War and the Bosnian and Kosovan conflict, Calais became a centre for those rejected at the UK border and those waiting to cross into the UK. Michel Agier et al. (2018) have produced a detailed account of the area around Calais, from the Sangatte centre (1999–2002), the Le Touquet treaty of 2003 which facilitated border controls at all the sea ports on the Channel and North Sea, to the closing of squats and encampments, most notably the Jungle of Calais in 2009. They also cover the opening of the 'New Jungle' in April 2015 and its eventual destruction in October 2016. Estimated numbers in this period ranged from 5,000 to 10,000, and a town grew up with shops, restaurants and a street theatre which became the 'Good Chance' theatre. Various nationalities occupied different spaces on the site. Dwellings varied from tents, makeshift shelters to more substantial accommodation. Far from the image of the pitiful, hapless refugee, the French authorities expressed considerable anxiety in relation to what was perceived as the self-management drift of the shanty town. This will be explored further in the graphic narrative and the film, as will the presence and sometimes contested role of volunteers, and the public authorities. Tightened border controls also meant the proliferation of smugglers. As has been shown elsewhere in this book (see Chapters 1 and 5 especially) migrants are the embodiment of mobility, but also of immobility as evidenced by the waiting in Calais, in detention centres, in airports and at borders. In many of these spaces, migrants politicised themselves or, perhaps more accurately, articulated already existing political awareness based on their countries of origin, and on their experiences in the world of migration. Always, at different stages in their journey, the migrant faces a border: borders thus become an 'elsewhere', that is, at the same time close at hand *and* distant because difficult to access. Very close to these camps in this logic of exclusion are the dead (40,000 dead on the borders of Europe between 1993 and 2017) and the subject of death itself. This proximity/distance dialectic will be seen especially in Melilla/Morocco in my next chapter (Fig. 4.1).

Agier's study of the 'Jungle' was developed from an anthropological perspective. Complementing this approach was *Lande: The Calais 'Jungle' and Beyond* (2019) an in-depth study by Dan Hicks and Sarah Mallet, which takes a historical approach, tracing what they call "militarist colonialism" as one source of the legacies at Calais. Combined with this

Fig. 4.1 An aerial view of the Jungle Refugee camp, Calais (Reproduced by courtesy of Daniel Vernon/Alamy)

is an approach through contemporary archaeology which, linked with the exhibit, La Lande, at the Pitt Rivers Museum, Oxford, in 2019, raised "cross-disciplinary questions around the material, environmental, temporal and visual dimensions of La Lande as a place of dehumanising borderwork, governance and violence on the one hand, and on the other as a 'space of appearance and protest', and as a site for comparison" (Hicks and Mallet 2019, vi). The *Campe de La Lande* was, they explain, "the controversial and euphemistic name used by the French authorities for the site of the 'Jungle'" (ibid., 2). It was, in fact, as they say, a dehumanising space as will be seen in the graphic narrative and the film.

I shall be drawing upon both these books for my analysis of the graphic narrative, or 'comic', and film.

Framing the Dispossessed

Kate Evans is a graphic artist, with an activist background, who visited the 'Jungle' on three occasions over a period of 10 days altogether. She explained in interviews that the first 14-page comic was posted on her blog in October 2015. She said that the drawings were rough and ready at first, a collage style which suited the subject matter, but 12,000 copies were crowdfunded and sold for Refugees Support Group. Although there were many different nationalities in the camp, she decided to focus on those from Afghanistan and Iraq, given the British market, both recent conflicts there and the longer colonial history. She used different colour backgrounds in an initial comedic style as a way of marking off the different sections, and three different colour tones for the diverse ethnic faces. There is no attempt at consistency in the book as panel sizes vary, lettering is uneven and often fragmented, and linearity is set aside as figures are introduced in one sequence or panel and then, after an interval, occur again.

No claim is made for objectivity as she insists on this as subjective experience. She draws herself into her narrative in a not very flattering way, with unkempt, punkish hair, and she is present throughout as witness, storyteller, interviewer and listener, both chronicler and documentarist. She is not only there as an artist but also as an activist, bringing blankets and other supplies, helping with construction (somewhat ineptly) and in other practical ways. The participatory observation, often witty and self-deprecating, personalises what is 'objectively' a grim situation. She does not dwell on this but the Refugee Rights Report, "The Long Wait: Filling Data Gaps Relating to Refugees and Displaced People in the Calais Camp", provides a statistical analysis of the insanitary conditions, the absence of effective shelter from cold and rain, overcrowding and the lack of space, health and safety insecurities, fear and experience of police violence, local instances of physical and verbal racism, and human rights violations.

The role of the Report is to tabulate, record and tell, whereas that of the graphic narrative is to *show*, to visualise in such a way that the reader can see, decode and interpret the evidence in human form: embodied through gesture, expression, pose, posture and body language. In a sense, the still image, the drawing, is animated in conjunction, or partnership, with the reader. The drawings give an immersive effect, density and a physical presence. At the same time, however, the artist acknowledges her own white privilege and detachment, able to distance herself from the camp.

The structure of the book came about as a result of a visit the author made to a local museum. Evans discovered on a visit to the Calais museum the vital role of the lace industry in the history of the town. Accordingly, she uses lace imagery in the end papers and in the gutters as a visual metaphor throughout, starting with the barbed wire, three-metre high fences/walls which weave their way from the port to facilitate the movement of transport and exclude the refugees. In the larger, page-sized opening panel the steel wall is transformed into lacework being hand-crafted by women depicted in historical costume. This is echoed in the endpapers which, after the destruction of the camp, show two women, dressed in traditional weaver's costume, putting together a wall, the lace fabric of which is seen as issuing from a traditional, mechanised loom and being transformed into brick. The caption says, "The British government begins construction of a £2 million, four-metre high wall around the port of Calais" (Evans 2017, 176). The enclosure is a metre higher than on the opening end-page emphasising the increased containment of the refugees. The delicate nature of the lace and its historical fashion use in the context of class contradicts throughout the ramshackle and impoverished camp inhabitants. At the start, the type print font is dispersed across both sides of the wall—on the port side, the story is confined to the details of the fences, on the city side is the backstory of lacemaking in Calais, with the reader left to put together the sequence of the lettering. This is one of the main techniques of the book as the reader is required to organise a narrative from fragments, time-shifts and contrasting/conflicting styles. The next two pages consist of six panels, with the first an overview of the camp, partnered with a panel showing a Russian fighter jet, bombing opponents of the Assad regime. We are left to make the obvious connection. The page is used as the edge of the horizontal panels; elsewhere there are panels of uneven size, with each one on the right-hand page overlapping and breaking into/up adjacent frames. Lace images are used as gutters. The form of the narrative is critical because its disjunctions and interruptions are unsettling, never coming to rest with any one approach. This also helps to undermine any tendency towards a sentimental response but, instead, is in keeping with "humanitarian empathy".

There is a division between the 'voice-over' commentary, typewritten inside variously shaped speech-frames, with the dialogue hand-drawn in black lettering. The panels are fairly crowded with a range of figures sketched in crayon, giving a representative overview of characters in the camp public spaces by age and ethnicity, but exclusively male in the opening pages. Emphasis is on everyday life, with examples of construction going on and an introduction to scarcity, a recurring theme. Kate (as she styles herself) and her friend enter the camp and are warmly greeted.

The reader has to organise the narrative from the threads and fragments placed at several different angles in the panels. The overall effect is of simultaneous/overlapping activity.

The opening pages establish the pattern for the distribution of panel sizes, fragmented into horizontals, overlapping squares, with text abutting into panels, and the irregularly shaped lace gutters. On the page after the introduction, there are various action sequences, and panels which enact the distance between Kate and the refugees. In her holiday apartment, Kate sits disconsolately with corkscrew, French cheese and wine, while, in the same panel, refugee children appear to share the space but not the very large table. In the previous panel there is a telling juxtaposition between a malignant-looking caricature of Marine Le Pen, architect of much of French anti-immigrant attitudes, addressing a local crowd as "You brave resistance fighters", battling the Muslim invasion, and the white, privileged volunteer (Kate) unlocking her apartment door, secure against the 'invaders'. Earlier, while distributing tools and equipment, she has had to refuse a padlock to an African migrant—again, emphasising the separation between refugee and volunteer. Later, a panel matching the Le Pen one shows Theresa May, then UK Home Secretary, in equally malevolent pose, the politician who coined the phrase 'hostile environment' as a way of describing the government's attitude to immigrants. Panels often cross-refer in this way.

The world separating the refugee from the volunteers is shown in sharp contrast between a full page in which a number of refugees are shown attempting to take down the fences at the Channel Tunnel which is shown by their pushing what looks like a lace-friezed roll of material, a visual 'pun'. At the tunnel, the men are depicted as stick-like figures, then more distinctively as they are beaten by police. The different colouring of the panels (browns, blacks and greys) makes it difficult to work out the sequence, but this is the point. There are no bright colours, and the refugees and the volunteers are both drawn in black and white, but whereas the volunteers are sketched sharply, the refugees are seen as shadows in the fog, begging lorries to stop. As the 'voice-over' informs us the asylum-processing office in Calais closed in 2002, so the only route to England is clandestine. Again, the lettering is varied, some set in small frames, others variously hand-drawn. The refugees are not only indistinct but voiceless, with all speech the province of the volunteers and a statement issuing from the Eurotunnel speaker system. The proximity of the volunteers, listening on the car radio to the statement, implicates them with the authorities. The next page focuses on the logistics of the aid process, the lorry, the forklift, the sorting of the supplies by the volunteers. The scene is chaotic but, in contrast, the previous page is drawn in very bright primary colours.

These early pages are designed to establish the basic framework/structure of the narrative, panelling, colour, lettering, and contrast between the limits of the refugee, encamped and policed, and the volunteers, vitally necessary but also, in Kate's case, aware of all kinds of contradiction. The narrative momentum thereafter is based on a wide range of events, encounters and characters in an interactive narrative. As she arrived initially at the camp as a volunteer, rather than as a professional cartoonist, Kate did not gain the consent of people she interviewed to use names or backgrounds, hence the characters and identities portrayed are composite figures, names are generic and stories are indicative, with incidents sometimes specific, sometimes symptomatic. Above all, as in so many of the cases cited in this book, all the refugees experience the sense of temporariness.

The opening pages are prefatory in the sense that they set up the rhythm of the encoding strategies for what is to follow, much of which graphically enacts the condition of the camp as detailed in the Refugee Rights Report (2016). I shall now look at a selection of indicative representations as a way of showing how the artist responds, metaphorically, to the ethical question posed by Lynne Huffer: "How can the other reappear at the site of her inscriptional effacement?" (Huffer 2001, 4). How is the spatial grammar/syntax of comics deployed in what Hillary Chute calls the form of a counter-inscription? How does she overcome the "risk of representation"?

The constant variation in panel size and shape, the 'haphazard' lettering, the refusal of symmetry in design are all linked to questions of narrative closure and the ethics of listening as a political practice. What *Threads* does is work against the idea that the narrator can envision herself as 'other' and make no attempt to conceal differences in power. If anything, the book over-stresses this 'distance'. What it does is work with the concept of "asymmetrical reciprocity", a dialogical exchange, an active listening to, and 'figuring of' the 'other', with the artist as interpreter, at times leaving little space for the voice or viewpoint of the refugee. At such times, she over-represents herself as 'knower', although she shares insights into the reasons why so many of the refugees have fled their countries—rape, persecution and other forms of violence.

As far as the authorities are concerned, the refugees in the encampment are figures of excess, left over and surplus to the nation-citizen. As Joseph Pugliese has argued, the logic of the camp causes "refugees to fall back on the one resource left to them in the midst of the violence of indefinite incarceration: their bodies. Even as the body is bounded and imprisoned, it can exercise a power that will elude the mechanisms of repression and the desire for absolute control" (Pugliese 2002, 12). This embodiment is a feature of the examples I have selected to examine, as it also testifies to the resilience and endurance shown in constructing dwellings, however insecure and rudimentary.

The body is, of course, also the site of violence and one incident represents this graphically in a way that words alone would not be able to do. It is a seven-panel sequence in which a pregnant woman is attacked by the police. It starts with the police in full riot gear, looking like stormtroopers from a Marvel comic, storming into the woman's home and trashing it. The woman is shown cowering and trying to protect her three small children, while begging the police not to photograph them as once photographed or registered, the UK refuses entry or asylum claim. Four panels trace the action in which the woman is slapped about the face and body by one of the militarised police. In the process her blouse is torn open and her distended, pregnant stomach is exposed, while two of the children crouch down beside her, hands clasped over their heads in fear. Apart from the physical scale which shows the disparity between the man and the woman, the blackness of the man's large, gloved hands is emphasised and set against the bright colours of the woman's clothing and that of her children as they are shown in full on each panel while only the police officer's screened helmet and violent arms are shown. Coloniality is gendered in this way, the man simply an instrument of the power of the state, without any identifiable features, robotic and unquestioning of his role.

Young's theory of "asymmetrical reciprocity" works with the idea that "A condition of our communication is that we acknowledge the difference, interval, that others drag behind them ... shadows and histories, scars and traces, that do not become present in our communication" (Young 1997, 53). The formal design of the book seeks to enact this, with the gutters, the intervals, gesturing towards these shadows and traces. The graphic form makes comics a medium of visibility, of presences, but *Threads* is also very much a text of absences—unaccompanied children, husbands from wives, wives from husbands and parents from their children. As Khosravi says at one point: "Exilic life is the constant presence of the absent" (Khosravi 2011, 74). These absences are visualised through expressions, gestures, silences and empty spaces. From the perspective of the reader, our ability to see and hear the 'other' is part of our process of reading and decoding. Treating the body of the refugee as excess, outwith the nation-state, is a sign of effacement. The function of the artist-activist is to fill "the empty inscriptional space of the other" who has been erased: "the notion of a haunting absence-as-presence that Levinas calls the question of the other" (Huffer 2001, 4). Huffer, in this context, suggests a provisional definition of ethics as "the readable site of an inscriptional relation to an other". The challenge for the artist is to render the unthinkable condition of the camp as a 'readable site' against rhetorical closures or narrative coherences, and through performative ruptures and fragmentations. In this way, the 'other' is no longer a given, a pre-narrative subject but becomes a subject through the process of asymmetrical reciprocity. So, the narrator/artist is both inside and outside the frame.

As I have said, contextualisation is part of the memoir/diary; on one page there is a panel which draws a range of men walking around the litter-strewn camp, with Kate wondering what the site would be like with 95 percent women not 95 percent men. As has been noted, the men tend to be drawn in an infantilised way, whereas the women are almost always shown in a caring or parenting role (Manea and Precup 2020, 2). The men are shown without role or function, perhaps this reflects a cultural gender deficit. Manea and Precup see this visual representation of childlikeness as a means of presenting them as less threatening to Western audiences but, on the contrary, it could be a reflection of their emasculation and infantilisation by the asylum process, as was discussed in the previous chapter. There is also a sequence shown where a group of men share delight in using colouring pencils which could be seen as a way of portraying them in a new, progressive light, freed from the burden of 'masculinity' and its performances.

Below the speculation about what a camp with 95 percent women would look like, a large, three-quarter-page panel counters the above reflections about childlikeness with a diptych divided by a flowing text which separates young men conscripted into weaponry from a parallel scene with the same men, shown now in their full bodies, with blood-stained shirts in postures of death or agonies of dying. This shows graphically the circumstances of their lack of choice—conscription or extermination. The young men are pictured meeting an ageing Afghan man, his wounds taped up with an old plastic bag, fearful, like so many others, of giving his name to the medical authorities because his asylum claim would be compromised under the Dublin Convention. This moment is juxtaposed with a wider context, a scene, coloured in dark browns and blacks, of US forces repeatedly bombing the MSF hospital in Kunduz, Afghanistan. No comment is made but the panel is left as a 'news' item.

The contrast between conditions of deprivation and the level of improvisation and ingenuity is featured throughout, as is the frequent instances of hospitality and food sharing, the animated young children and the unsettled and 'rebellious' teenagers.

A whole white page interrupts the narrative sequence with a drawing of a radio in black and white announcing the death of a migrant hit by a train. This is just one instance among many: "It could have been any one of them". There is no melodrama, simple reportage.

This is followed by one of many excerpts from Kate's iPhone presented through the image of a mobile phone placed horizontally on a deep brown lacework background, with a typed message (tweet) on the screen bearing a right-wing criticism of her cartoon blog. A similar format of lace, phone and tweet is on the following page, of one of her critics acknowledging the problems in the world, but citing the lack of resources in England, and making accusations of fake humanitarianism: this is part of the commonsense lexicon of anti-immigration, and milder than some of the far-right trolling she also presents, either from tweets received directly on her own phone or on others gathered elsewhere online. Without explicitly addressing this, on the facing page there is an example of self-critique as she is shown, in a monitoring role—refusing entry to a clothing tent to a man—as patronising and insensitive.

One of the mobile tweets mentions that the men are safe in Calais and should apply for asylum there. The response to this is a reported incident: "Midnight. 21st January 2016. Three Syrian refugees are walking through the suburbs of Calais". They are cornered by six men with guns and iron bars. There are a few words only, as the attack is conveyed by scale, size and positioning, the dark blue clothing of the masked men, shown in various poses of animation, contrasted with the terrified eyes of the Syrians, their bodies overwhelmed. The power of the blows is registered by swinging arms and legs, attacking heads, genitals and bodies. The scarlet blood is picked out against the blacks and browns of the scene. The 'bulging' of the lace gutters and the bleeding of the panel visually enacts the disturbance. It is an emblematic event—one of more than fifty in the past year, we are told. The attackers were possibly police with their ID emblems removed.

Informal games and more formal art workshops constitute part of the camp's infrastructure of activity and one two-page spread shows Kate's felt-tip and crayon sketches copied from the men's efforts.

Responding to a call for action, Kate and a friend return to Calais on a second visit to help with supplies and moving 2,000 people from the edge of the camp. The camp has been transformed by caravans and houses, and water points, rubbish collections, a warehouse and workshop space for prefabricated houses, and a '3-star hotel', but with a lot more restriction in terms of dwelling spaces.

Continuing the practice of self-critique, Kate attempts to distance herself from 'voluntourism' and closes in on a particular story—that of Hoshyar, a composite story but with sufficient specificity to register a not untypical situation. He has been at Calais for 120 nights and becomes a recurring link in the narrative. Kate and her husband are introduced to Hoshyar by a midwife friend, Jet. Their exchange takes place over several pages. His experience is indicative—cramped in an eight-foot shack with his friend, Alaz, with just a broken sliver of shaving mirror each and an eighteen-inch kitchen. With characteristic hospitality he cooks for them, and they exchange family photographs taken on their mobile phones, his spacious home in Iraq contrasting with the limited space in the camp: the number of small and uneven panels suggests the sense of enclosure: "washing dishes with baby wipes".

The last few panels of the sequence feature Hoshyar on his own against a dull brown interior, with his few possessions drained of colour, even the red of the kettle is muted. Despite this, and aware of the politics of the situation, he is sure that the politicians will come up with a solution. As he speaks with enthusiasm, his guests sit despondently and express their misgivings and the attitudes towards refugees. Except that they don't, as their thoughts are framed in the 'commentary' slots, and not expressed in the in-frame, ink-dialogue lettering: "That's what we don't say". Hoshyar's story is one of the few close-ups in the book. After six months, his chances of joining his uncle in Croydon are diminishing. He also faces eviction, his dwelling is to be demolished, and there are very few places left in the shipping containers in the camp.

After seeing so much negativity and inspired by Hoshyar's optimism, we see Kate, in full colour, seated in her studio with pencil in mouth, with a small sheet of white paper with the words 'fairy tale' printed on it. What follows is a hypothetical scenario in which she drives Hoshyar to the ferry port, where he moves through passport control with ease, enjoys a full meal on board the ferry, watches the cliffs of Dover from the deck, 'sails' through UK passport controls and is driven to his uncle's house in Croydon. The next panel reverses this narrative, shows Kate and Hoshyar being arrested, with Kate facing a prison sentence for people trafficking, and her children being taken away by their grandmother after a prison visit. The next full-page panel mirrors the earlier one in her studio, except that instead of bright colour, there is a range of browns, an empty office chair and a blank drawing board. This scenario is the more likely outcome.

Kate and her friends move on to the wet, muddy camp of Dunkirk where police confiscate their blankets and sleeping bags as there was an embargo on dry bedding. The camp is comprised of tents only, no wooden structures. In the camp they meet up with the little girl, Evser, that Kate had played ball with for an hour at Calais, now living in a mouldy pit with her mother, her earlier animation diminished. The old Afghan man also turns up again.

They return to Calais and meet up with Hoshyar. One of the 'restaurants' shows a film with people smugglers getting beaten up. That page is light and many-coloured. By contrast, the opposite page is entitled "Let's Talk about People Smugglers" and is sepia-tinted, drained of people and colour, with only a single image—a tap and an overflowing pedestal basin—but a lot of text, horizontal, vertical, and some morphed from the overflowing water drops. The eye has to move rapidly in response to a series of fragmented text-straps discoursing on the background to the refugees' stories, warfare and conflict, Daesh and the Taliban, the market in people smuggling, and the 'securitisation' of borders at enormous cost. The next page is brightly lit and features a man, met earlier, with his family waiting to join his brother in Wolverhampton. There is also a profile of a composite people smuggler. Hoshyar returns to the frame, echoing the words of the earlier panel, he and his friend robbed by smugglers demanding £5,000. Smugglers have also been involved in shooting in the camp.

In February 2016, Kate and her husband return as volunteers. Kate has brought her paint brushes and inks and she plans to draw portraits. This proves very popular, particularly with the young men as they are given positive images of themselves. This, however, is short-lived as, following a tweet saying "We need to purge this scum with fire theres no other choice" (the venom and the illiteracy fairly typical of this kind of trolling), the next few panels show the burning down of the migrants' dwellings, with only the structures created by the European volunteers left intact; a distinction which characterises the coloniality of power discussed earlier. Riot police were sent in to evict the migrants. Kate is not present but we see her and her daughter at breakfast watching the scenes of devastation on television. She continues watching the footage as she takes her daughter to school and the teargas-filled streets of the camp are in sharp contrast with the relaxed parents and children at the school. A final image on the phone is of an adult and child emerging on the street, their profile blackened. In response to the destruction, some of the men sew their lips together in protest, their lives destroyed yet again, not just their shelters but also their minds.

With the eviction over, a decision is taken to keep the art space open and use up all the materials. Rows of paper cut-out figures are hung on lengths of red tape between power lines, images of the emptied lives of the camp residents. It is recorded that 129 lone children disappeared from the camp during the evictions, with no knowledge of what happened to them afterwards. The dispassionate tone, as so often in the narrative, underlines the pathos of the camp without sensationalising it.

The final panels offer some images of hope and optimism with children, including the now-lively again Evser playing excitedly on the areas of the new and well-equipped Dunkirk camp, and on the next two pages men are shown playing an improvised game of cricket on the bulldozed flatlands of the Calais camp, the ruins of their former homes.

The penultimate two panels, entitled 'Hope', are given over entirely to print with type print font lettering, as in newsprint, spaced out horizontally across the page and outlining the economic argument for allowing refugees into the UK, in response to a mobile message which, in a representative way, speaks of the lack of resources available for refugees. The problem with the economic argument is that it appeals to rationality, for example: "mathematical modelling shows that removing all national barriers to migration would *double* global GDP" (Clemens and Pritchett 2016, 174) whereas the tabloid and right-wing opposition to immigration is based upon a delusional nationalism and an imperial nostalgia. On the next page, in response to a familiar comment about the effects of austerity (while not calling it that), shortages, waiting lists and 'looking after our own', the rational argument which follows outlines how resources are available for bombing raids, and for subsidising the arms industry, and shows how inequality weakens democracy and fuels the far-right. An attempt is made to break the austerity/immigration link. As in the earlier argument, sources are cited as part of what, from a liberal perspective, would be seen as a logical argument. This conclusion renders in discursive form what had been shown graphically, but with little commentary, in the earlier pages. In this respect, like many of the other texts examined in this book, it is a work of advocacy. This point is confirmed by a quotation from the former Shadow Chancellor, John McDonnell: "Inevitably in this century we will have open borders … the movement of peoples across the globe will mean that borders are … going to become irrelevant" (cited in Clemens and Pritchett 2016, 175). This was said at the beginning of 2016 but, as is now known, the premise of that prediction, perhaps seen as a threat by some, was overwhelmingly rejected in the December 2019 General Election in the UK.

The next section also deals with Calais but in the form of a documentary film which, instead of the distillations and condensations of the graphic narratives, clearly situates individual figures in a context of displacement and powerlessness but also with signs of resourcefulness and with articulate voices.

In the Grey Zones

In Shahram Khosravi's *'Illegal' Traveller: An Auto-Ethnography of Borders,* he says that "One aspect of migrant illegality is that one's life is unsettled, unpredictable and erratic. Migrant illegality means abrupt and dramatic interruptions in one's life, interruptions such as detention, deportation or simply sudden opportunities to move" (Khosravi 2011, 69). Later, in the same chapter, he makes a comment which applies almost to every figure covered in this book: "The border exposes me to a gaze that does not *see* me as an individual but *reads* me as a type" (ibid., 76; italics in original). Not just a type but also a *racialised* type. I am raising these points by way of a prelude to a discussion of a film which inverts that border gaze and sees the 'illegal' migrant, not as a type, but in terms of a unique singularity. *May They Rest in Revolt* (2010), directed by Sylvain George, is sub-titled "Figures of War" because the men which are at the centre of the film are, in many cases, in flight from war but also as 'illegals' they are engaged in a constant war with the state authorities—the omnipresent police vans symbolise this. George spent three years filming the lives of male migrants in Calais, living on the margins of the city and at the edges of the camp. In another context, the journalist and photographer, Caroline Gregory, said something which could describe George's approach to film: "This kind of visual activism, documenting ordinary life in an extraordinary landscape, could only be achieved by long-term immersion …The media response, much like the academic field of Refugee Studies, is overdetermined by 'emergency', but only by taking our time and looking beyond the urgency can we really understand La Lande in all its contradictions" (Hicks and Mallet 2019, ix). I would add that the men in the film somehow manage to turn their extraordinary life into a semblance of the quotidian. The director worked over three years on filming the camp.

The opening image of the film is of Mount Sinai, designed to announce the trope of exodus which is the theme of the film, taking it out of its immediate context in contemporary France and linking it to continuing histories of flight from oppression. It is a fragmentary composition, filmed in black and white and in contrasting styles—long takes, short, speeded-up frames, observing at a distance or from close up. The design of the film does not follow any particular logic but places its emphasis on affect, producing an *inline* of the lives of men caught between borders. The director is concerned with the ethics of production and makes sure that he secures the consent of anyone filmed. The focus throughout is on faces and voices, on presence.[4] George speaks of film as a dialectical tool, not as something which is always exterior and synonymous with oppression and domination. He stresses the necessity of working with the interior of lives, hence the frequent close-ups, the spaces left for people to speak and interact, with the camera as unobtrusive as possible. In the text accompanying the DVD he speaks of filming in 'bursts'—bursts of voices, bursts of laughter, bursts of anger. Calais is seen as a front line, as if of a war. The film does not impose a message on the viewer but, instead, leaves its fragments, its snippets of words, images and memories to compose the narrative. Images are not predetermined but, on the contrary, work within a field of immanence, subjective and restless, unsettled and unsettling.

The men are all from North Africa, the Middle East and sub-Saharan Africa, some, having already been deported, making multiple attempts to claim asylum, and in the process travelling across numerous borders and many countries. By focusing on these men, the director bears witness to the reasons why people become 'illegal' migrants and to the policies deployed by modern states. These states, as evidenced in other chapters in the book, have created myriad grey zones where the exception and the rule have become indistinct from one another.

When asked why he chose to shoot in black and white, George says, "Because this allows me to work and question the concepts of document, archive, preservation. Because doing so establishes a historical distance from displayed events that are in keeping with what's very important, what's indeed very red hot news. Black and white also conjures up an aesthetic and poetic dimension fully relevant to the film" (*Diagonal Thoughts* 2011, n.p.). Perhaps another one of the reasons he chose to film in black and white was to point up the spaces which become grey zones, spaces of indeterminacy. Another reason could be that images can be made 'blacker' or 'whiter' for emphasis, as are shots of skin or teeth, for example: "For instance, you'll get some overexposed sequences where whites are burnt out and blacks very deep" (ibid.). This helps to produce what George calls singular space-times which explode clock-time, 'temporal bombs'. At various intervals, a clock can be heard striking but, as the film concentrates on the daily life of the men, this time is seen to be irrelevant as, apart from sleep, they follow no time-based routine but live in discontinuity and disruption. They are surrounded by the sight and amplified sounds of transportation—trains, lorries, ferries, cruise liners—all of which, except in clandestine and opportunistic ways, are denied to them. One man is shown making repeated attempts to gain access to a passing lorry heading for the port, and finally succeeds. Other men are seen balancing precariously on railroad tracks as they walk a path they will never travel and attempt to surmount fences and barriers erected to prevent their movement, reminders of their exclusion.

The immobility, or aimless wandering of the men, is contrasted with local people or tourists moving purposefully. The wandering is not entirely aimless as they have to maintain constant vigilance to escape police raids; frequent arrests are shown. Running is seen as purposeful, but it is running from and never running towards a specific target; they are the hunted of the modern world. In contrast to the police are the food supplies and the treatment of injuries offered by local volunteers, defying the orders of the state. Later in the film, with the focus on the destruction of the Calais camp and the police brutality, a similar volunteer presence opposed to deportations and to borders is shown in support of the migrants.

The men are shown in a range of various daily situations, washing in the river, shaving, queuing for food or blankets, just sitting by the roadside or hiding from the police in woodland. The washing and the shaving are significant because they indicate a refusal by the men to accept their ascription as waste, or surplus, to yield to the conditions of indigence forced upon them. There is an emphasis on time passing and on images of the incoming tide, the changing seasons, on the poetic and not just the immiseration of the men who are described at one point by one of them as living and not living, existing and not existing, an in-between life. This is said as the camera pans round a row of gravestones. Earlier, in contrast with this, a small group of young Ethiopian men are filmed singing and at prayer, their faces exuding a certain joy despite their circumstances.

Apart from the long sequences where two men, one from Ghana and one from Nigeria, are granted space on camera to articulate their specific situations and, in the process, point to some of the reasons why people are forced to leave their countries, generally the men are simply observed or interacted with. Reasons for leaving include the need to provide for families, to fund education, to pay rent often in circumstances of extreme deprivation, which, apart from internecine strife, motivate the oldest young person in the family to migrate in order to send remittances back to sustain the family. The man from Ghana had already been deported back to his country but, after a circuitous journey, is making a second attempt to reach the UK. The other man, apart from needing to support his family, is hoping to return to Nigeria and resume his studies. These lengthy cameos illustrate not just the plight of two individuals but, as was argued at the end of *Threads*, the waste of human resources, of people who could work and contribute to society. These are not just generic migrants given thirty seconds on camera but are men who are enabled to share their stories at length.

The most 'iconic' sequence in the film is where a group of men are shown lighting a fire in order to heat screws to remove skin from their fingers so that their fingerprints cannot be used against them at any application for asylum. Close-ups are also shown of razors being used to scrape the skin from fingers. This removal of fingerprint traces, also shown in *On the Bride's Side*, is with reference to the Dublin regulation (now in its third revision) which requires refugees to apply for asylum in the country where they first 'illegally' entered EU territory—so-called Dubliners (see Picozza 2017). Several close-ups are shown of the scarred fingers which resemble the branding of cattle as well as tribal scarification but, here, in an entirely negative context because all the men are in flight from the so-called competent state where their fingerprints had been taken for the assessment of an asylum claim. The black and white close-ups emphasise the striations and would have been far less effective in colour. George's work edges towards the allegorical and, in a sense, this erasure of fingerprints is a way of these particular men, but also of all others in similar circumstances, enacting a form of refusal, saying to the 'coloniality of power', fingerprints are your indices of identity, the mark of the criminal, but not ours. The men are not seen as victims but as people capable of organising their lives, despite their circumstances.

The lengthy concluding scenes focus on the destruction of the camp, with George's camera a meditative presence among what has become a media circus. The scenes are allowed to speak for themselves as the, at times, unstable camera captures the chaos of bulldozers, police brutality, exaggerated high-pitched sounds, the noise, resistance and slogans of protesters—migrant and European voices joined together—with bureaucrats, politicians and government officials jostled as they try to justify the unjustifiable. The almost noiseless intervals point up the devastation more sharply.

No attempt is made to produce an effect of realism as the film is quite deliberately an intervention, politically radical and cinematically poetic, evident in its fractured editing, the frequent fades and dissolves, and its discontinuities pointing up the artifice and mediation of the filmic process. The director is interested in a cinema which interrogates the plastic resources (*les ressources plastique*) of the medium, of image, sound and colour, a heretical, refractory cinema, made up of spaces and interstices, above all a cinema which challenges the existing grammar of the documentary film. George says about his film that "Politically speaking, it is about standing up, contesting these grey zones, these spaces or cracks like Calais standing somewhere between the exception and the rule, beyond the scope of law, where law is suspended, where individuals are deprived, stripped of their most fundamental rights" (George 2016).

This is a cinema of witness, of activism and advocacy, of testimony and of deliberate disorientation, designed to unsettle preconceptions about the overlooked, *those who do not count*. He also wants the film to do more than just document a specific, or local, set of circumstances, so he used voice-over (infrequently) "not so much to bring extra factual info but rather to generate distance, to play on other layers of temporalities, to open up the times and film to anything that may go through it ..."

(ibid.). He is not attempting to do something as banal as to make the film 'universal' but to point to something beyond its immediate time and space, other temporalities, so that, for example, during the final credits, there is what George calls some "singing from the Outside" in the form of Archie Shepp humming "Strange Fruit" recorded by the actual camera used in filming, the haunting song which recalls the lynching of black men in another era, other racialised men treated as less than human in the Global North.

The phrase 'those who do not count' is taken from the work of Jacques Rancière. The politics of George's films are close to some of the theoretical positions taken by Rancière who says, at one point, "This is the most profound politics of Sylvain George's films: not only in showing the capacity of 'the wretched of the earth, to live and think in accordance with the violence they are subjected to, but also in making them antecedently inhabit this world that is refused to them, the world where everyone has access to everything including the superfluent and the artificial" (Rancière quoted in George 2016). The removal of the fingerprints by the men is their refusal of the violence they are subjected to and a claim to inhabit the world from which they are excluded or, rather, to which they are not allowed to belong.

George's film counts that which cannot be counted, those who, in Rancière's words, have no part. The film works against the prescriptions of the dominant, it turns representation (of the other) into presentation *by* the other, a mode of subjectivation which makes the act of filming a matter of reciprocity and equality, along lines similar to *On the Bride's Side*. Refusing the consensual order, George resists it by, using a concept from Rancière, 'staging dissensus'. This is the claim just referred to, by those who have no part in a social order—the *sans-papiers*, for example, or the so-called illegal—but assert their right to participate in that order. By washing in the river, shaving and inhabiting the spaces of Calais, the men are appropriating these spaces as part of their 'claim' to be recognised. The camera acts in accordance, colludes, with this appropriation giving the men face, voice, name and presence—singularity is the word used earlier. In Rancière's words, "their actions are manifestations of a dissensus; that is, the making contentious of the givens of a particular situation" (Rancière 2000, 124). To comply with the 'givens', the men would have to retrace their journey back to their place of origin, consent to the description of them as 'illegals'. Alternatively, what George's film produces is "certain subjects that do not count [who] create a common polemical scene where they put into contention the objective status of what is 'given' and impose an examination and discussion of those things that were not 'visible', that were not accounted for previously" (ibid.).

All of the texts discussed in this chapter, to a greater or lesser extent, and deploying a range of different techniques, make present things that were not 'visible', raising questions about the objective status of the hegemonic narrative, whatever shape it might take and challenging the representational clichés of clandestine migration. In the next chapter, an outline is presented of some of the characteristics of the far-right response in Europe to the claims made by asylum seekers, African in this case, to inhabit a world that is increasingly refused to them, followed by an analysis of texts which put the 'givens' of the European narrative on immigration into contention.

Notes

1. There is a considerable amount of controversy among both practitioners and academic theorists about what to call these image-text productions. "Graphic novel" is used but is also disliked by many practitioners as a publishing and marketing tool. Hillary Chute, one of the leading theorists of the genre, uses "comics" as a singular noun, while she and others find the term "graphic narrative" acceptable (Chute 2017, 2, 18, 19). Not being an expert in this field, I have opted to use the latter term.
2. This phrase is taken from an interview with Shaun Tan by Harriet Earle (Earle 2016, 395).
3. I should like to thank Ghazal Mosadeq for assistance with the translation of the Neyestani text and Hicham Yezza for help with this text and the Sylvain George film.
4. There is an illuminating article on the 'face' in George's films by Jiewon Baek (2016).

References

Agier, Michel. 2008. *Managing the Undesirables: Refugee Camps and Humanitarian Government*. Cambridge, UK: Polity Press.

Agier, Michel. 2011. *On the Margins of the World: The Refugee Experience Today*. Cambridge: Polity Press.

Agier, Michel, et al. 2018. *The Jungle: Calais's Camps and Migrants*. Cambridge, UK: Polity Press.

Baek, Jiewon. 2016. "Turning Toward the Other: The Face of Humans, the Face of Things and the Face of Language in the Documentaries of Sylvain George." *Studies in French Cinema* 16 (1): 61–77. https://doi.org/10.1080/14715880.2016.1138719.

Banerjee, B. 2016. "Creating a 'Well-Fitted Habitus.' Material Culture, Homemaking and Diasporic Belonging in Shaun Tan's *The Arrival*." *Journal of Graphic Novels and Comics* 7 (1): 53–69.

Chute, Hillary. 2017. *Why Comics? From Underground to Everywhere*. New York: Harper Perennial.

Clemens, Michael, and Lant Pritchett. 2016. "The New Economic Case for Migration Restrictions." Working Papers 423, Center for Global Development.

Diagonal Thoughts. 2011. *Artist in Focus: Sylvain George in the Context of the Courtisane Festival*. www.diagonalthoughts.com

Earle, Harriet. 2016. "Strange Migrations: An Essay/Interview with Shaun Tan." *Journal of Postcolonial Writing* 52 (4): 385–98. http://shura.shu.ac.uk/information.html.

Ek, R. 2006. "Giorgio Agamben and the Spatiality of the Camp: An Introduction." *Geografiska Annaler* 88 (4): 363–86.

Evans, Kate. 2017. *Threads from the Refugee Crisis*. London: Verson.

Foster, Michelle. 2012. *International Refugee Law and Socio-Economic Rights: Refuge from Deprivation*. Cambridge: Cambridge University Press. Excerpt retrieved April 17, 2016. http://assets.cambridge.org/97805218/70177/excerpt/9780521870177_excerpt.htm.

George, Sylvain. 2010. *Qu'ils Repose en Révolte/Des Figures de Guerre (May They Rest in Revolt/Figures of War)*. Directed by Sylvain George. Paris: PODNOIR.

George, Sylvain. 2016. "Dissent." *Auguste Orts*. www.augusteorts.be/discourse/33/DISSENT-Sylvain-George.

Godin, Marie, Katrine Møller Hansen, Aura Lounasmaa, Corinne Squire, and Zaman Tahir, eds. 2017. *Voices from the Jungle: Stories from the Calais Refugee Camp*. London: Pluto Press.

Hicks, Dan, and Sarah Mallet. 2019. *Lande: The Calais 'Jungle' and Beyond*. Bristol: Bristol University Press.

Huffer, Lynne. 2001. "'There Is No Gomorrah': Narrative Ethics in Feminist and Queer Theory." *Differences: A Journal of Feminist Cultural Studies* 12 (3): 1–32.

Khosravi, Shamsan. 2011 [2010]. *'Illegal' Traveller: An Auto-Ethnography of Borders*. Basingstoke: Palgrave Macmillan.

Kinstler, L. 2015. "An Iranian Graphic Novelist Updates a Classic WW2 Guide for Migrants." *Quartz*, June 23. http://qz.com/435129/an-iranian-graphic-novelist-updates-a-classic-wwii-guide-for-migrants/.

Maldonado-Torres, N. 2007. "On the Coloniality of Being." *Cultural Studies* 21 (2): 240–47.

Manea, Dragos, and Mihaela Precup,. 2020. "Infantilising the Refugee: On the Mobilising of Empathy in Kate Evans' *Threads from the Refugee Crisis.*" *a/b: Auto/biography Studies* 35 (2). https://doi.org/10.1080/08989575.2020.1738078.

Nail, T. 2005. *The Figure of the Migrant*. Stanford, CA: Stanford University Press.

Neyestani, M. 2015. *Petit Manuel du Parfait Réfugié Politique*. Paris: ARTE editions/çà et là.

Picozza, Fiorenza. 2017. "Dubliners: Unthinking Displacement, Illegality, and Refugeeness Within Europe's Geographies of Asylum." In *Borders of 'Europe': Autonomy of Migration, Tactics of Bordering*, edited by Nicholas De Genova, 233–54.

Pugliese, Joseph. 2002. "Penal Asylum: Refugees, Ethics, Hospitality."*Borderlands* 1 (1) [Online]. http://www.borderlands.net.au/vol 1 no1/pugliese.html. Accessed May 25, 2020.

Rancière, Jacques. 2000. "Dissenting Words: A Conversation with Jacques Rancière: Jacques Rancière and Davide Panagia." *Diacritics* 30 (2): 113–26. https://www.jstor.org/stable/1566474.

Rancière, Jacques. 2016. "Dissent." *Auguste Orts*. www.augusteorts.be/discourse/33/DISSENT-Sylvain-George.

Refugee Info Bus. 2018. *Police Violence in Calais: Abusive and Illegal Practices by Law Enforcement Officers*. Observations and testimonies: 1 November 2017–1 November 2018.

Refugee Rights Europe. 2016. *The Long Wait: Filling Data Gaps Relating to Refugees and Displaced People in the Calais Camp*. London: Refugee Rights Europe.

Richmond, Anthony H. 1993. "Reactive Migration: Sociological Perspectives on Refugee Movements." *Journal of Refugee Studies* 6 (1): 7–24.

Tan, S. 2006. *The Arrival*. Melbourne: Hachette.

Tan, S. 2010. *Sketches from a Nameless Land*. Melbourne: Hachette.

Ticktin, Miriam. 2016. "Calais: Containment Politics in the 'Jungle.'" *Funambulist Magazine* 5 (May–June): 29–33.

Young, Iris Marion. 1997. *Intersecting Voices: Dilemmas of Gender, Political Philosophy, and Policy*. Durham, NC and London: Duke University Press.

CHAPTER 5

Restaging the Colonial Encounter: Far-Right Narratives of Europe and African Migrant Responses

All the chapters in this book so far have been, in some ways, concerned with borders. This chapter and the next one are focused on borders in the form of walls, fences and checkpoints. This chapter concentrates on the EU/Africa border in Melilla, the Spanish enclave in Northern Morocco; the next on the Wall, checkpoints and roadblocks in the West Bank of Palestine/Israel.

Apart from the COVID-19 pandemic and climate change, arguably, the most urgent narratives in the contemporary world are political in the widest sense of the term. It seems to me, certainly from a European perspective, that there are two major, conflicting political narratives at the moment: a European one from a white nationalist, Identitarian perspective, seeing itself in danger of being displaced by migrants, challenged by a narrative from the Global South, itself constructed by those in flight from war, poverty, and exploitation. Both, in a profound sense, are linked by displacement, one metaphorical/symbolic, and the other emergent and actual. In this chapter, I want to concentrate upon this particular European (or, more precisely perhaps, Euro-American) far-right narrative which, if not exactly dominant, is certainly gaining currency and is manifested in populist politics. The principal target of this narrative is immigration, specifically refugees; its main adversary is the "lickspittle

© The Author(s), under exclusive license to Springer Nature Switzerland AG 2021
R. Bromley, *Narratives of Forced Mobility and Displacement in Contemporary Literature and Culture*, Studies in Mobilities, Literature, and Culture, https://doi.org/10.1007/978-3-030-73596-8_5

mentality" of liberalism which has, it is claimed, nurtured the "ethnic invasion" threatening Europe. In attempting to locate the sources of this discourse in the concept of racialisation, an analysis derived from decolonial thinking will be presented. In the second part of the chapter, I will look briefly at three texts (literary and cinematic) which have contributed to a counter-narrative about forced migration and actual physical, and psychological, displacement, rather than the metaphorical displacement of European 'nativism'. This counter-narrative, it will be argued, is primarily imagined from the perspective of migrants/refugees on the borders of Europe in many senses.

In this chapter, I shall outline the main themes and tropes of far-right, or extreme right, narratives in Europe today and then will attempt to locate the origins of these narratives in colonial discourses. My argument will be that ideology is most effective when structured like a narrative, a convincing story. A number of these far-right 'stories' will be outlined. In a sense, this outline of the far-right could have been situated in any of my chapters but, since in terms of the 'great replacement'(see below) the 'replacers' are seen as mostly coming from Africa, and very often as Muslims, I have decided to place the outline in the context of an analysis of three African texts. Finally, I shall look briefly at these texts, all of which seek to place the migrant/refugee at the symbolic centre of the contemporary world in order to produce an alternative form of cultural resistance, the potential for a counter-narrative.

In February 2018, Viktor Orban, Prime Minister of Hungary, called for a global alliance against migration as he began campaigning for the April election: "Christianity is Europe's last hope". He went on to add that with mass immigration especially from Africa, "our worst nightmares can come true. The West falls as it fails to see Europe being overrun" (*The Guardian*, February 2018). This speech summarises one dominant strand of what I am calling the far-right narrative in Europe. This narrative takes almost as many forms as the far-right itself which is composed, broadly, of the following components: the electoral or parliamentary approach, the intellectual and conceptual, and the 'street' with its varying levels of violence. These narratives are often contradictory. The New Right (Nouvelle Droite) in France, for example, especially its leading intellectual, Alain De Benoist, opposes Christianity and the Judaeo-Christian tradition and favours a 5,000-year-old, Indo-European, pagan legacy (see de Benoist 2016). Renaud Camus, Steve Bannon and others insist upon a

2,000-year-old Christian (mainly Catholic) tradition as being at the heart of European, and Euro-American, identity.

In the conflict of interpretation over the current crisis in Europe, which are the narratives that dominate and how can they be countered? Who is setting the agenda and claiming ownership of particular issues? For all the differences among those on the far-right, one common denominator is opposition to immigration or, more precisely, non-white immigration. According to Michael O'Meara in his book on Guillaume Faye, "immigration is also code for Third World colonisation and Islamisation" (O'Meara 2013, 123). How do we go about developing new constitutive stories, alternative narratives? How can we find a narrative space beyond the increasingly dominant far-right frame: the space of the migrant? Edward Said, in his book *Covering Islam*, refers to the ways in which Islam is framed by representations in which "a handful of reckless generalizations and repeatedly deployed clichés" (Said 1997, li) come to constitute a public discourse of negativity. A repertoire of similar, recurring images makes up this fairly recent European narrative, shaped after 9/11 and sharpened since 2015, against which the 'Other' has to seek permission to narrate, in Said's phrase. In *Time and the Other*, the anthropologist, Johannes Fabian, calls this "the denial of coevals": "a persistent and systematic tendency to place the referent(s) of anthropology in a Time other than the present of the producer of anthropological discourse—the 'otherer'" (Fabian 1983, 31). Islam is, in other words, seen as out of time, unchanging, fixed and backward, pre-Modern, othered.

The intellectual roots of the far-right are fairly easy to locate but the impetus to the growth of the far-right narrative has come not only from 9/11, the most spectacular and horrific example of Islamist terrorism, but also from the role of Al-Qaeda and Daesh (ISIS in popular media) in the Middle East, and the Islamist bombings in Madrid (2004), London (2005, so-called 7/7), Paris (November 2015), Brussels (2016), the 'Charlie Hebdo' killings in Paris (January 2015) and the Manchester suicide bombings of May 2017. Until October 16, 2020, with the beheading of a teacher just outside Paris, the stabbings of three people in a church in Nice (October 26, 2020) and, as I write (November 2, 2020), the killing of four people in Vienna, all allegedly by 'Islamist terrorists', attention seemed to have shifted to incidents of 'white' terrorism in the US and, most recently, in New Zealand (referred to below). The 'Islamist' bombings appeared to give 'respectability' to Islamophobia at many levels, and to unproven claims about terrorists gaining entry as refugees. This put the focus on young, single men who, for a time, constituted the largest group of asylum seekers. Since the civil war in Syria, families have come to dominate the asylum seeker population and far less is heard about the refugee/terrorist narrative, especially as in the US and the UK, it is recognised by the security services that far-right terrorism poses a greater threat than Islamist fundamentalism.

WHITE GENOCIDE

In Europe, there is a war on immigration, mainly, but not only, articulated by, and shared by most of, the right. However the opposition to migrants/refugees is formulated or coded, it is primarily a white nationalist, or nativist, narrative, and something shared with similar groups in the US, although there are different inflections and referents. Also shared is the idea that Europe/the US is being overrun by migrants, specifically Muslims, and the Islamification of Europe or the threat of Eurabia is often invoked: Guillaume Faye speaks of "a massive colonisation settlement of the West by peoples from the Global South" (Faye 2016, Introduction). On a visit to the UK in 2018, the then-US President Donald Trump said, "Immigrants are stripping Europe of its culture".[1]

Another enemy of the right is multiculturalism and de Benoist advocates the 'right to difference' by which he means the establishment of separate civilisations and cultures, what he calls ethnopluralism, in which organic, ethnic cultures/communities live independently of each other in an 'empire of the regions'. Richard Spencer, the US alt-right leader, speaks of 'operation Homeland', the establishment of separate homelands dominated by those of white, European descent. The term 'homelands' is also commonly used by the Identitarian movement in Europe and the US. *Generation Identitaire* was formed in France as the youth wing of the Bloc Identitaire and has spread across Europe. Identitarianism is a pan-European movement, primarily a cultural narrative—'our way of life'. Identitarian activists set up a 'Defend Europe' campaign in 2017 and chartered a ship in order to prevent migrants coming by sea from Libya, and to disrupt NGO rescue vessels. Since that time, the new populist Italian government coalition seemed to be following a similar course of action to exclude migrants, until Matteo Salvini, deputy prime minister and leader of La Lega, left office in September 2019.

For all their differences, what is also common to all shades of far-right opinion is opposition to cultural homogenisation, the product, it is claimed, of elite global capitalism. In addition to this, the most frequently reiterated targets are liberalism, consumerism, Islam, the left, feminism, LGBT+ politics, political correctness and so-called cultural Marxism. The intellectuals of the right see themselves as engaged in metapolitics—a cultural and ideological 'war of position', the winning of hearts and minds, the idea that cultural change needs to precede political change. This is a concept borrowed from the Italian Marxist intellectual and activist, Antonio Gramsci. de Benoist speaks of 'Right Gramscianism'. This is part of resistance to what is perceived as the conquest of Europe by migrants, a reverse colonisation.

The right sees itself as engaged in a reconquest (*Reconquista* was the term used in fifteenth-century Spain to refer to the period from 718 to 1492 which led the Christian defeat of Islam)—the defence of Europe against the diminishing of ethnic purity, its demographic and cultural decline, betrayed by left-liberalism and globalisation. *Reconquista Germania* is an extreme-right channel on the gaming app Discord; 'Make Europe Great Again' is the official motto of the German AfD far-right party. There is an existential fear that the political and demographic character of the West will be altered forever by the influx ('flood' is often used) of migrants.

The essence of this liberal modernity, it is claimed, is the idea of conquest formulated in a phrase, and the title of a book in 2017 by Renaud Camus, called 'The Great Replacement' (*Le Grand Emplacement*), which is probably the most important narrative theme of the right in recent times. This theme is also called *A Global Coup* by Guillaume Faye (2017), another, founding, New Right intellectual who broke with the group in the 1980s. Another book of his was called *The Colonisation of Europe*. Together these three phrases—replacement, coup, colonisation—constitute the core ideological precepts of the nativist, far-right narrative, along with 'ethnic submersion' and 'change of people'. In this scenario, the dispossessed majority in Europe faces the possibility of extinction—'white genocide' in US right discourse—and will be substituted by immigrant hordes: 'global substitutionism' (*remplacisme global*) is the phrase used by Renaud Camus. Camus even goes so far as to claim that Europe is far more colonised by Africa than Europe ever colonised Africa and is worse because it involves *demographic change*.

This paranoid narrative, the idea of the sacred nation, brings to mind the mystical and mythical, 'blood and soil', at the root of much white nationalist ideology. I say 'paranoid' because it is predicted that by

2030, the Muslim population of Europe will only comprise 7 percent of the continent. It is currently 4 percent. It is hard not to see the Muslim stereotype as a pretext, a symptom of a much deeper anxiety and uncertainty. With elimination becoming the key factor in a ruthless, financialised capitalism which has led to precarity in employment (the 'gig' economy) and housing, and produced an ever-increasing debt economy, it is not hard to see how the 'left behind' or abandoned working and lower middle class might turn to identities that seem to promise security and meaning and "do not involve competition, such as nationality, ethnicity, language, religion, and gender [and] become more and more attractive as sources of meaning, self-esteem, and efficacy" (Salmela and von Scheve 2017, 594). This is a vast and complex subject which cannot be covered here, but it does help to explain the virulent, and often violent, response from the far-right in Europe and the US to the 'Black Lives Matter' political and social movement which gathered renewed momentum in July 2020. According to a report by *Hope Not Hate*, the movement was being reacted to by a rising white nationalism at the level of the street and in social media (Murdoch 2020). The recent "Patriotic Alternative" (PA) group in the UK, described by *Hope Not Hate* as a "fascist, anti-semitic white nationalist organisation launched in September 2019 by Mark Collett, former director of publicity for the British National Party" (ibid.), is designed to bring together the numerous splinter groups on the far-right in the UK and seems to have achieved some success in this respect. I am always hesitant to use the term 'fascist' but, in this case, it would appear that their antisemitism, Holocaust denial, and Nazi salutes at demonstrations, seem to justify its use here. PA claims that "Native British people are set to become a minority by 2066" (www.patrioticalternative.org.uk). The group seems on a continuum from the 'great replacement' trope. Another recent, and increasingly popular, far-right group is QAnon, a conspiracy theory organisation started in the US but also active in the UK, which sees Donald Trump leading the fight against the 'deep state' and is associated with acts of extreme violence and anti-semitism but also with an emotional appeal constructed around 'saving' children from paedophile gangs. It has gained currency also from anti-lockdown campaigns during the COVID-19 pandemic.

The title of a book by Thilo Sarrazin, published in August 2018, is *Hostile Takeover: How Islam Hampers Progress and Threatens Society*, a title which sums up one particular, and increasingly dominant, feature of the far-right. Generation Identity describes the Great Replacement theory as "the process by which the indigenous European population is replaced by non-European migrants. Employing similar rhetoric, Brenton Tarrant, the white supremacist who killed 50 people at two New Zealand mosques on March 15, 2019, entitled his manifesto "The Great Replacement" and wrote about the "crisis of mass immigration and … assault on the European people that, if not combated, will ultimately result in the complete racial and cultural replacement of the European people" (*Counter Extremism Project* 2020).

In Charlottesville, Virginia in August 2017, the 'Unite the Right', white nationalist, neo-fascist rally chanted 'you will not replace us' and 'the Jews will not replace us' echoing the 'Great Replacement' claim, with a sharper anti-Semitic edge than is currently deployed publicly in Europe. The fightback against this 'replacement' has its violent, street manifestations but is also articulated in right intellectual circles through publications such as *Manifesto for a European Renaissance* (de Benoist), *A New European Renaissance* (Faye), and *The Real Right Returns: A Handbook for the True Opposition* (Friberg), all published by ARKTOS, the publishing house of the far-right, set up to circulate: "those ideas and values which were taken for granted in Europe prior to the advent of Liberalism" (Friberg 2015, ix). These are ideas, one might argue, which have leaked into mainstream discourse since the recession of 2008, as well as gaining considerable exposure in social media. An American far-right website (Daily Stormer) speaks of weaponising Internet culture, of coordinating media disruption strategies.

There is a website called 'European Civil War' which articulates how this supposed conflict is seen, a conflict which many on the far-right see as being resolved by what is called 'EuroSiberia' (the reunification of all peoples of European origin), or 'EurAsia' which is a formulation produced by looking to Putin and Russia for leadership, a federation of white ethno-states. The overall framing narrative consists of a belief in order and structure, hierarchy, leadership and authoritarianism. It is anti-egalitarian. In its street manifestations, it revolves around a vitalist ethic of the body, of Nordic masculinity. Generation Identity attacks the 68ers (the 1968 generation) for taking the 'manliness out of man'. Richard Spencer urges his followers to 'become who you are'. So, we can add 'masculinism' to the right narrative I am trying to develop, a response to what they term the emasculation and enfeeblement of the 'white race'. Most of the groups emphasise the importance of collective narratives, rituals and symbolic repertoires, and stress the aesthetic and the affective in what is a rhetoric of belonging and the anxiety of unbelonging: the overarching narrative of displacement which comes to occupy a xenophobic polemical space:

> Most importantly, right-wing populism does not only relate to the *form* of rhetoric, but to its specific contents: such parties … construct fear and—related to various real or imagined dangers—propose scapegoats that are blamed for threatening or actually damaging *our* societies, in Europe and beyond. (Wodak 2015, 2, my italics)

For all the far-right rhetoric which claims to speak for the grassroots and demonises the elites, Peter Geoghegan has shown how many of the populist parties and leaders have been funded by wealthy transatlantic networks funnelling 'dark money' into Europe's nativist movements, for example, the Vox party in Spain, the AfD party in Germany, and the World Congress for Families (Geoghegan 2020). The far-right narrative is derived from ideologies of nation and concepts of national sovereignty:

> The doctrine of nationalism which crystallized in 1848 gives a geographic imperative to the concept of culture itself: habit, faith, pleasure, and ritual—all depend upon enactment in a particular territory. More, the place which nourishes rituals is a place composed of people like oneself, people with whom one can share without explaining. Territory thus becomes synonymous with identity. (Sennett 2011, 58)

At a time, since the 2008 recession, when the 'European' narrative is ceasing to make sense, cohere, motivate or hold people together at the economic, social or political level, mainly because of neoliberalism and globalisation, it is being re-assembled symbolically/discursively on a negative construction of immigration. This is true for a number of countries in Europe where far-right parties are gaining prominence on the basis of opposition to immigration. The explicitly neo-Nazi, ethno-nationalist party in Greece, Golden Dawn, is violently opposed to immigration and what its statutes call the 'demographic alteration'; the party gained 18 seats in the June 2012 Greek elections. The immigrant is mapped against an already existing, fixed, and (so the story goes) socially cohesive national culture—the symbols, stories and legends of the deeper normative notions and images that underlie the 'social imaginary', those once-common understandings and a widely-shared sense of legitimacy produced by the conversion and transformation processes brought about by nineteenth-

and twentieth-century hegemony—a partly conscious, partly unconscious repertoire. The Golden Dawn predicates its statutes upon the assumption that what they call the 'People' is not just an arithmetic total of individuals but the *qualitative* composition of humans with the same biological and cultural heritage. This 'tribal' definition would most probably find echoes in the majority of far-right parties in Europe. While the far-right is growing electorally in Poland, Croatia, Macedonia and Slovenia, the Freedom party in Austria has lost all its seats in parliament, as has the Golden Dawn. Recently (October 7, 2020), 69 members of Golden Dawn—including its 18 elected (but suspended) MPs—were found guilty of orchestrating murder, arson, assault and weapons possession, and of being a criminal organisation.

A struggle for recognition is taking place which is deep, complex and, partly, at the level of the unconscious. Claims of Britishness, Frenchness or Danishness (the three countries where right parties led the EU elections in 2014) form the basis on which refugee and migrant issues are used as organising principles for the social critique of other political issues: "The originality and richness of the human heritages of this world are nourished by their differences and their deviations, which surprise and fascinate as soon as one passes from the culture of one people to another. These originalities can find protection, in turn, only in the homogeneous ethno-cultural space that is proper to them" (Krebs 1997, 8). The title of Krebs's book is *Fighting for the Essence: Western Ethnosuicide or European Renaissance* and the word 'essence' is crucial here, that same biological and cultural heritage just referred to. Krebs is one of the intellectuals of the 'New Right' and exercises considerable influence on theories of ethno-nationalism. For example, the Danish People's Party speaks of Denmark as belonging exclusively to the Danes and argues that a multi-ethnic Denmark would dilute the so-called homogeneous society by the introduction of reactionary and backward cultural habits.

The post-Cold War period has seen the "dismantling of ideological, political, social and identification reference points" (Laïdi 1998, 2), readily available dyadic symbolic forms, and, as a consequence, the nation has come up against the limits of its being and meaningfulness, its representational currencies; what in psychoanalysis would be called its 'narcissistic self-enclosure', hence the preoccupation with borders and security. There is a crisis at the boundary of articulation. As de Benoist puts it: "once upon a time borders played a significant role: they guaranteed the continuation of collective identities" (de Benoist 2004, 37).

Beppe Grillo, of The Five Star Movement (in Italy) said at one point that the borders of what he called the 'Fatherland' were once regarded as sacred, but they had been sacrileged by politicians. The use of the word 'Fatherland' here has sinister echoes, and blaming politicians (in Italian, *La Casta*) is a core feature of right populism. A coming ethnic civil war is predicted as Europe is overwhelmed through its porous borders, so the rhetoric goes.

How can refugees be represented other than as vulnerable or pitiable? One way is through *recognition* enabling them to become, in terms already referred to, 'grievable subjects'. With more than a thousand people having drowned crossing the Mediterranean in the first six months of 2018, despite the number of refugees seeking entry to Europe having fallen sharply since 2015/2016, *The Guardian* newspaper decided on World Refugee Day (June 20, 2018) to make available a list of the 34,361 migrants and refugees *known* to have died in the attempt to reach the borders of Europe. The key word in that sentence is 'known', that is, reported deaths, as there may well be countless others. The list was compiled by United for Intercultural Action, a European network of 550 anti-racist organisations drawn from 48 countries. Banu Cennetoglu, an artist working in Istanbul, has incorporated the list in her work for the past sixteen years. She had an exhibition at the Chisenhale Gallery, London from June to August 2018, and the current edition of the list was commissioned and produced by the Gallery; it also featured as part of the Liverpool Biennial of Contemporary Art. The name of the refugee, country of origin, year, cause and source of death constituted the database of the list.

In itself, the list as a compilation of data cannot make the particular individual 'grievable' but its existence and its distribution in a range of public places, rather like other public forms of commemoration, has an anamnesic effect—bringing to mind, to visibility and to memorability, those who might otherwise be disregarded. By disseminating the list at bus stops, on billboards, in advertising columns in major European cities, on a wall in Los Angeles, and a public screen on top of Istanbul's Marmara Pera hotel, the artist is creating a form of public declaration, metaphorically restoring to a visual reckoning those who do not count, an attempt to interpellate, bind, 'those whose lives matter' (as a result of colonial and racialised computations) with those who have been, and continue to be, erased.

I have dwelt upon this list at length because it seems to me to offer a framework for potential recognition and reciprocity, a revaluation of those subject to the 'failure of regard' (Butler 2009, 25). It is never easy to measure the effects of a work of public art (which the *distribution* of the list effectively becomes) or of literature, but I wish to conclude this argument by examining three cultural productions—a film and two novels—which attempt to place migrants and refugees as 'grievable subjects' at the centre of their own narratives because, as Daniel Trilling has said, "often they are given no story at all, reduced to a shadow that occasionally flits across European vision" (Trilling 2018, 9). A decolonial narrative is one which attempts to give that story back.

The Southern Gaze

Reference was made earlier to Guillaume Faye's comment about "a massive colonisation settlement of the West by peoples from the Global South", and in the next sections, drawing upon decolonial thinking, I shall examine three texts from the Global South: the film *Those who Jump* (2016) and the novels *The Gurugu Pledge* (2017) and *African Titanics* (2014 [2008]). On the African continent, the "coloniality of power" can be seen as "a crucial structuring process in the modern colonial/world-system" (Grosfoguel 2007, 219–20). Notionally independent and decolonised, most African countries experience, at a range of levels—epistemological and structural—continuities from the colonial past in the form of neocolonialism. There is already extensive material on anti-colonialism in African literature, dating from the early part of the twentieth century and gaining momentum in the 1950s and 1960s (Achebe, wa Thiong'o, Soyinka and many others) under the impetus of decolonisation. Stimulated by Edward Said's *Orientalism* (1978) Western scholars developed postcolonial theories which were applied to texts from the majority world. *The Empire Writes Back* (Ashcroft et al. 1989) and *Colonial Discourse and Postcolonial Theory* (Williams and Chrisman 1993) were pioneering works in this area, and since that time the field has grown exponentially. As my focus is on the representation of forced migration and displacement in *contemporary* literature and culture, the basis of this chapter is on a limited number of sub-Saharan texts which deal specifically with refugees in the broad sense in which I have been using the term. Despite Western extensive media coverage of overcrowded boats and drowning bodies, there is not very much evidence as yet of cultural fictions by refugees.

In the most comprehensive recent coverage of refugee research across the Humanities, *Refugee Imaginaries* (Cox et al. 2020), only two of the thirty-two chapters deal substantially with African literature or culture, and none of the texts analysed is produced by refugees. I shall attempt to approach my selected texts through the lens of coloniality, introduced in Chapter 1 and referred to elsewhere. The Peruvian scholar Anibal Quijano argued that "European culture was made seductive: it gave access to power … European culture became a universal cultural model". It is this continuing cultural hegemony which means that the 'imaginary' in non-European cultures could hardly exist today and, above all, reproduce itself outside of these colonial relations. In order to offer fresh interpretations of refugee representation, and to account for dehumanisation and indifference to their destitution or death, theoretical resources drawn from the Global South will be deployed. The Global South in this formulation is not seen as a geographical space, or spaces, but as a repository of ideas, practices and epistemologies which challenge the universals of Western modernity and global corporate capitalism, and the need for delinking from hegemonic Western narratives by means of 'epistemic disobedience'. In the words of Chakrabarty, it is to "provincialise Europe" (Chakrabarty 2000). For Chakrabarty, "European historicism allows only one trajectory to non-Western societies if they are to be recognised as part of the grand human story: they must undergo a visible metamorphosis—fast or slow, effective or otherwise—to Western capitalist modernity" (quoted in Comaroff and Comaroff 2016, 3). Where the missionaries set out to convert the non-Western 'other' to one of the major narratives of Europe, colonial scholarship, and the coloniality of knowledge, seek to convert non-Western societies to European modernity. Although I would not claim that the texts included in this chapter succeed in rewriting the 'grand human story', at least they offer significant challenges to ways of reading that story. Novelist Ngugi wa Thiong'o has been a force in African literature for decades: since the 1970s, when he gave up the English language to commit himself to writing in African languages, his foremost concern has been the critical importance of language to culture. In *Something Torn and New* (2009), Ngugi explores Africa's historical, economic and cultural fragmentation by slavery, colonialism and globalisation. Throughout this tragic history, a constant and irrepressible force was Europhonism: the replacement of native names, languages, and identities with European ones. The result was the dismemberment of African memory. Seeking to remember language in order to revitalise it, Ngugi's quest is for wholeness. Wide-ranging, erudite, and hopeful, *Something Torn and New* is a cri de coeur to save Africa's cultural future.

The first two texts are both based on Mount Gurugu in Morocco, the site of an informal, refugee camp inhabited by between 500 and 1,000 people, mainly young men, from West Africa. To screen its squalor, the men ironically name it 'the residence'. The camp is situated two kilometres from the Spanish autonomous, and anomalous, enclave of Melilla, which is on the African continent yet marks Europe's border with the Global South. It is structurally liminal but actively signified as 'European', with "Europe as a master signifier in discourses of exclusion and deportation zones" (Soto Bermant 2017, 138). Melilla, with its eleven-kilometre long, six-metre-high, three-tiered, razor-wired fence, represents in microcosm the conflict of which I have been speaking, that narrative encounter between entitlement and disposability. This representation of the border, marked by Melilla, is symbolic, physical, and historical. It was captured by Spain from the Moors in 1497 and established as a military outpost. This enclave, in addition to its fence, has 106 fixed cameras for video surveillance, and helicopters are also used for surveillance. It epitomises the militarisation of security on EU borders and also the externalisation of migration management to the extent that "Africa's sub-Saharan countries have become EU's southern border" (Ceriani 2009, 2). Its CETI (Centre for the Temporary Stay of Migrants) holds hundreds of migrants/refugees: the enemy *almost* within. The EU gives Spain and Morocco millions of euros each year to maintain this border. Laurie has argued that decolonial approaches attempt "to politicise epistemology from the experiences of those on the border" (Laurie 2012, 13). Hence, Melilla and Gurugu are appropriate sites for texts which take apart the logic of coloniality and seek to imagine the possibilities of decolonial societies.

The title of the film *Those who Jump* syntactically enacts the subjectivity and agency of the refugees with its active verb. The idea for the film arose from a decision by two young filmmakers to hand over a camera to Abou, a university graduate from Mali who had been living in the camp for fourteen months, in the hope that he could produce an insider's view of the daily experience of those living there. In the course of filming, Abou, in a sense, becomes the camera: "I feel that I exist when I film". It is this presence of an active existence which moves the representation of the refugee away from the object of pity, the hapless victim. He, like all the others, *is* a victim, of repressive regimes, of hunger, poverty and unemployment, but the film reverses the European gaze and presents the active point of view of those held in time by the proximity of the fence and the desire to jump it. The temporariness, and the improvised quality, of their lives feature throughout the film. We see men cooking food over an open fire, clothes hanging out to dry on trees, with plastic and cardboard sheets the only bedding. Men scavenging for food and water in the nearby city of Nador hover between hope and despair, death and life. One voicemail message left by Abou is to the mother of a friend who died in the camp: Mustafa. The unstable, handheld camera at times embodies the endangered lives of the men, particularly in a sequence showing the men being pursued by helicopter and armed police.

There are long-distance shots of Melilla which represent the tantalising, frustrated perceptions of the camp dwellers and an image of a plane coming into land mocks the immobility of the watching men. One of the figures interviewed says: "Every day I see my future in front of me but I cannot reach it". Abou had been on Gurugu for fourteen months and attempted to climb the fence countless times. His journey began with forty euros and his dream was to join his brother who reached Europe in 2015. The film underscores the fact that lives are at risk from a number of perspectives. The scale of the danger involved is revealed by night-time, black-and-white editorial inserts of border surveillance images showing the vast numbers of men approaching the fence in ordered, single file.

Far from being passive, Mehdi Alioua has shown, from his fieldwork research, that sub-Saharan *transmigrants*, who have crossed several borders on their journey to the Maghreb, have formed social networks, irrespective of languages spoken or nations of origin, and have established complex organisational structures and impressive mutual aid collectives. In the face of Western ideologies of individualism, they construct models of cooperation, something reflected in the makeshift forest camps. In some, committees are set up and elections take place. Strategies are also devised whereby certain groups function as diversions, or decoys, for those trying to climb the fence in relay fashion, with members of these decoy groups becoming fence climbers next time. As Alioua shows, given the conditions of conflict and deprivation in which most of the migrants live, "from the outset their life is guided by mobility … their life is migration" (Alioua 2006, 5); migration becomes a project defined by the "act of crossing". A collective consciousness develops as mobile phone networks are set up, migrants act as guides for those coming after them, and information is shared. In Alioua's words, "These Africans conceptualize 'elsewhere' as 'the universe of possibilities'" and, in a crucial phrase which resonates across all the chapters in this book, "The border they want to cross is the one that in their perception separates the world of waiting and immobility from the world of action and innovation" (ibid., 10).

As well as featuring 'the world of waiting and immobility', the film indicates the makeshift nature of the camp, its rocky terrain, and focuses on the everyday: the first aid applied with care and precision to those injured by police, the numerous dogs roaming the camp, and a passionately engaged football match between Mali and the Ivory Coast. Humour is also evident throughout—the match is played at the Maracana stadium (in Rio de Janeiro) one man mockingly comments. 'Makeshift', maybe, but also evident is the way in which the different nationalities organise their own administration and regulations, and plan action around the fence jumps and camp organisation. Rule One for all, it is stressed, is 'we will all enter Europe', so their whole existence is predicated on this, to become an African in Europe. Although each nationality has its space and structure set out, there is also a commonality in which versatility is a key aspect, with roles from the past—doctor, lawyer—changed by the exigencies of their condition. Resourcefulness and improvisation are also manifested by the construction of devices designed to aid the climb in the darkness. Frequent shots of the bright lights of the city below are a contrasting provocation to the watchers above. There is very little in the way of polemic or back story, but the hellish journey through the desert is remarked upon as is the fact that, with their countries having been exploited for years, Europeans cannot expect to take everything away from African people and expect to keep them outside. The men are aware of the hazardous nature of their lives and pray that they will never become anonymous corpses. This touches upon a key aspect of the film—the men are rescued from anonymity, given identities, and positions to speak from: subjects who act in unison, knowing that behind the fence lies the future. It is also recognised that this future may not be all that is hoped for, so they may dream but they are not illusioned.

In the final sequences of the film, fog shrouds the mountain as the men are shown approaching the fence and the film ends in a blaze of colour and on a collective note of song and dance as a number of men are shown celebrating in Melilla having successfully surmounted the fence and evaded the police. Abou, the filmmaker, is one of them and he is now living in Germany with temporary leave to remain, having survived living on the borders but still subject to time waiting.

Elsewhere and Here: Revisiting the Colonial Encounter

Unlike almost any other work of its kind, *The Gurugu Pledge* (Laurel 2017) only exists in published form as a translation into English of an unpublished collection of typed manuscripts in Spanish, the colonial language of the writer, Juan Tomás Ávila Laurel, from Equatorial Guinea. I stress 'colonial' language because the novel is an exemplary instance of decolonial thinking in which a group of refugees and migrants from Anglophone and Francophone (both terms derived from the 'New Imperialism' of the late nineteenth century formulated at the 1884–1885 Berlin conference which saw the carving up of Africa by European powers) African countries are confined on Mount Gurugu, a volcanic mountain two kilometres southwest of Melilla, a Spanish territory in Northern Morocco: "the backdoor to cherished Europe" (Laurel 2017, 45). The word 'cherished' is crucial because it articulates the colonised mentality which had driven the residents of Gurugu to the threshold of Europe; a mentality which is not able to envisage any other alternative to their desperate plight in their own countries, other than reaching the wealth and power of Europe. The novel reveals how exclusive this wealth and power is and shows how the journey to Europe, even if successful, may be illusory. Wordless and rendered worthless, these men and women communicate in the imposed languages of the coloniser (Ngugi's 'Europhony'), and the camp itself is divided in ways which reflect this linguistic hegemony and the discourses of power which control their subjectivities and knowledge. From these voiceless and fragmented identities, the novel opens up spaces for their stories as ways of countering the epistemic violence of coloniality (Fig. 5.1).

The narrative is multi-voiced with many shifts in register, tense and mode of writing. It often deploys a satiric form by magnifying the follies of those complicit with neocolonialism into grotesque and absurd behaviour. Examples of this are the former aide of Idi Amin, bloated into obesity by greed and gluttony and leading three hundred men to

5 RESTAGING THE COLONIAL ENCOUNTER … 157

Fig. 5.1 African migrants climb a border fence between Morocco and Spain's North African enclave of Melilla (Reproduced by courtesy of Reuters/Alamy)

their deaths at the Victoria Falls, and also through the lengthy, and absurd, backstory of Omar Salango, a brutal former soldier, who arrives at Gurugu and continues his violence and exploitation of women. Some of the stories follow a realist trajectory, while others are more irrealist in the sense that they edge towards fable and folk tale, the tall tale, in an attempt to replicate African oral traditions. Although each character has a name and their story is distinctive, there is a sense also that both characters and stories are generic, as is much in the novel. Specific incidents and journeys are illustrative, exempla in the medieval sense, as the novel has a metonymic structure. Even Melilla becomes more than a place on a map as its 'border spectacle' is not just a local staging of the Europe/Global South division but comes to synthesise the historical colonial encounter and its political, economic, and cultural violence. In synoptic form, it represents the fences and walls in almost seventy countries, designed to prevent the flow of migrants.

The first-person narrator opens and closes the novel but, episodically, hands over the narrative to other voices, as well as intermittently adopting both third- and second-person stances. The overall narrative is punctuated by speculative discourses, like the lengthy one on football in an African context (discussed below), and others which subjunctively propose dialogues between scholars, conspicuously absent from, and uninterested in, the plight of the people in the camp. The scholars, wedded to European forms of knowledge, are presented as elite beneficiaries of colonialism, or neocolonialism, immured in their academic privilege, arguing over arcane and obscure topics. These imagined dialogues are one of many critiques in the text of neocolonialism in contemporary Africa, contrasted with the immiseration of those forced to flee from their countries:

> Instead of bringing a political response to the structural causes of the poverty and destitution spreading through the African continent, and which are the result of structural adjustment policies and the neocolonial pillage of strategic resources by multinational companies, Europe continues to build barbed-wire fences. Immense strategic wealth … is shamelessly plundered, while the victims of this, namely the great majority of Africans, are forbidden to enter the Schengen area… (from the "Declaration on the Repression of African Immigrants," quoted in Lecadet 2017, 149)

Although, as I have said, the novel individualises each person's flight, the novel gives fictional shape to the situation of poverty and destitution described, as well as to the plundering of gold, oil, and other mineral resources which have devastated the African continent and produced the perilous and tortuous journeys which have culminated in Gurugu.

The subjunctive interludes introduce an irrealist mood which contrasts sharply with the wretchedness of the indicative mood, the quotidian reality, which 'entangles' the refugees. I conflate refugee and undocumented migrant because, whatever the motivation for flight, all have been rejected, abandoned and neglected, the marginalised in their country for whom leaving is the only option. The journey to the European border is not only a flight from the residues of the colonial but from what has been termed 'the postcolonial neocolonised' world of the Global South (Ndlovu-Gatsheni 2013, 28). According to Mbembe, what he has called the 'Postcolony' is a composite of past, present and the future which has created an 'entanglement' which is interpenetrating and intersecting—Africa in Europe, Europe in Africa (Mbembe 2008, 4). It is this 'entanglement' which the novel seeks to articulate fictionally with its allusions to the colonial past, references to the violence of neocolonial dictatorships (with Idi Amin the paradigm case), and the fantasy of the People's Republic of Samuel Eto'o founded by 'disregarded subjects' from a range of West African countries on Mount Gurugu (Laurel 2017, 60).

Africa is not romanticised, as is evidenced by the extended, if humorous, critique of Amin and of two disruptive figures in the camp (Omar and Aliko), nor is the novel simply anti-colonial, but it works with the idea of the coloniality of power: "the heterogeneous and multiple global structures put in place over a period of 450 years did not evaporate with the … decolonisation of the periphery over the past 50 years. We continue to live under the same 'colonial power matrix' … We moved from a period of 'global colonialism' to the current period of 'global coloniality'" (Grosfoguel 2007, 219). Grosfoguel is referring primarily to Latin America but, in broad terms, much of what he says can be applied to the African continent where the "coloniality of power" can be seen as "a crucial structuring process in the modern colonial/world-system" (ibid., 219–20).

By way of placing the novel in its wider context of decolonial thinking, I will draw upon the outline of what is meant by the coloniality of power introduced in Chapter 1. There, I used Sylvia Wynter's idea of the master code whereby Western man *over-represented* himself as being within the genre of the human—what she calls the fiction of *homo oeconomicus*—to an extent that the colonised subject could find no space in that genre but was represented as less than human: "The colonial encounter determines not just the black colonial subject's familial structure or social and physical mobility and such, but colours his or her very being as he-or-she-which-is-not-quite human" (Weheliye 2014, 26). This is the context in which Europe becomes the destination of the African migrant, unable to think outside the framework of coloniality but, to understand this, and challenge it, Wynter insists "that the material and historical specificities of dehumanised life under the coloniality of Being provide the only possible sites from which to read *grammars of resistance* to coloniality's hegemonic hold on human life" (Tsantsoulas 2018, 175–76, my italics). The novels and film under discussion here, with their counter-hegemonic narratives are part of this "grammar of resistance".

As an imperialising force, Western Europe practised extensive forms of exclusion and also developed an accompanying ideological narrative related to this, of which Wynter and Weheliye speak and which persists today. As James Baldwin wrote, "the great force of history comes from the fact that we carry it within us, are unconsciously controlled by it in many ways, and history is literally present in all that we do" (Baldwin 1965). Nationalism, the corollary of imperialism, is one way in Europe in which history is still present in all we think and do.

In order to resist seeing the refugee as a knowing subject, with autonomy and agency, many Europeans essentialise the 'other', reduce them to a set of invariable and negative characteristics and this enables them to regard their deaths with *indifference*. How this indifference, this disengagement and emotional disidentification can be challenged is partly by coming to *terms* with narratives that originate beyond the coloniality of power, or which interrogate this, such as *The Gurugu Pledge*. It might be argued that the refugee crisis has a lot to do with nations, in search of their '*not selves*', only secure in the knowledge that 'out there' there are still the barbarians of myth, displaced from '*our*' identity. To dehumanise others is a form of displacement, to remove them from their identity (and 'ours') so that you can be reassured that those who drown or are killed are not your own kind, but sub-human. As Mbembe has commented:

> It is now widely acknowledged that Africa as an idea, a concept, has historically served, and continues to serve, as a polemical argument for the West's desperate desire to assert its difference from the rest of the world. In several respects, Africa still constitutes one of the metaphors through which the West represents the origin of its own norms, develops a self-image, and integrates this image into the set of signifiers asserting what it supposes to be its identity. (Mbembe 2003, 2)

In the argument which follows, it will be shown how this Western metaphor of Africa has imprinted itself deeply on African consciousness and undermined attempts to create a self-image and distinctive, complex and diverse African identity. It will be claimed that one of the achievements of *The Gurugu Pledge* is its challenge to this concept of Africa and the deconstruction of the Western signifiers. The search for what is described critically in the novel as a "brilliant future in Europe" is the product of "the colonisation of African imagination and displacement of African knowledges" (Ndlovu-Gatsheni 2013, xi) and is only partly ironic because it refers to the fact that "European culture was made seductive: it gave access to power … European culture became a universal cultural model" (Quijano 2007, 169). European football, to cite an example from the novel, has today become a universal cultural model at the expense of African football. It is this continuing European hegemony which means that "The imaginary in the non-European cultures could hardly exist today and, above all, reproduce itself outside of these [colonial] relations" (Quijano 2007, 169).

The novel is constructed as an 'entanglement' of two imaginaries. One is that indicated by Quijano, the continuing seduction of Europe (*Elsewhere*), the other is the tentative and speculative emergent African imaginary proposed in the subjunctive interludes which I spoke of earlier and which the novel as a whole represents, the re-casting of an alternative African imaginary (*Here*).

Here is Mount Gurugu, symbolically condensing the experiences of the colonised and neocolonised African Continent; *Elsewhere* is Melilla, Europe's border with Africa in which is conflated the cartography, ideology, and coloniality of Europe:

> For a space and a life where they feel they are going somewhere as opposed to nowhere, or at least, a space where the quality of their "going-ness" is better than what it is in the space they are leaving behind. More often than not, what is referred to as 'voluntary migration' then is either an inability or unwillingness to endure and 'wait out' a crisis of existential mobility. (Hage 2009, 98)

In the novel, this 'waiting out' forms part of its resolution.

Storytelling, playing football, scavenging for food and water, and preparing to jump the fence comprise an active existence which moves the representation of the refugee away from the object of pity, the hapless victim. They *are* victims, of repressive regimes, of hunger, war, poverty and unemployment but the narrative reverses the European gaze and presents the active point of view of those held in time by the proximity of the fence and the desire to jump it.

The narrative underscores the fact that lives are at risk from a number of perspectives, from the police who raid the camp and burn all the meagre possessions of the inhabitants, and also attack them, as well as the clandestine journey to the fence and the obvious hazards of the attempt to scale the fence. The shared strategy of the men is to approach the fence en masse, so as to outnumber the police. The sense of collective solidarity is shown, without sentimentality or romanticisation, as also shown is the 'trial' of the men who exploited and violated a woman resident which, after much discussion, leads to a verdict which "departs from the logic of vengeance" (Mbembe 2008, 11), an important break with neocolonial law.

The Gurugu Pledge shows Fanon's 'wretched of the earth' as subjects. The novel gives fictional form to what Ndlovu-Gatsheni has described as "a dominant Western power backed up by Euro-American epistemologies which resulted in the colonisation of African imagination and displacement of African knowledges" (Ndlovu-Gatsheni 2013, xi). The fact that everyone in the 'residence' is displaced from the heart of Africa and had a past, but also spoke in French or English and are in thrall to Europe (a phone call or a letter from a European address would be a high point) articulates this hegemonic colonial legacy. All of the people on Mount Gurugu have a life and a story which Europe cannot ignore, and the novel gives them subjectivity and agency. In Mbembe's words, "the colonized person is a living, talking, conscious, active individual whose identity arises from a three-pronged movement of violation, erasure and self-writing" (Mbembe 2008, 4). The novel articulates this violation, writes against the erasure by the European gaze and presents an opportunity for self-storying. It begins with a first-person narrator who then hands over to the stories of a range of other men, stories which are related with frequent interruptions, often witty and ribald, by the listeners. Although each story is different, there is a narrative convergence in the sense that they share a metaphorical 'neighbourhood' of displacement and deprivation, the racialisation of the Black 'other', driven from their home countries by, variously, religious bigotry, violence, poverty, hunger, superstition and lack of work. Added to this are the cronyism, violence and corruption of African dictatorships, with Idi Amin singled out as the representative, neocolonised figure, and the more recent build-up of armaments, the desertification of Africa, the destruction of biodiversity, and reduction of African agricultural knowledge and expertise to the service of corporate capitalism. The narrator's role is to make sure the stories will cross the sea and be told on the other shore.

The inhabitants are divided into language groups: "eat or *manger* according to whichever History *the whites chose for you*" (Laurel 2017, 65, my italics). The passivity of the syntax emphasises that, literally and metaphorically, these are 'disregarded, discarded subjects'; they live in the colonial present. The appropriation of classic English styles such as Miltonic sentences, circumlocution, hyperbole, and proprietary, is a way of undercutting the colonial, linguistic hegemony. In the words of one man, "they told me I no longer have a country, that's what they said at the border: you've no country any more, now you're just black" (Laurel 2017, 75). This epitomises the racialised abjection, the precarity and lack of value experienced by the migrant.

The lengthy sequence on football is of interest in envisioning an alternative to Europe:

> People played football on Gurugu to keep warm and busy, for the hours were long and football enabled them to lose track of time, but in *a different set of circumstances*, they'd have read all day and into the night. And in *a different reality*, a team of African scholars would have come to Gurugu mountain to talk to the inhabitants and ask them to comment on Peter's father's poem. (Laurel 2017, 87, my italics)

The italicised phrases indicate what has been called 'epistemic injustice'. I take this concept from Miranda Fricker's book of that name (Fricker 2009) to describe the ways in which both colonisers and African elites, complicit in the relationship between knowledge, prejudice and power, have withheld forms of knowledge from the majority of African peoples, leaving a negative space in which reading and intelligent discussion are largely absent. The 'different set of circumstances' and 'the different reality' refer to the challenge for the Global South to raise the profile and credibility of knowers and knowledges marginalised by the West.

Peter is one of the mountain dwellers whose family had lost their social status years before because his father had written a poem, in a *Conceptismo* (later sixteenth/early seventeenth century) Spanish style, for which he had been expelled for its supposed indecency. This issue is treated in mocking style through euphemism and rather 'coy' circumlocution. That the inhabitants of Gurugu would have been able to discuss such an arcane poem indicates a different, non-colonial, reality in which learning and dignity would have been possible. It also posits an image of African identity beyond the categories imposed by Europe. The scholars did not come but, the narrator suggests, a positive image might have caused some of the refugees to retrace their steps and return to their country of origin.

In an earlier, and unpublished, novel, called *Ahmed the Arab, or the Desert's Embrace*, Laurel wrote of a group of African migrants who, with the help of a millionaire, founded a city in the desert. Some of the men in *The Gurugu Pledge* fantasise that if they owned Mount Gurugu they could cultivate it, grow food, and become self-sufficient; in other words, produce an Africa, in miniature, free from exploitation and the coloniser, which they wouldn't have to leave. The republic created would be called the Republic of Samuel Eto'o (the world-famous Cameroon player) as football is the one preoccupation which distracts them from their wretchedness and is, at this stage, the limit of their cultural knowledge. The exodus of African footballers to Europe (e.g. the current 'hero' Mohammed Salah) is held up as a model of their own ambition and names of players and European clubs are reeled off like sacred icons. What these footballers have is what is known as *exit capacity*, the mobility denied to those stuck on the mountain. The narrative is critical of these models of aspiration, as the only value they represent is that of the market and a focus on the exceptional; according to Laurel, football has the capacity to interfere with African lives. Football is a sustaining, if illusory, fantasy, with men keeping fit until signed by a European club, but with no ambitions to stay and play in Africa, underlining a residual colonial legacy and the persistence of colonial rhetorics and practices, including the 'importing' by European clubs of teenage footballers who are left to fend for themselves if they don't succeed. As it is, on the mountain, football is the only available reality and is more than just the opium of the people, but, in different circumstances of their own choosing, other realities might have prevailed. These are key features of the novel, its refutation of the dehumanising colonial argument that the Africans were naturally inferior, and its gestures towards other potentialities.

The novel does not sentimentalise the figures in the camp, as blackmail and corruption are shown, and the few women are used and sexually abused. However, compared with the journey most of the residents have endured, including violence at 'bandit' African checkpoints, the mountain is the least racist place they have experienced, and "it's the place they live with the most dignity on their migratory journeys" in the view of the author (Laurel 2018). Despite the appalling conditions, there are traces of conviviality and reciprocity. Some of the stories told are like moral parables, they synthesise qualities or faults which are generic. For example, the illness of one of the two women featured in the text, and her subsequent miscarriage, encapsulates the shared narrative of hope, renewal and despair. What is also shared are the humiliations and terrors faced, the common perilous journey across hundreds of miles of inhospitable terrain: "the rule of thumb was that the closer you get to the gates of Europe, the more you disposed of linking you to a concrete African country" (Laurel 2017, 90). Tactically, this makes sense, but it also marks the emptying out of a *repertoire of identities* as well as the emptying out of a continent in order to go to another one. As one other person comments, "the closer we get to the finishing line, none of us is from anywhere" (121). What the novel shows critically is the existence of dependent voices combined with seeds of independent thinking: "Until we show them any different, what's written in books will be what's read out on the radio, day and night" (120). This is an argument for alternative voices, counter-narratives, no longer hooked on Europe.

The Gurugu pledge itself is a collective action—contrary to the individualism of neoliberalism—an act of unified solidarity, a mass stamping on the ground prior to an attempted scaling of the fence, during which the men and women speak of the colonial history of Africa. The novel concludes with this scaling and shows a certain generosity of spirit and evidence of a collective African identity. The Melilla Africans, the African in Spain, come to the fence to hail those in the act of climbing but this particular attempt fails, the failure synopsised by the shape of two figures, out of the hundreds, stuck with one leg either side of the fence. In an act of self-sacrifice and altruism, those who failed the climb take two sick women to the top of the fence in the hope that they will be rescued and given medical help. This act of solidarity undercuts the patriarchy and misogyny shown earlier in the text, a form of overcoming in itself.

The final chapter—"The Beginning and the End"—departs radically from many similar narratives in that the first-person narrator steps forward to tell his own story with a different outcome. "I'm African", he declares and what follows is in keeping with one of the main themes of the novel: the construction of a potential African identity, complex and diverse, freed from the chains of dependence on Europe. This is a reminder that the people on Gurugu are not only, but also much more than, refugees. What they share is the lack of exit capacity, to use marketing jargon.

The ill-treatment of a fellow teacher of the narrator—an albino—and the irrationality of followers of the occult who had damaged the man, caused the narrator to set out on "the long road to nowhere". On the mountain he decided, after an earlier failed attempt, not to join in the attempt to scale the fence and abandoned his quest to reach Europe. Images of Africans dead on a Spanish beach confirmed him in his decision. He reflects on the impunity with which Africans are killed in Europe and on the lack of respect for their lives: "They didn't kill you for not having papers, that was just the excuse they used" (Laurel 2017, 180). This brings to mind a point made by Tiffany Tsantsoulas in respect of

Sylvia Wynter's work: "The imperative point being that the production of deprived and depraved humanity—symbolic death—is essential to the fiction of *homo oeconomicus*" (Tsantsoulas 2018, 169). The narrator was, of course, speaking of actual death. Symbolically, he makes his way to the mountain's southern face, to the sides where the lights of Europe do not reach and his story becomes a narrative of decolonial thinking from the Global South: "I chose the *southern face*, that my gaze was turned towards the River Zambezi" (*Gurugu Pledge*, 183, my italics). As has been argued, "Claiming a voice as a refugee also means exposing the continuing and evolving forms of the colonial gaze that permeates the discourse of forced migration" (Brant et al. 2017, 627). The narrator's choice of the southern gaze lays bare and makes visible the European narrative of power and casts the whole preceding narrative as "a committed epistemological resistance against epistemic violence that had prevented imaginations of the world and freedom from knowledges and cosmologies of the Global South!" (Ndlovu Gatsheni 2013, 264). An act of epistemic and embodied disobedience, the narrator's decision to stay on the mountain is linked to the hope that he will be able 'to make the story known', and perhaps inhabit a different reality which others might also strive for. The story is the one we have just read which is both a personal story and a symptomatic one generated by a critical, decolonial lens

Silenced Deaths

Having outlined aspects of decoloniality, I should now like to turn to another African novel which demonstrates, among a range of other things, features of the coloniality of mind and the coloniality of knowledge. *African Titanics* was published in Arabic in 2008 and translated into English in 2014. The author, Abu Bakr Khaal, is an Eritrean who now lives in Denmark, but, as a member of the Eritrean Liberation Front, was expelled from Eritrea and sought refuge in Libya for a number of years until, during the civil war, he fled to Tunisia where he spent two months in a refugee camp. Khaal combines local politics with colonial and postcolonial histories in a narrative which draws extensively upon African cultural traditions and histories. It might be called a work of 'epistemological regard': "Coloniality of knowledge is useful in enabling decolonial thinkers to understand how endogenous and indigenous knowledges have been pushed to what came to be deemed as 'the barbarian margins of society' where they subsist as folklore and superstitions" (Ndlovu-Gatsheni 2015, 33). This novel is a 'writing back' from those margins.

Eritrea, Sudan, Libya and Tunisia all figure in the novel but it is not autobiographical although it has a first-person narrator who, some way through the novel, we learn is called Abdar. The narration is both participatory, first-hand, and reported, second-hand. The text is full of ruptures and dislocations which create multiple shifts in temporality and spatiality, almost like a 'handheld' form of writing, a kind of discontinuous present tense. It is not possible to establish a precise timescale except that the main story is contemporary. Logical sequencing is eschewed. Several examples of prolepsis and analepsis occur—we are told about an event which is then retold at a later time. For example, "One day I relayed my musings to Malouk, a Liberian whose fate was deeply entangled with mine for some time, and whose departure left a deep well of sadness within that still torments me to this day" (Khaal 2014, 5). We are told this on page 5, then Malouk is not mentioned again for a considerable time until he reappears and his death is narrated. The narrator is a chronicler but there are several events of which he hears but does not experience or witness.

The novel begins with a statement: "Migration came flooding through Africa, a turbulent swell sweeping everything along in its wake" (3). The narrator describes this 'flooding' (a word, incidentally, used in anti-migrant discourse over many years) as a pandemic, a plague which he attributes to a dark sorcerer promising paradise. The use of the word 'sorcerer' also mirrors European views of African forms of knowledge. It is used ironically because the actual source of the migration 'bug' is the colonising of mind/psyche which has invaded the core imaginary of Africans, as mentioned earlier. This is the point where the word 'seductive' is most apt to describe the urge to migrate. I stress the word here because Abdar, dismissive of the lure of migration for five years, finally elects to follow the migrant path.

Abdar had resisted the seductive appeal of migration, "until I was plucked from Eritrea, swept across the Sudanese border, and on into Libya ... I was lost, and almost perished in the desert, before slipping through into Tunisia" (3). The passivity of the syntax suggests that he was in thrall, helpless to a superior power/force. The sentence is also proleptic in the sense that it summarises, in a few words, the trajectory of his journey which will occupy much of the narrative, with frequent digressions and detours. The passivity also emphasises a lack of agency, or of migrant subjectivity, although Abdar speaks sceptically of African-in-Europe success stories which prioritise money, women, and cars and relegate achievements in the realm of knowledge—for example, degrees awarded—suggesting that migrant 'success' is only valued in terms of European models of consumerism.

The narrator's friend, Malouk tells an African story which he had copied out, *The Adventures of Kaji*, about a man, Kaji, who tried to protect his nephew from the migration bug. Malouk, with his treasured guitar, is the carrier of African stories and songs in the novel, forms of indigenous knowledge.

Listening to tales of migration, Kaji is sceptical about whether ships ever reached Lampedusa—a foreshadowing of later events in the novel. He tries to cure his nephew of the migration bug by means of his songs. One song is the *Song of Joy*, which is, in effect, an origin story—an African first-man-on-earth myth who, through the medium of magic, creates a female companion. In his Homeric verse novel, *The Perfect Nine: the epic of Gikuyu and Mumbi* (2018), Ngugi Wa Thiong'o produces an origin myth, a 're-writing' of a Kenyan creation story in the form of a feminist narrative. Ngugi is writing against the 'dismemberment' of African cultures by the inscription of "Europhonism [which] took the form of mapping, owning and naming" (Ndlovu-Gatsheni 2015, 32). In Kaji's tale the man is the first artist, founder of Africa's earliest musical and narrative heritage. It is a song which will recur throughout the narrative. This is the first of several references in the text to forms of African creativity, knowledge and cultural traditions, a cultural response to the marginalisation mentioned previously. The point of the story is to emphasise that Africans are capable of producing knowledge (demeaned by Europeans as irrational, folkloric, etc.) and of exercising imagination and the power of art to overcome sorcery (the lure of coloniality)—the migrant trap. This challenges what Santos calls 'abyssal thinking'.

The opening sections of the novel establish much of the scaffolding of the narrative which becomes both a commemoration and a kind of wake: "Living in the wake on a global level means living the disastrous time and effects of continued marked migrations, Mediterranean and Caribbean, trans-American and -African migration, structural adjustment imposed by the International Monetary Fund that continues imperialisms/colonialisms and more" (Sharpe 2016, 15). What the novel does is produce both a generic and specific migrant narrative—each of the components of which reproduce a familiar story of people smuggling, terrifying desert journeys in unsuitable vehicles, payments for crossings, and a perilous sea voyage in unseaworthy vessels. As one of the characters, Terhas, says at one point to the narrator, Abdar: "Weren't we together in the Desert of Death and the Smuggler's Den? And preparing for the Sea Voyage?" (Khaal 2014, 78). The three core features mentioned by Terhas constitute the main tropes of the novel and give it an allegorical framework. Each feature is a familiar component of Western media narratives of migration but is seldom written from the inside, so to speak, from the perspective of the migrant.

I want to relate this novel to something Mbembe has said as it fits it very precisely: "the colonized person is a living, talking, conscious, active individual whose identity arises from a three-pronged movement of violation, erasure and self-writing" (Mbembe 2003, 8). Along with Quijano's word 'seductive', used earlier, I want to keep in mind the word 'erasure' throughout, as the two terms represent the contrapuntal texture of the novel.

The narrative is generic in the sense that it articulates a number of well-known refugee journey tropes, as I have said, a kind of outline or synopsis of the migrant/refugee condition. However what the narrative does is also present an *inline*, by taking each of these generic tropes and personalising them into specific experiences by naming the nameless, rejecting the European dehumanising anonymity of refugee deaths, and constructing identities with 'grievable selves', bearing in mind my discussion in Chapter 1 of Judith Butler's concept of the 'ungrievable': "lives regarded as disposable" (Butler 2014, 35). This is the core issue of value which I will return to later in the discussion.

The specificity begins with Abdar's move to Khartoum and takes shape through his endless search for people smugglers to take him, and others, across the Sahara. He gathers extensive information about smuggling by land, sea, and air, and keeps track of all the ironically named Titanics, so-called because of their propensity to sink: a joke is made of a tragic fact but it also undermines the Western narrative of invincibility and superior knowledge/power, given the history of the original 'Titanic' in 1912. He has up-to-date knowledge of all the boats likely to be used and of the bribery and corruption involved. This is what I mean by *specificity*, as in the European narrative of migration there is no space for these extensive preparation stages, the networks involved, and the costs.

Specificity is also part of the construction of identifiers, unique, named persons with whom the narrator travels and/or relates to; they are made knowable, beyond subjection. Chapter 3 introduces Naji, the driver who will take Abdar and others from Omdurman to Kufia in Libya. This detail, together with the precise number of 23 people in the grossly overcrowded Range Rover, are further examples of specificity. On the journey, the driver has to bribe various people and he de-romanticises the desert (of orientalist myth) and stresses its perils as well as those of the sea. We witness these slowly emerging dangers—fuel shortages, losing the way, health issues, climate hazards, bandits, dehydration, hallucinations—all narrated in an indirect/oblique way and dispassionate tone so as not to render them sensationalist or melodramatic. Such details of the desert crossing are mostly absent from the hegemonic narrative: people dying on the journey here are named, shown in close-up, localised. One particular instance encapsulates the desert plight of the migrant, in this case an Eritrean, Assegdom Mesfin, hovering between life and death, in that it points to the absurdity of the Eritrean/Ethiopian war, which produced so many refugees and arose from what was a legacy of colonial times:

> We were identical … the lot of us … our features, our clothes … and we all knew the enemy's language … and when we fought in the dark … their army would attack each other and we'd fight each other too … we buried their dead beside ours … because they couldn't tell them apart … they did the same. (Khaal 2014, 33)

The pronominal use underscores the futility. There is another specific instant which shows the power of affect, something usually seen as not part of the Global South:

> People were dropping like flies. Assegdom Mesfin, another young Eritrean was hovering between life and death. Terhas (a young Eritrean woman) diligently cleaned the sand from his mouth as he lay unconscious, his head resting on her lap. Pushing her finger through his lips, she unclogged it of sand before leaning over and transferring her saliva into his mouth … throughout that scorching day, she moistened his tongue with her spit, determined not to give up. (Khaal 2014, 32)

She also, we are told, poured the acrid drops of her, painfully produced, urine down his throat. This is cinematic in its minute attention to detail. There is no evidence of any relationship between them and these actions, framed by the precision of the active syntax, are evidence of her capacity for agency denied to the African 'primitive' by the abyssal narrative. The detail, completed by "we laid the body in a shallow grave" is another example of closely observed personalisation in the text, which includes the positioning of Mesfin, the precision of Terhas's finger and the bodying of her care. She becomes a subject, the centre of the narrative at this point, the subjective embodiment of the frequently anonymised African. It might be claimed that this is a case of a gendered cliché but I would argue that the attention to the lips, throat, tongue, spit, saliva and urine embodies something far more intense. The dispassionate and 'itemised' style underpins this. The whole extended moment captures in synoptic fashion the desert journey of the migrant—it is, like so much in the novel, indicative, symptomatic, metonymic even. It has the quality of parable. What it also shows is *embodied* care, the rejection of what has been called 'value abjection' (Müller 2019, 6), where values of relationality, interdependence, and mutuality predominate over those of the individualism and competition of financialised capitalism which prevail in the Europe to which the migrants are seduced. Terhas works with the unclean, the improper bodily waste, those features of the human excluded and expelled from the values of the West, relegated to the margins, the work of low-paid migrants, usually female. Here, Terhas revalues the abject and demonstrates an ethical model of care, rebelling against the abject identity of the marginalised. Her action is exemplary in the literal sense, disinterested and relational, a refusal of the subordination of reproduction to production. In the process, she stakes a claim to be 'human' against the abyssal category of 'less than human', 'other'. She is neither pitiable, hapless migrant nor terrorist of Western media myth but she carves out an alternative identity, an independent imaginary.

I have stressed this narrative of care and relationality because it recurs at different intervals in the text, against the predation of smugglers and forms of Western devaluation—for example, the later refusal to rescue drowning migrants.

The International Organisation for Migration has shown that, in the period from 2013 to 2018, 6,600 African migrants have died on the journey to Europe, mostly while crossing the Sahara desert, and this figure is regarded as a gross underestimate (GMDAC 2018). Since 2014 more than 4,000 fatalities have been recorded annually on migrant routes worldwide, and, in the past twenty-five years, 75,000 migrant deaths have been recorded.

The next phase in the journey is the prelude to the sea voyage, another stage of precarity and uncertainty. In Tripoli, Abdar seeks out smugglers for the boat journey and is made aware of the $1,000 cost of the crossing. He is with a group of twenty-five Eritreans plus a few other nationalities. They contact smugglers and are locked in a hideout prior to boarding. In the hideout are the discarded clothes and belongings of earlier migrants, and, as they await departure, Abdar finds a love letter from a previous migrant who recounts a journey similar to the one just experienced. The pathos lies in the fact that the letter never reached his lover, Malfanita. The name and the date, March 12, 1998 is another one of the specifying features I have mentioned. Similarly, on the walls of the hideout, Terhas and Abdar read messages left by previous migrants in a range of African languages. One such message is dated, another has a specific address. The messages stress separation—the signatures of the wretched of the earth— but they are also inscriptions, marks of subjugation of what Ranciere calls those who do not count in the global order of inequality. Defiantly, these are projections of memorials into public space. In Rancière's terms, the police, by which he means the ordering of authority, "is an order of bodies that defines the allocation of ways of doing, ways of being, and ways of seeing … an order of the visible and the sayable" (Rancière 1999, 26). This order excludes the refugee who is deemed to be invisible and voiceless, because they have nothing worth saying in the European narrative of modernity. The migrants' signatures are a claim for the expansion of that field of a possible narrative, for inclusion as more than passive objects— invisible and silenced. They are reminiscent of the discarded clothes and of the names scratched on the wall in *On the Bride's Side* (discussed in Chapter 2).

Prior to boarding, the waiting period of immobility—a common experience for migrants—is punctuated by anxiety over the weather, and about television reports of "shipwrecks and images of men and women plucked from the waves. Rows of drowned corpses were routinely displayed, carelessly covered over as though victims of a street brawl" (Khaal 2014, 59). The words "routinely displayed" suggest a commonplace experience, as does "carelessly covered over"—drawn from the lexicon of the grammar of global indifference, in sharp contrast with the care shown by the migrants to Mesfin. It is yet another instance of the devaluation of which I have been speaking, the *carelessness* of twenty-first-century capitalism. In this waiting period, evidence of the collective role of these transnational migrants is demonstrated, their relationality; even though they are separated by many different languages, they bond together in their shared experience of hope and also fear.

The narrator describes the terror which precedes the departure of a boat and the deathly silence on departure. He speculates on the possible fate of a boat in a generic sense—"you become fixated upon an idea"— as he does not actually make such a journey; it is one of many such speculations and generalisations about fear, hunger, thirst, drifting off course, and death; the arising of conflicts in which people, once part of a shared migrant community, act out the dehumanisation attributed to them by Europe, by robbing dead bodies of "random, valueless objects". Once again, the narrator uses the second-person pronoun to close the gap between reader and discourse, and to hypothesise about something only experienced second hand: "You grow paranoid, convincing yourself they are feeding off the bodies themselves. You watch them fighting to the death, bent on destruction with every fibre of their beings. They have become animals and you fear that you have become one too" (Khaal 2014, 62).

This is another example of the projection of a generic 'you', a form of interpellation in which both reader and narrator are constituted as 'refugee'—a moment of empathy, identification. It is also prefigurative as will be seen.

Among the second cohort to arrive at the smugglers' hideout is Malouk, who had been introduced a lot earlier, a musician and poet who can trace his ancestry back sixteen generations to another Malouk who was dedicated to building a ship to sail and rescue his wife, captured by pirates. This never happened because he died before the ship was built. Abdar tells Malouk about a boat which sank with 170 people on board, including a friend of his, with the bodies washed up on the Tunisian coast. This is another generic incident and, when Malouk and Abdar are joined by an Ethiopian, Malkita, there is another proleptic moment in which the narrator tells of the sinking of the boat in which Malouk and Malkita will sink.

Apart from 'Captain' Attiah, a pharmacist, Malouk, Abdar and Terhas decide to head for Tunisia rather than take the much longer journey from Libya to Sicily. Attiah does make it to Lampedusa and then to Norway where he works as a pharmacist until, after 9/11, he is reported as a terrorist (he is seen praying) and he is deported. This is a brief passage in the novel but it points to one of the key hazards faced by migrants since 2001, the criminalisation of migrants in a new culture of securitisation.

Terhas, Malouk and Abdar, together with two Eritreans, Uthman Yasin and Anfira, negotiate the checkpoints and barbed wire of the Libya/Tunisia border and find a man to drive them to Tunis. They stay in a hotel but, undocumented, they are still liable to arrest. Malouk hands

Abdar a bundle of papers entitled 'Malouk the Second'. This Malouk became a famous storyteller. One original story, 'The Stone that only Spoke Once', tells of events which would take place in the future and speaks of Africans complicit in their own oppression because of colonialism. The tale became a myth, in time. Malouk does not set much store by these gods and idols but acknowledges them as part of his rich heritage of rituals and mantras, a feature of African knowledge dismissed by the West, forgetting its own legacy of rituals and ceremonies in Jewish and Christian tradition, something I will return to.

Malouk's music, poetry and stories are emblems of Santos's post-abyssal culture, that which is derogated by the Global North. Terhas at one point refers to her and Abdar's experience as if it were part of an epic tale—the Desert of Death, the Smugglers' Den, and the Sea Voyage, indicative features of the narrative as described earlier. The novel has twelve chapters which mimic the classical epic structure of Western culture. Malouk's poem, 'Crossing', enacts the passage of the migrants through numerous obstacles.

Unequal Mobility Regime

The penultimate chapter opens with Abdar and his companions meeting with a large group of 170 fellow migrants waiting to set sail in three days' time. There are so many languages spoken that mime is needed; this emphasises the complex African linguistic heritage. Abdar meets up with a former friend—Ali Khayrat, a fisherman and goods smuggler—who is to be the boat's captain despite a total lack of experience at this level, another generic feature of many of the boats used to smuggle migrants. This particular boat and journey has been prefigured earlier and is now repeated as a cautionary tale as Abdar speaks of the 'fate of the unlucky boat', as if it were a tale, before he actually narrates the story of the actual voyage. The boat's structure, with its holes, oil and dirt, also has generic characteristics. Ali has volunteered as skipper as a way of avoiding the $1,000 fee which he cannot afford. He has a rudimentary grasp of steering but fails to understand the GPS system.

The fatal journey is told from the perspective of Ali, and Malouk, who is on board, witnesses the boat falling apart and taking on water. This is all narrated in a fairly matter of fact way, with the engine failing and people dying, as if it were a predictable, almost inevitable occurrence. Ali is confident that, as they are in international waters, they would be rescued. On the eighth day (the expected duration of the journey) "a massive oil tanker hove into view" (Khaal 2014, 110), ironically carrying something they were running out of. This moment is one of the most iconic, and horrifying, in the book and has that generic quality mentioned already but also with a tragic specificity. The migrants waved desperately and threw a dead woman's body in the water to indicate their plight but all they saw was "a small group of sailors grouped motionlessly on its deck, surveying them in silence" (110). This posture suggests the stance of the European border regime. The tanker, in a sense, mirrors the migrants' boat as it is what we might call in shorthand an encounter between the Global North and the Global South, the people who count and those who do not count, those possessed with ungrievable lives: "The sailors made no response [...] But the steamer continued on its course and the sailors remained on deck, their arms folded across their chests, smiling and sniggering" (110). It is a tableau of indifference as the phrase "their arms folded" emphasises their racialised refusal to intervene, as it is these unfolded arms that could have been used for rescue.

This section is remarkably prescient, written as it is in 2008, as it links to the 'Left-to-Die Boat' case during 2011 in which sixty-three migrants who had left Tripoli on March 27 died during fourteen days of drift on the open sea despite having made contact with the Italian coastguard, several aerial and military naval assets and some fishermen's boats. There were only nine survivors. This story can be found in *Forensic Oceanography*'s report on the 'Left-to-Die Boat' and in the brief film, *Liquid Traces*. *Forensic Oceanography* reconstructed the 'liquid traces' of this event which formed the basis of a report which was used in a number of legal complaints (Heller and Pezzani 2012). This was but one instance, among hundreds, perhaps thousands, which illustrates what Charles Heller and Lorenzo Pezzani called "a selective and unequal mobility regime [which] emerged across the Mediterranean" (Heller and Pezzani 2018). It is this regime, exercising the coloniality of power, which is responsible for the violence of borders, so much the common experience of the contemporary world and not just in Europe. It could be argued that these transnational migrants are invisible to the coloniality of being but highly visible to the coloniality of power.

The dispassionate, third-person style used to relate the indifference of the ship's crew shifts to a closer, interior 'shot' of the boat, focusing on a man committing suicide, "fish nibbling at the woman's breast" in the sea—the ultimate dehumanisation—and moves near to Malouk, floating on a plank in the sea trying to recall the moment when they set sail and, in keeping with his role in the text, "fragments of Rimbaud flashed through his mind" contradicting the objectified image of the uneducated African 'other'. "In my mind, the narrator says, I hear Malouk reciting verses", and he shifts from a generic boat tragedy to a specific imagining, consonant with his image of Malouk. The poem of Rimbaud would most probably be "The Drunken Boat" ("Le Bateau Ivre") and the narrator proceeds to construct, or fictively reconstruct, a poem by Malouk which is both immediate—"Their unnamed boats / their Unmarked graves"— and analeptic—"As city walls bounce them back [...] The bones of their corpses / Abandoned / In the desert; Civilization crucifies them / Above the border's barbs" (Khaal 2014, 114).

The poem enacts the erasure of the migrant—"unnamed", "unmarked"—recalls the desert journey and, very tellingly, juxtaposes "civilisation" with "crucifies", which does not just simplistically link the refugee to Christ but crucially suggests that it is a specifically Christian Europe, self-styling itself as civilisation, which constructs "the border's barbs". In a sense, it takes apart the whole preceding narrative by erasing the subjectivities it has established. It might be argued that Abdar with his passion for the poetry of Shelley and Malouk with his love of Rimbaud (gun-running in Africa) are in thrall to European culture but it is noticeable that both the chosen poets were outsider figures, rebels against European norms.

Not only are Abdar and Malouk educated, contrary to the Western media's image of the 'uncivilised migrant', but Terhas also has "extensive reading of lawyers, judges and prisoners of conscience in the developed world" (Khaal 2014, 117), those resistant to, and disaffected by, the West. Before they could board the ship, Abdar, Terhas, and others in the hostel are arrested and thrown into prison: "places for violence and humiliation" where they are interrogated for hours, beaten and kicked. They had claimed that they were travelling from Europe but a dropped Libyan banknote betrayed them. The face on the note was that of Omar al-Mukhtar, a Libyan national hero who fought against Italian colonialism—yet another naming of a figure who resisted the European claim to superiority.

The experience of prison is yet one more feature of the migrant journey—immobility—which is abruptly aborted when Abdar and Terhas are deported to Libya and then to Eritrea. Deportation is, of course, one of the many ways in which Europe controls the mobility of the migrant. Towards the end of the narrative we learn, in yet another of the temporal switches, that Malouk had escaped when Terhas and Abdar were arrested, hence he made it to the boat which sank. The wreck was retrieved together with the body of Ali Khayrat but not that of Malouk.

Malouk becomes a figure of legend, with tales from Rome, India and elsewhere attesting to his mythical status: "A man standing abreast two waves, carrying a guitar on his back". He was, in these tales, rescued from the waters, "apparently walking on the crest of a wave as calmly as people walk on land". This is another obvious Christ reference but I am not sure if it is ironic, recruiting Christ to the ranks of those who do not count, alluding to the role of missionaries in Africa, or asserting the validity of this recent African myth alongside the Christian myth of European civilisation. A song heard on the boat is attributed to Malouk, giving him an oracular legacy, the role of witness: "To all the pounding hearts / In feverish boats / I will cut / Through these paths / With my own liberated heart / And tell my soul / To shout of your silenced deaths / And fill / Palms of dust with morning dew / And song" (Khaal 2014, 122).

Each of the texts examined in this chapter has been seen as contributing towards a 'grammar of resistance', of claiming a space for the voice of the African migrant as she/he confronts the hazards of precarious journeys across desert, land and sea, constantly thwarted by the continuing presence of the coloniality of power in the form of violent border regimes. In the following chapter, the displaced and the 'less than human' face very different journeys, within their own land yet checked, diverted, and re-routed by walls, fences, permits and roadblocks which constitute the physical and psychological barriers of more than fifty years of occupation. A range of texts will be analysed which seek both to articulate this experience and to challenge the conditions of its existence.

Note

1. [Former President] Donald Trump, *The Sun*, July 13, 2018.

References

Alioua, Mehdi. 2006. "Silence! People Are Dying on the Southern Borders of Europe." Translated by Brian Holmes. In *The Maghreb Connection: Movements*

of Life Across North Africa, edited by Ursula Biemann and Brian Holmes, 1–17. Barcelona: ACTAR.
Ashcroft, Bill, et al. 1989. *The Empire Writes Back: Theory and Practice in Postcolonial Literature*. London: Routledge.
Baldwin, James. 2016 [1965]. "James Baldwin on History." American Historical Association. http://t.co/TXAMyBVG5. Accessed May 5, 2018.
Boffey, Daniel. 2018. "Orban claims Hungary is last bastion against 'Islamisation of Europe'". *The Guardian*, 18 February, 2018.
Brant, Clare, Tobias Heinrich, and Monica Soeting. 2017. "The Placing of Displaced Lives: Refugee Narratives." *Auto/Biography Studies* 32 (3): 624–28. https://doi.org/10.1080/08989575.2017.1339996.
Butler, Judith. 2014. "Ordinary, Incredulous." In *The Humanities and Public Life*, edited by Peter Brooks and Hilary Jewett, 15–37. New York: Fordham University Press.
Camus, Renaud. 2017 [2012]. *Le Grand Remplacement*. Paris: Lulu Books.
Ceriani, Pablo, et al. 2009. "Report on the Situation on the Euro-Mediterranean Borders." *Work Package* 9 [University of Barcelona], April 27.
Chakrabarty, Dipesh. 2000. *Provincializing Europe: Postcolonial Thought and Historical Difference*. Princeton and Oxford: Princeton University Press.
Comaroff, Jean, and John L. Comaroff. 2016. *Theory from the South Or, How Euro-America Is Evolving Toward Africa*. Abingdon: Routledge.
Counter Extremism Project. 2020. Executive Summary: "European Ethno-Nationalist and White Supremacy Groups." (n.p.).
Cox, Emma, et al., eds. 2020. *Refugee Imaginaries: Research Across the Humanities*. Edinburgh: Edinburgh University Press.
de Benoist, Alain. 2004. "On Identity." *Telos* 128: 9–64.
de Benoist, Alain. 2016 [1966, 1996]. *The Indo-Europeans: In Search of the Homeland*. London: Arktos Media Ltd.
Fabian, Johannes.1983. *Time and the Other: How Anthropology Makes its Object*. New York: Columbia University Press.
Faye, Guillaume. 2016 [2002]. *The Colonisation of Europe*. London: Arktos Media Ltd.
Faye, Guillaume. 2017. *A Global Coup*. London: Arktos Media Ltd.
Friberg, Daniel. 2015. *The Real Right Returns: A Handbook for the True Opposition*. Stockholm: Arktos Media Ltd.
Fricker, Miranda. 2009. *Epistemic Injustice: Power and the Ethics of Knowing*. New York: Oxford University Press.
GMDAC. 2018. "Over 6,600 Migration Deaths Recorded in Africa Since 2013—Just the Tip of the Iceberg." *International Organisation for Migration*. December 18. https://www.iom.int/news/gmdac-over-6600-migration-deaths-recorded-africa-2013-just-tip-iceberg. Accessed September 10, 2020.

Geoghegan, Peter. 2020. "Funding Hate." *New Humanist*, Autumn.
Grosfoguel, Ramon. 2007. "The Epistemic Decolonial Town: Beyond Political-Economy Paradigms." *Cultural Studies* 21 (2/3): 203–46.
Hage, G. 2009. "Waiting Out the Crisis: On Stuckedness and Governmentality." In *Waiting*, edited by Ghassan Hage, 97–106. Carlton, VIC: Melbourne University Press.
Heller, Charles, and Lorenzo Pezzani. 2012. "Report on the 'Left-To-Die-Boat'." *Forensic Oceanography*. London: Goldsmiths, University of London. www.forensic-architecture.org. Accessed February 7, 2020.
Heller, Charles, and Lorenzo Pezzani. 2018. "The Mediterranean Mobility Conflict: Violence and Anti-Violence at the Borders of Europe." *Humanity Journal*: 1–16.
Khaal, Abu Bakr. 2014 [2008]. *African Titanics*. London: DARF Publishers.
Krebs, Pierre. 1997. *Fighting for the Essence: Western Ethno-Suicide or European Renaissance*. London: Arktos Media Ltd.
Laïdi, Zaki. 1998. *A World Without Meaning: The Crisis of Meaning in International Politics*. London: Routledge.
Laurel, Juan Tomás Ávila. 2017. *The Gurugu Pledge*. Translated by Jethro Soutar. Sheffield: And Other Stories.
Laurie, Timothy. 2012. "Epistemology as Politics and the Double-Bind of Border Thinking: Levi-Strauss, Deleuze and Guattari, Mignolo." *Journal of Multidisciplinary International Studies* 9 (2): 1–20.
Lecadet, Clara. 2017. "Europe Confronted by its Expelled Migrants." In *The Borders of "Europe": Autonomy of Migration, Tactics of Bordering*, edited by Nicholas De Genova, 141–64. Durham, NC: Duke University Press.
Mbembe, Achile. 2003. "Necropolitics." Translated by Libby Meintje. *Public Culture* 15 (1): 11–40.
Mbembe, Achile. 2008. "What Is Postcolonial Thinking? An Interview with Achille Mbembe." *Eurozine*, January 9: 1–31.
Müller, Beatrice, 2019. "The Careless Society—Dependency and Care Work in Capitalist Societies." *Frontiers in Sociology*, January: 1–10. https://doi.org/10.3389/fsoc.2018.00044.
Murdoch, Simon. 2020. "Patriotic Alternative: Uniting the Fascist Right." *Hope Not Hate*, August 17. www.hopenothate.org.uk.
Ndlovu-Gatsheni, Sabelo J. 2013. *Coloniality of Power in Postcolonial Africa: Myths of Decolonization*. Dakar: Codestria.
Ndlovu-Gatsheni, Sabelo. 2015. "Decoloniality in Africa: A Continuing Search for a New World Order." *ARAS* 36 (2) (December): 22–50.
Ngugi wa Thiong'o. 2009. *Something Torn and New: An African Renaissance*. New York: Basic Civitas Books.
O'Meara, Michael. 2013. *Guillaume Faye and the Battle of Europe*. Budapest: Arktos Media.

Quijano, Anibal. 2007. "Coloniality and Modernity/Rationality." *Cultural Studies* 21 (2/3): 168–78.
Rancière, Jacques. 1999. *Disagreement: Politics and Philosophy*. Translated by Jacqueline Rose. Minneapolis and London: University of Minnesota Press.
Said, Edward. 1978. *Orientalism*. New York: Pantheon Books.
Said, Edward. 1997. *Covering Islam: How the Media and the Experts Determine How We See the Rest of the World*. London: Vintage.
Salmela, Mikko, and Christian von Scheve. 2017. "Emotional Roots of Right-Wing Political Populism." *Social Science Information* 56 (4): 567–95.
Sennett, Richard. 2011. *The Foreigner: Two Essays on Exile*. London: Notting Hill Editions.
Sharpe, Christina. 2016. *In the Wake: On Blackness and Being*. Durham, NC: Duke University Press.
Siebert, Moritz, Estephan Wagner, and Abou Bakar Sidibe (directors). 2016. *Those Who Jump (Les Sauteurs)*. Copenhagen: *Final Cut for Real* Productions.
Soto Bermant, Laia. 2017. "The Mediterranean Question." In *The Borders of "Europe": Autonomy of Migration Tactics of Bordering*, edited by Nicholas De Genova, 121–40. Durham, NC: Duke University Press.
Trilling, Daniel. 2018. "Five Myths About the Refugee Crisis." *The Guardian*, June 6: 9–11.
Tsantsoulas, Tiffany. 2018. "Sylvia Wynter's Decolonial Rejoinder to Judith Butler's Ethics of Vulnerability." *Symposium* 22 (2): 158–77.
Weheliye, Alexander G. 2014. *Habeas Viscus: Racialising Assemblages, Biopolitics, and Black Feminist Theories of the Human*. Durham, NC: Duke University Press.
Williams, Patrick, and Laura Chrisman, eds. 1993. *Colonial Discourse and Postcolonial Theory: A Reader*. London: Routledge.
Wodak, Ruth. 2015. *The Politics of Fear: What Right-wing Populist Discourses Mean*. London: Sage.

CHAPTER 6

Fragmented Spaces/Broken Time: Restoring the Absence of Story in the West Bank of Palestine

Zionism is the last remaining active settler-colonialist project or movement. Settler colonialism is, in a nutshell, a project of replacement, settlement and expulsion. (Pappé 2016)

In the preceding chapters, displacement has been a feature of many of the texts discussed. The focus of this chapter is on all the features of settler colonialism outlined by Pappé, and it takes as its starting point something said by Eyal Weizman and colleagues: "According to the regional plans of politicians, suburban homes, industrial zones, infrastructure and roads are designed and built with the self-proclaimed aim of bisecting, disturbing and squeezing out Palestinian communities … Planning and building in the West Bank is effectively executing a political agenda through spatial manipulations" (Segal and Weizman 2003, 19). 'Spatial manipulations' are at the core of all the narratives which will be explored in this chapter.

It is not the purpose of this chapter to attempt to add to the already extensive literature on the politics of the Occupation but simply to examine its impact in terms of literary and cultural representations in the form of memoir, short story and novel. What will become evident, in the course of the argument, is that whim and impunity are characteristics of many of the practices of the Occupation. Some of these practices are common to settler colonialism regimes elsewhere but others are unique

© The Author(s), under exclusive license to Springer Nature Switzerland AG 2021
R. Bromley, *Narratives of Forced Mobility and Displacement in Contemporary Literature and Culture*, Studies in Mobilities, Literature, and Culture, https://doi.org/10.1007/978-3-030-73596-8_6

to Israeli governance. Separation, displacement, subjugation/obedience, without rights, control and surveillance of mobility and the colonisation of time and space are all prominent features of the regime.

In keeping with what the Israelis call 'facts on the ground' (since the 1967 Occupation, the colonisation of Palestine by settlements and other measures), displacement is an ongoing and dynamic narrative, varying in its intensity, and in the case of the West Bank of Palestine—the subject of this chapter—there is a long-standing 'war of narratives', which, simply put, is between 'law' and 'right' in so far as so many of the conflicting narratives are predicated upon the 'law of return' (Israeli) and the 'right of return' (Palestinian). Not surprisingly, 'return' is at the core of most displacement narratives but this varies from situation to situation and from generation to generation—from keys and deeds retained to a more metaphorical idea of return. The historic forced migration of Palestinians was in 1948 when 750,000 were expelled but this continued over years on a different scale; for example, from 1967 to 1992, 1,522 Palestinian residents of the Occupied Palestinian Territory (OPT) were deported by Israel, mostly to Jordan and Lebanon (Shafir 2017, 37). Not everyone wants to return but the idea tends to dominate what might be called displacement narratives of the oppressed. For the Palestinian situation, Edward Said's "Permission to Narrate" (1984) is seminal and I want to briefly comment on this later. As important is something Mourid Barghouti says in *I Was Born There, I was Born Here* (2012)—the title itself referencing a frequent dialectic in displacement narratives:

> The cruellest degree of exile is invisibility, being forbidden to tell one's story for oneself. We, the Palestinian people, are narrated by our enemies, in keeping with their presence and our absence. They label us as suits them. The weaker party in any conflict is allowed to scream, allowed to complain … but never allowed to tell his own story. The conflict over the land becomes the conflict over the story … In this sense the entire Palestinian people is exiled through an absence of its story. (Barghouti 2012, 144)

The weak, the other, is always already narrated. Storying, I would argue, is a form of hope. In Mahmoud Darwish's monumental prose-poem, *Memory for Forgetfulness, August, Beirut, 1982*, he says at one point, "For here [Beirut], where we are, is the tent for wandering meanings and words gone astray and the orphaned fight, scattered and banished from the centre" (Darwish 1995, 11). How that tent (with its refugee camp link) might become a narrative is the theme of Said's "Permission to Narrate", in which he says the West has suppressed and denied the authority of the Palestinian narrative of dispossession and by so doing "has revoked the permission to narrate the Palestinian experience", a narrative pointed towards 'self-determination', and based upon a narrative of displacement (he is speaking after 1982). This communal narrative is the restoring/the restorying of an historical story to its place of origin and future resolution in Palestine. What is needed, he says, and this is true of all the narratives I shall examine, is "an enabling vocabulary, a narrative entailing a homeland" (Said 1984, 253). As Darwish said in another context, the Palestinian people, since 1948, have been "redundant shadows exiled from space and time" (a theme to be developed in this chapter) and the Nakba "is an extended present that promises to continue in the future" (Darwish 2001, translation of broadcast speech, 15 May).

Time, Space and Mobility

Erasure—evictions, displacements, seizures of land and demolitions—was/is part of the 'spatial strangulation' (Pappé 2016), with Palestinians in Israel known as 'present absentee aliens' and a systematic process of ex-nomination set in place with Arabic place names replaced by Hebrew or Biblical names (e.g. Lod for Lydda; Judea and Samaria for the West Bank). So, land, name and narrative deterritorialisation were produced by Israeli 'transfers', ethnic cleansing, occupation post-1967 and the colonial settler paradigm. A process of fragmented mapping has occurred in which continuity and contiguity in Palestinian territory have been broken up both by settlements and, since 2004, the so-called Security Fence.[1] I will talk about the ways in which space and time are orchestrated negatively for Palestinians, but one post-Oslo example will suffice at this point. Julie Peteet in *Landscape of Hope and Despair: Palestinian Refugee Camps* (2009) explains that a Palestinian leaving Jenin in the north (of the West Bank) would have to change zones fifty times in order to reach Hebron in the south—although both are in Area A (Palestinian Authority area); an Israeli could cross the entire West Bank from north to south or east to west without leaving Area C (Israeli controlled). As Camille Mansour says, "this cartography scarred their daily landscape with countless signs of military control: watchtowers, barbed wire, forced detours, concrete block barriers, zigzagging tracks, flying checkpoints" (Mansour 2001, 83). This is a concise summary of the conditions of internal displacement reprised on a daily basis in the West Bank.

All of these physical, spatial barriers combined with the "circulation of affect … the continuous accumulation of hurts and humiliations of occupation", the "everyday exercise of the power to humiliate", as Meron Benvenisti calls it, adding that the purpose of checkpoints "is to send a message of force and authority, to inspire fear, and to symbolize the downtrodden nature and inferiority of those under occupation", remind us that displacement always has symbolic, psychological and material characteristics which are often internalised to the point of abjection (Benvenisti, quoted in Gregory 2004, 119). This is explored in Ramzy Baroud's *The Last Earth* (2018), written against dominant narratives, a form of history from below.

Dysrhythmia is precisely what this cartography of displacement produces: "a violent fragmentation and recombination of time and space, which is nothing less than a concerted attempt to disturb and derange the normal rhythms of Palestinian life" (Gregory 2004, 126). This is a feature of the narratives I shall be examining, all of which document the frustrations and absurdities of occupation. As Adi Ophir notes, 'Temporariness is now the law of occupation' with the occupier playing with time—"on borrowed time, in fact on stolen time, other people's time" (Ophir 2002, 60). Mobile frontiers, shifting borders—displacing activities—immobilise the ebb and flow of transit instead of regulating it. As Barghouti says, "The soldier of the Occupation stands on a piece of land he has confiscated and calls it 'here', and I, its owner, exiled to a distant country, call it 'there'" (Barghouti 2012, 80).

As has been argued powerfully:

> The refugee camps. The very mark of our condition, the [continuing] sign of the original deed which catapulted us all into this unending journey, the embodiment of what might have been, what was, what could be, the body which must be dismembered for so many [Israelis] to breathe lightly, rest back in comfort.
>
> This body within our body, the representation of our memory. (Jayyusi 2003, 127)

Jayyusi speaks also of "the decades long project of undoing an entire society" and it is this 'project' which frames the arguments in this chapter, "An occupation that persists and increasingly insists on consuming and appropriating place and space, land, air and water. An occupation in the service of a colonial order, of a colonial will to erase, marginalise, silence, replace and dispose at will" (Jayyusi 2003, 127, 128). In what follows, an emphasis will be placed on the expropriation of Palestinian land, the erasure of place and memory, the displacement and disposability of people, but also on the unmasking of this colonial order through resistance, in Jayyusi's memorable phrase: "by an indigenous population awoken to its own rhythms" (2003, 126).

De Certeau argues that "Every story is a travel story—a spatial practice" (de Certeau 1984, 115), and this is doubly true of stories of displacement in which orientation/disorientation/re-orientation becomes the story itself, so much so that the narrative is not simply the record of a past experience but is seen as actively creating experience. In this way, displacement is ongoing and dynamic, not just a nostalgic longing for what was but also constituting a belonging which might be—the stories give memory a future, developing fresh discursive resources out of the complex dialectic of here and there, then and now; as Freeman says, "as a general rule we don't just live lines, moving inexorably through one thing after another, we live spirals of remembrance and return, repetition and reconfiguration, under the spell of ... mythopoeic desire" (Freeman 1998, 47).

In this context, it is worth remembering what Darwish says in respect of loss: "Everything here is proof of loss and impairment. Everything here is a painful contrast with what was there. The thing that wounds you most is the fact that 'there' is close to 'here'" (Darwish 2006, 30). 'There' may be close to 'here' geographically but separated by years of conflict, legislation and ideology. Not surprisingly, displacement focuses a lot on place so that memory is spatialised in terms of specific sites but also of objects associated with those sites—mosque, church, olive, fig, lemon tree, etc.

It is not possible, of course, to speak of a Palestinian narrative but of multiple, complex and contradictory narratives often inflected by both generation and gender. Some of the narratives are crudely nationalist, some strategically nationalist, others speak of a bi-national co-existence, but almost all are articulated in terms of land and landscape—imagined and real—loss and dispossession. For each generation in different historical conjunctures, the narrative shifts in emphasis from the Nakba (1948) to the first intifada (1987–1993), to experiences of the refugee camps set up after 1948, the Sabra and Shatila massacres of September 1982 in Lebanon, the Oslo Accords (1993–1995), the second intifada (2000–2005), and Operation Cast Lead (known as the 'Gaza massacre' in the Muslim world, this was the three-week armed conflict between the IDF and Gaza, in which more than one thousand Palestinians were killed, including many children and civilians, and thirteen Israelis lost their lives, four from 'friendly fire'). With these shifts in emphasis also come changes in narrativisation, style, use of metaphor, paradigm, trope and tone. Every telling is a re-telling, a new kind of narrative giving rise to an alternative imaginary.

In the book quoted from earlier, Barghouti argues that the Occupation (nineteen refugee camps in the West Bank) "imprisons time inside space" and I want to use this to give focus to the chapter, as "A politics of time is concerned with the appropriation of the time of others, the institutionalization of a dominant time, and the legitimation of power by means of this control".

Time is used in the Occupation as a technology of power through the means of border, checkpoint and curfew which are also spatial constructs. Linked to this is the repeated exercise of humiliation to demean people's cultural identity, social esteem and sense of worth. All of these—time, space and humiliation—are material aspects of everyday life: waiting, frustration, endless delays, permits, circuitous and interrupted journeys (a ten-minute bus journey can take four hours), lengthy diversions and re-routings—instances of forced immobility but which also exist at the level of the symbolic, mental and affective. A curfew, for example, disrupts transactional life and mobility both temporally and spatially. All of this is designed to manipulate relations of power and dependency.

Time and space are both bearers of significance and classification, carriers of hierarchies of meaning. The dominant rhythms of Israeli life—freedom of movement, high quality roads, ease of transportation—exclude the Palestinians. Time and space are part of a codification and command culture with power over duration and spatial sequence and logic—the methodology of dispossession. Circulation and scheduling are Israeli-controlled—how is it possible to plan a journey or a daily routine in the face of checkpoints and curfews? The powerful divide the powerless from routine, schedule, norm and rhythm by disorganisation and dislocation of the everyday through a process of irregularity, arbitrariness and unpredictability. Disruption is a mode of control and the lack of predictability is crucial because most of us experience time in a taken for granted, almost unconscious, way with our daily routines following timetables, schedules and automatic procedures. We inhabit an internalised grid of expectation. Certainty and security are removed from the Palestinian who is denied co-evalness and is 'othered' through a discourse of power in a relation of inequality. It is what I call 'ideological time' and is part of a larger concept of temporality in which Zionism was seen as modernity and progress, Palestine feudal and backward, immobilised in time: distanced, separated and asymmetrical, at a standstill, defined as an absence ('a land without a people for a people without a land').

These temporal/spatial arrangements of what Eyal Weizman calls "the architecture of occupation" are designed to de-mobilise the Palestinians through a master/ing narrative of power to colonise their lives and their imagination through what is a form of terror, a relationship of violence. Rashid Khalidi gives a very early example of the plan to colonise Palestine from an extract of Theodor Herzl, widely regarded as the founder of modern political Zionism and author of *Der Judenstaat* (The Jewish State, 1896), writing in his diary in 1895:

> We must expropriate gently the private property on the estates assigned to us. We shall try to spirit the penniless population across the border by procuring employment for it in the transit countries, while denying it employment in our own country. The property owners will come over to our side. Both the process of expropriation and the removal of the poor must be carried out discreetly and circumspectly. (Herzl 1960 [1895], 88–89)

Suad Amiry's fictionalised memoir, a work of refusal and resistance, uses a combination of satire, mockery and irony to magnify the excesses of Israeli occupation—Herzl's "process of expropriation"—and their impact upon the time and space of everyday life in the West Bank (Amiry 2005). For many living in the West Bank, the following description by Fanon might seem apposite. Fanon describes the native town as "without spaciousness, men live there on top of each other. The native town is a hungry town, starved of bread, meat, of shoes, of coal, of light. The native town is a crouching village, a town on its knees" (Fanon 2001 [1965], 30). This describes the physical and psychological condition of the refugee camp, towns and villages in the West Bank, and it is embodied in the military posts and roadblocks, the curfews that imprison hundreds of thousands on a regular basis and in soldiers closing down borders with impunity.

This summarises a culture of terror, impunity and whim. Weizman has shown how colonial occupation operates through schemes of over and underpasses, a separation of the airspace from the ground. He describes settlements (mostly built on hilltops/slopes) as "urban optical devices for surveillance and the exercise of power" (Weizman 2002, sec. 5, para. 5). This spatial power is enhanced by a network of fast bypass roads, bridges and tunnels that weave over and under one another in an attempt at maintaining the Fanonian 'principle of reciprocal exclusivity': "the bypass roads attempt to separate Israeli traffic networks from Palestinian ones, preferably without ever allowing them to cross" (Weizman 2002, sec. 10, para. 4). This is the overlapping of two separate geographies that inhabit the same landscape. There are also, as I have been saying, two overlapping narratives which rarely cross. As Weizman shows, Israeli sovereignty would seem to be based upon a perception that the existence of the 'other' represents a threat to the life of the Israeli citizen, and that their life would be enhanced and made secure by the elimination of the Palestinian. On the basis of this perception, land, water and airspace resources are appropriated, and bulldozers are deployed to demolish houses, uproot trees, dig up roads, destroy transformers, tear up airport runways, and break up village boundaries for the Security Fence.

All of this spatial activity has been described as infrastructural warfare and is featured in narrative after narrative alongside the watchtowers, the militarised checkpoints, and the barbed wire fences—time imprisoned in space in a culture of humiliation and impunity. In order to explore this culture of securitisation/imprisonment, Simone Bitton's film documenting the construction of the security fence, *Wall* (2004) will be referred to (see Note 1).

Naziheen, the Displaced Ones

Borders and curfews are both spatial and temporal; the checkpoint slows down time by waiting and delay, curfew speeds it up in a sense by forcing people to operate at a faster pace in order to get things done in time. On the other hand, it has been reported how a young man took what was once a two and a half hour trip from Ramallah to Jenin in 16 plus hours and he never reached Jenin. This is just one story among thousands of the expropriation of time by the zoning of space through permit and checkpoint—visible signifiers of hierarchy and power, of 'topographic control'.

A very significant spatial and temporal memoir is presented by Mourid Barghouti's *I Saw Ramallah* (2005 [2000]), described by Edward Said as "one of the finest existential accounts of Palestinian displacement that we now have" (Preface to Barghouti 2005, vii). This memoir is shaped by both macro- and micro-time as Barghouti spent thirty years in exile from 1967 when he was banned from his homeland. What he sees (*saw* not visited) in Ramallah is objects, structures in space imprinted by time, a time both of absence and presence. Shahram Khosravi has described exilic life as the constant presence of the absent and what Barghouti has to come to terms with is both presence and absence—the absence of the present—hence the constant shifts in tense and time, the varying grammar of memory. In a sense what can be seen designates what is no longer there, as the narrator inhabits a palimpsest of time and space—a place of displacement, no longer readable but only as a metaphorical city. What orients it, situates it, temporalises it, and makes it function as a lived place is no longer there; there is an unbridgeable gap between the 'being-there' of 1967 and the 'being-there' of 1996—two poles of different experience.

The narrative activity of the book is initially founded on two tropes: the frontier and the bridge which mark the interior and exterior boundaries of the space to be entered literally, as well as being the signifiers of displacement which negated the possibility of encounter and exchange: a site of both conjunction and disjunction. The frontier has a mediating role and this is also what the narrative is designed to do—to mediate the temporality and spatiality of Ramallah, here and there, now and then. The bridge and the river are the markers of continuity in the context of a thirty-year displacement. The frontier becomes a crossing, an opening up, not just for the author but for thousands of displaced at that post-Oslo moment, a moment of re-emergence. The narrative re-organises Ramallah, it is itself a bridge that opens the inside to the other. In a sense, Ramallah is 'displaced' by the memoir—it is mobilised into a dynamic litany of past memories and also of present limitations and restrictions, but produces resources for a journey of hope: 'his Palestine'. Nevertheless, as Said points out, it is an account of loss and new forms of displacement: "it re-enacts exile rather than repatriation" (Preface to Barghouti 2005, xi): "A mist envelops what I see, what I expect, what I remember. The view here shimmers with scenes that span a lifetime: a lifetime spent trying to get here" (Barghouti 2005, 1).

These visual metaphors shape the narrative: mist and shimmer are symptomatic of the memory narrative, displaced in and by time, a subjective lens: "Behind me the world, ahead of me my world" (1) but, of course, that possessive is problematised throughout. The displaced live permanently in shifting tenses, shifting pronouns. In 1967, "Ramallah is no longer mine" and "I became that displaced stranger whom I had always thought was someone else". The text then changes person from *I* to *he*, *mine* to *his* in a sentence which enacts displacement grammatically—"the stranger is the person who renews his Residence permit ... he is the one whose relationship with places is distorted" (Barghouti 2005, 3) and the memoir is itself a form of distortion—a spatial, temporal and visual disfigurement. He is the one who cannot tell his story in a continuous narrative but is a creature of discontinuity: "At noon on that Monday I was struck by displacement"—it is like a disease, "a person gets displacement as he gets asthma" (4). Barghouti adds that "the world finds a name for us. They called us *naziheen*, the displaced ones" (3). He is on the boundary—in liminal drift—between two times, 1967 and 1996 which anchor the narrative. The encounter at the border—Palestine is metres away but deferred in an endless period of waiting which mocks and mimics the thirty-year time lapse; bridge time is metonymous—is like an exchange of spies (a sense of his double life): "You wait here until we receive a signal from them, then you cross the bridge" (5). The Occupied Territory, once an abstraction for the author is now physically present: "what is so special about it except that we have lost it ... our song is not for some sacred thing of the past but for our current self-respect that is violated anew every day by the Occupation" (6, 7). His memoir is a song against the humiliation of dispossession and displacement; it is also a memorial for his dead brother who was twice refused entry across the same bridge which "is no longer than a few meters of wood and thirty years of exile" (9)—space becomes time and time becomes space.

These time/space conflations are frequent throughout the narrative—they hinge and unhinge it: "The summer of 1966, and immediately after, no slowing down, the summer of 1996" (Barghouti 2005, 10). The phrase 'no slowing down' is illusory; it comes at a moment when the narrative is enacting the crossing. Barghouti's narrative is part of "people's need to have their voice heard through listening to it from the voice of another", a "voice outside themselves expressing what is inside them" (11), and this is what the memoir attempts in its double voicing, its pronominal shifts—standing back and closing in, stepping outside the frame, like Suad Amiry. Such narratives are needed when people are unable to speak or act. The memoir gives a narratable identity to the displaced: "And now I pass from exile to their ... homeland. My homeland? The West Bank and Gaza? The Occupied Territories? The Areas? Judea and Samaria? The Autonomous Government? Israel? Palestine? Is there any other country in the world that so perplexes you with its names?" (Barghouti 2005, 13). The book is filled with such questing, questioning.

Barghouti silently apostrophises the Israeli soldier at the border: "His gun is my personal history. It is the history of my estrangement. His gun took from us the land of the poem and left us with the poem of the land" (13). He is "the guard guarding our country—against us" (14).

In one extensive paragraph, he enumerates the things taken by Israel and the phrase 'they took' is repeated to mesmeric effect. Finally, he says "Rabin has taken everything, even the story of our death" (Barghouti 2005, 177) and this ties in with what I was saying earlier about the refusal to allow, or to hear, the story of the displaced and the struggle to reclaim that narrative at all kinds of level, through dance, song, film and theatre. Reclaiming that narrative has been made especially difficult because of the ways, until perhaps in the last decade or so, in which Israel has recruited world opinion, particularly the USA, to a narrative of victimhood. Speaking of Rabin, Barghouti says: "This leader knew how to demand that the world should respect Israeli blood, the blood of every Israeli individual without exception. He knew how to demand that the world should respect Israeli tears, and he was able to present as the victim of a crime perpetrated by us. He changed facts, he altered the order of things, he presented us as the initiators of violence in the Middle East and said what he said with eloquence, with clarity and conviction" (Barghouti 2005, 177–78). While the Palestinian tactic of suicide bombing continued, its 'spectacularity' and devastation made it hard to refute that narrative. The abandonment of the tactic is perhaps one reason why international understanding of the Palestinian situation has shifted in a more positive direction.

Barghouti locates the rhetorical strategy of Rabin very astutely by pinpointing a specific technique which he refers to as *secondly*: "It is easy to blur the truth with a simple linguistic trick: start your story from 'Secondly'... He simply neglected to speak of what happened first" (178). He illustrates this analysis with reference to the responses to violence of Native American Indians, the Vietnamese, Black/White conflicts and Victor Jara's songs in Chile.

To live displacement is always to live 'temporarily,' suspended in time, once uprooted always uprooted, *temporary*. In writing of displacement, Barghouti sees writing as a displacement, from the habitual, the partisan, the unconditional, from the dominant used language, what I have called the always already narrated—to a "language that speaks itself for the first time". The challenge for narratives of displacement is to shape a language that speaks itself for the first time, not just to produce narratives of substitution, of replacement, but narratives of hope in which, as Bhargouti says, "we do not want to regain the past but to regain the future and to push tomorrow into the day after", to re-appropriate a Palestinian time and a Palestinian story of bodies, dreams, people, homes, land and trees in which to 'give memory a future'. However, he has to recognise his limitations as a writer:

> I tried to put the displacement between parentheses, to put a last period in a long sentence of the sadness of history, personal and public history. *But I see nothing except commas. I want to sew the times together*. I want to attach one moment to another, to attach childhood to age, to attach the present to the absent and all presents to all absences, to attach exiles to the homeland and to attach what I have imagined to what I see now. (Barghouti 2005, 163, my italics)

I have focused mainly on the opening and closing chapters because that border moment, out of which Barghouti creates a number of metaphorical ripples, is itself one of the commas which separates time and place, and time from time, place from place—the poetry of displacement. The repetition of the word *attach* five times underlines the impossibility in that moment of 'sewing the times together'. It encapsulates not just a personal situation but synoptically enacts the broader Palestinian history of Occupation, a story of *detachment* at so many levels in the form of broken times and scattered fragments, material and psychological: "I crossed the forbidden bridge and suddenly I bent to collect my scattered fragments as I would collect the flaps of my coat together on an icy day" (Barghouti 2005, 182). It is this act of 'trespassing' which has opened up trauma, nostalgia, anger and reflection, and having offered an analysis of the physical and personal displacements of 'his country', he is left posing a deep philosophical and political question in the last line of the book: "*What deprives the spirit of its colours / What is it other than the bullets of the invaders that have hit the body?"* (182). In the following section, I shall be looking at a novel by Adania Shibli, *Minor Detail* (2017) which in many ways provides the 'firstly' narrative which precedes the 'secondly' of Barghouti's argument.

The Architecture of Occupation

As the primary themes of this book are separation, displacement and im/mobility, I now want to turn to providing a fuller background to one of the most egregious instances of these, the Occupation of the West Bank and East Jerusalem of Palestine-Israel. The Palestinian Authority (PA), formed in 1994 as one of the outcomes of the Oslo Accords, notionally had governance over the West Bank in the first instance, until this was extended to control of the Gaza Strip also in 2005. I say 'notionally' because the PA had exclusive control over security-related and civilian issues in Palestinian urban areas (Area A) and only civilian control over Palestinian rural areas (Area B), the substantial remainder of the territories, including Israeli settlements, the Jordan Valley region and bypass roads between Palestinian communities remained under Israeli control (Area C), effectively giving Israel 60 percent military control of the West Bank. Gaza had nominal autonomy in 2005 but Israel controlled the crossing points, airspace and the waters off the Gaza Strip's coast. Although Hamas took over the territory in 2007, splitting from the PA, Gaza remains cut off from the West Bank, and virtually incarcerated by Israel in what Pappé (2016) calls 'spatial strangulation'.

Apart from the fragmentation of the Palestinian territory, displacement has meant 7.2 million Palestinian refugees worldwide, nineteen refugee camps still in the West Bank (in excess of 750,000 refugees) and well over a million refugees registered in eight camps in Gaza. Within Gaza, the population, technically, has more freedom of movement than those people in the West Bank, subject to checkpoints, official and random curfews, and the wasting of time in circuitous journeys on inferior roads, but the people of Gaza nevertheless regard themselves as living in a state of siege. It has been variously described as 'the world's largest prison camp', 'the world's largest open-air prison camp', and 'the largest concentration camp ever to exist'.

It is because of the multiple obstructions to mobility, symbolised, above all, in the wall, the fence or the security barrier, depending on whose perspective is adopted, that I have decided to focus on three memoirs, a short story and a novel, which focus primarily on West Bank experience. These are taken from the earlier part of the twenty-first century, through to the middle and most recent part of the past two decades. As recently as March 2020, the Israeli defence ministry approved plans for a road that would separate Palestinians and Israeli commuters east of Jerusalem, the latest move to establish an illegal settlement as part of the E1 settlement project. This plan will effectively cut the West Bank in half, only allowing Palestinian vehicles to pass through the illegal settlement of Ma'ale Adumim, along a tunnel-like wall, linking Palestinian villages south and north of Jerusalem. Not only would this compound the separation of the territory, increase hindrances to mobility and further displacement in the form of settler homes on Palestinian land, but also, and most importantly, cut West Bank residents off from access to occupied East Jerusalem, seen by most Palestinians as the capital of a future state. This is a prospect already seriously threatened by the move of the US Embassy to Jerusalem and the so-called deal of the century brokered by Trump.

"The occupation is understood here as an unstable set of technologies of power that open and limit a space of action and reaction for their subjects" (Ophir et al. 2009, 17). As technologies of power and control are a feature of many of the chapters in this book, I shall examine in this chapter what Ophir et al. summarise as "the regimentation of movement, the fragmentation of space, the checkpoint system, creeping colonization, and extrajudicial assassinations" (2009, 17). Curfews affect time and mobility, while incursions into Palestinian territory for the building of the wall and for matters, so claimed, of Israeli security disrupt everyday life. The Israeli state also has a monopoly of the means of violence and, even if not used, the omnipresence of armed police and military produces a sense of anxiety and uncertainty. One way of controlling a population is through unpredictability, so that it is rarely possible to know when a checkpoint is open, how long a waiting period might be, or when a military patrol might enter a village. Unpredictable displays of power are more effective in producing intimidation than are those which follow a regular pattern. This will be seen in the texts to be analysed. The many refugee camps in the Occupied Palestine Territory (OPT) will not be considered here but, as has been argued, "the most vivid expression perhaps of this protracted state of exception is the Palestinian refugee camp that currently functions as an experimental laboratory for control and surveillance exercised by

Israeli authorities and international agencies alike" (Ophir et al. 2009, 23). So, trialled in the camps used as 'laboratories', different modes of control are randomly introduced into the West Bank cities and villages and become a routine part of "normalization". Modes of control include, for instance, the withholding of permits to build and the labelling of constructions in defiance of this as 'illegal', as well as "house demolition", either in the interest of "operational needs", or because a property is deemed to belong to that of a 'terrorist'. According to the "Data on Demolition and Displacement in the West Bank" of The United Nations Office for the Coordination of Humanitarian Affairs (OCHA), 7,102 structures have been demolished since 2009 and 10,819 people displaced (OCHA, November 9, 2020). In August 2020 alone, eighty-two structures were demolished in the OPT.[2] Some years ago, one of my former Ph.D. students had his house demolished while he was in prison with only twenty minutes notice given to his family.

By keeping a population 'on its toes' in a climate of anxiety, dependency is gradually formed, augmented by immiseration, higher unemployment and poverty. Humiliation can generate both abjection and resistance, examples of which will be seen in the texts to be examined.

The most extensive treatments of the depth of control exercised by Israel are by Ariel Handel and Eyal Weizman, and I shall draw heavily on both in what follows. The title of Handel's essay "Where, Where to and When in the Occupied Territories: An Introduction to Geography of Disaster" (Ophir et al. 2009, 179) aptly summarises the spatial and temporal axis on which most of the people in the OPT depend. Weizman has written a number of books and articles on the Occupation, and I shall focus here on *Hollow Land: Israel's Architecture of Occupation* (2017 [2007]), specifically on the new edition which was published on the fiftieth anniversary of the Six-Day War of 1967.

In one of the epigraphs to his essay, Handel quotes Azmi Bishara's *Yearning in the Land of Checkpoints* (2006), in which Bishara speaks of the planning of weddings in Palestine that prepare invitations in which the wedding and its location are announced but a blank space is left for the day of the week, the date and time, because these are subject to the arbitrary use of the curfew. This is just one instance in which the control of time is imposed upon a subject population. Handel's concern is with the basic use of space: "how one can move in it", and how movement always includes time. I shall give examples in my textual analyses of the imbrication of space with time in the form of blockages, checkpoints, road checks and curfews, all of which put a hold on mobility. For example, I do not use a map to visit my local library as its location and my distance from it is built in to my 'cognitive map' through a process of habit, repetition and expectation, what Giddens calls my 'ontological security'. For the Palestinian inhabitant of the West Bank no such security exists because new regulations and reconfigurations of space restrict, and render unstable, movement possibilities. For the Israeli settlers no such instability exists as they enjoy unlimited access, modern super-fast highways and few impediments. In addition to the internal restrictions within the West Bank, further limits are placed on Palestinians gaining access to East Jerusalem, or on moving between the Gaza Strip and the West Bank. In addition to the separation wall (see Note 1) which has separated people from their land, place of work and schools, there are fifty-eight, or more, guarded checkpoints and 471 unstaffed roadblocks, and, on average, more than 100 surprise, or 'pop up' checkpoints each week. Physical barriers are erected, or taken down, on an irregular basis. Nightly IDF raids take place. There are some areas completely inaccessible. The West Bank is divided up into numerous cells and movement within much more of a distance than a few kilometres is difficult to predict or calculate. Handel has produced a series of maps of the division of OPT space and the hundred or more cells where people must get through specific checkpoints. The presence of checkpoints determines the choice of school and place of work. Israel has blocked Palestinians from using the majority of West Bank road space. Even the bypass and underpass roads enable access on only a conditional basis. The overall effect is one of discontinuity and the lack of contiguity, or spaces of enclosure. Where permits exist, they are severely restricted to a very small number (less than 0.5 percent).

As Handel points out, for a settler making a 17 km road journey, it can take 11 minutes, whereas for a Palestinian making a 24 km road journey (on an inferior road) it can take 3 hours, 24 minutes. This is just one local instance of the asymmetries of power; further examples will be discussed later. Distances and times can vary enormously depending on the distribution of checkpoints and waiting times. Handel concludes that Palestinians spend most of their time in movement, which includes endless spells of immobility within the framework of supposed movement. Almost all journeys for Palestinians are transgressive, a form of violation of the masses of regulation, so despite all the barriers, resistance does take place:

Checkpoint workers … constantly subverted physical boundaries: at night they stealthily pushed concrete Blocks a few more inches apart to make way for horse carriages, or trampled the edges of newly-made dirt Barriers so that porter carts could get to the other side. And through both necessity and ingenuity, they Reclaimed the space of the checkpoint from being purely a site of oppression and brutality into the one where livelihood, social life and even sociability could be recovered. (quoted in Handel 2009, 215)

"Separation, in space and law, is the most fundamental component of Israel's system of colonization" (Weizman 2017, xii). The most prominent manifestation of this separation is the 708 kilometres of the West Bank wall which, as has been noted, carved through Palestinian villages, separated people from their fields and olive trees and expropriated 10 percent of the territory for the settlement, at a cost of three billion US dollars. There are now almost eight hundred thousand Israeli Jewish settlers/colonists in the West Bank and occupied East Jerusalem. What Weizman calls 'the politics of verticality' refers to the division of the West Bank into three main political levels, or layers: "the *surface*, landlocked pockets were handed over to Palestinian control; the *subsoil*, including water and mineral resources; and the *airspace* above Palestinian areas, which was left in Israeli hands" (Weizman 2017, xvi) With 61 percent of the total area of the West Bank under Israeli control, not only are the Palestinians encircled but they are also dominated from above and below (Fig. 6.1).

The wall is variously described as a fence, a barrier or a wall; although only three kilometres in length, it is actually constructed of eight-metre high concrete slabs; the rest consists of electronic fences, barbed wire, radar observation towers, cameras, deep trenches and designated patrol roads. The wall is a site of conflict over territorial space, physical resources and demographic issues as well as having a literal and symbolic role in terms of identity, security and sovereignty. The extensive graffiti on the wall signifies a mode of resistance, however limited. The West Bank barrier cuts off Bethlehem from the rest of Israel. The IDF and the settlements/colonies have not had it all their own way as, on a few occasions, the HCJ (High Court of Justice) has ordered the state of Israel to reroute several sections of the wall because of the negative effect the proposed route would have on the Palestinians living in the adjacent areas. Nevertheless, considerable displacement has taken place with thousands

Fig. 6.1 Cultural resistance in the form of graffiti on the annexation wall in Bethlehem (*Photo* The author)

of Palestinians trapped in enclaves west of the wall in what have been designated as 'closed military zones'.

What Weizman calls "a new way of imagining space has emerged": "One is an upper-land—the land of the settlements—or scattering of well-tended hilltop neighbourhoods woven together by modern highways … The other, Palestine—crowded cities, towns and villages that inhabit the valleys between and underneath the hills, maintaining fragile connections on improvised underpasses" (Weizman 2017, 182). In this new space, there are separate security corridors, infrastructure, bridges and underground tunnels.

The impact of this extraordinarily complex political and territorial separation on Palestinians was shown above in Amiry and Barghouti's memoirs, and will be further illustrated here in a short story and the opening section of Mourid Barghouti's *I Was Born There, I Was Born Here*.

The confusing and contradictory positions which the wall and the checkpoints have thrust upon Palestinians are summed up by Nuha Khoury:

> Go inside, he ordered in hysterical broken English. Inside! I am already inside! It took me a few seconds to understand that this young soldier was redefining inside to mean anything that is not visible, to him at least. My being 'outside' within the 'inside' was bothering him. (quoted in Weizman 2017, 185)

This links with Fanon's comments on the colonised subject: "The colonised subject is constantly on his guard. Confused by the myriad signs of the colonial world he never knows whether he is out of line" (quoted in Kotef 2015, 153).

Khoury's article, with its title, "One Fine Curfew Day", announcing how curfew breaks up, and into, a fine day, describes the most crucial impact: "the stifling stillness of the long curfew hours, which is lifted once every four days for four hours, has *redefined the meaning of time and space*" (in Weizman 2017, 185, my italics). As well as redefining time and space, it arrests movement, rendering people motionless for days. However, rather than only subjugating a people, it actually mobilises forms of solidarity and resistance as evidenced by the actions of neighbours keeping watch over the soldiers as they help to negotiate Khoury's passage home through the backstreets when she was spotted on a friend's veranda during curfew.

Here Distances Always Measure the Same

This sub-heading is taken from the opening section of Mourid Barghouti's *I Was Born There, I Was Born Here*, "The Driver Mahmoud", which charts his journey by road from Ramallah to Jericho. He says that his suitcase was small because he knows that at each checkpoint it was likely to be opened and inspected. He is travelling with seven other people in a taxi driven by a young man called Mahmoud, on the day before the 2002 Israeli invasion of Ramallah. The journey is of unpredictable duration and distance because of road closure, flying checkpoints and other unforeseen obstacles to movement. Barghouti is surprised at the level of humour in the taxi but realises that this is a form of stoicism—*sumoud*—produced by the Occupation, a way of not giving in, of being able to live through oppression. Another way is the resourcefulness of the driver, dropping down into a field next to the road to avoid a flying checkpoint, an arbitrary technique of the oppressor. One man says the journey will take an hour while another says "What do you mean an hour? ... Make that two, three hours ... four. You heard what the man said. We may get there, we may not" (Barghouti 2012, 5). Barghouti no longer 'knows the geography of my land' so he does not recognise the numerous diversions and reversions along unknown roads which Mahmoud takes. Some of the route is through fields full of olive trees uprooted by Israeli bulldozers making way for the separation wall—olive trees with a deep symbolic resonance for Palestinians, signifiers of cultural identity and belonging. The point he is making is that each journey by road a Palestinian takes they are confronted by humiliation, an affront to their dignity and meaning, a disruption of the rhythm of life. If it is not a flying checkpoint, it is something else which causes delay or diversion on their journey, an Israeli tank in one instance, an army hideout in another. The most significant obstacle is an impassable, mud-filled trench met on their improvised route. The taxi had to be airlifted by a crane, apparently such a regular occurrence that the nearby villagers have a giant winch standing by and charge 100 shekels for each car. Barghouti reflects that life under Occupation means that actually arriving at a destination, finding a scarce item in a shop, or that the electricity is working, is a cause for celebration, an unexpected victory: "What matters is that for every obstacle the Occupation sets, Palestinian desperation finds a solution" (Barghouti 2011/12/13, 22).

After the 'airlift', Mahmoud announces what would be a commonplace in most other places but here is exceptional: "From here to Jericho there's no army, no checkpoints, no cranes, and no swings in the air" (24). The Occupation, however, is never ordinary or commonplace. "The Occupation distorts the distances between humans as much as between places" (24). This is a very apt summary of the Occupation; as much as it is a separation, a displacement and a dispossession, it is, perhaps above all, a *distortion* of relationships, of time, of space and of vision. This is underlined when, arriving in Jordan, Barghouti says, "distances always measure the same. You know how many minutes you need to get from one place to another" (29). When I was in Palestine in 2018, it took me some time to understand why no-one could ever tell us precisely how far a particular place was or how long it would take to reach. The fallback position, I learnt, was always to over-estimate so that if an estimated journey by taxi or bus of two hours took forty minutes, it was a small victory.

Liana Badr's short story, "Other Cities" (Badr 2006), is also about a journey through numerous obstacles, that of gender in particular. Barghouti's journey in "The Driver Mahmoud" was from Ramallah, that of Umm Hasan and her children in "Other Cities" is to Ramallah from old Hebron. This journey used to be a forty-minute drive, but now "it required an entire day of meandering from village to village along rocky, hilly roads" (Badr 2006, 43) as well as the prospect of security patrols making the trip impossible. Umm Hasan suffers under a double form of occupation—that of the Israeli Occupation and that of a patriarchal culture, in the form of an indifferent husband, thinking her plans to travel "typical of a woman's folly" and that "Mentally, however, she wasn't all there" even though she was beautiful, had given him sons and daughters, and managed her household well—all attributes of the 'perfect' wife in accordance with patriarchal norms. "Yet here she was, imprisoned in her own home by settlers' attacks, held hostage in her neighbourhood by constant military patrols, and kept a captive in Hebron because she couldn't go anywhere else without ID" (Badr 2006, 41).

Hebron is the only city in the West Bank in which Palestinians (30,000) live side by side with Israelis (800), but the Palestinians are hedged in by gates placed at the end of streets, endless curfews and other security measures, severe restrictions on movement and settler harassment.

Under the Oslo Accords the Old City was placed in the H2 area under the authority of strict Israeli military control.

So determined is Umm Hasan to visit Ramallah that she declares to heaven "May I be divorced if we don't go to Ramallah within the week". If her neighbours had seen her make this declaration, they would have deemed her insane, incredulous that any woman could swear by divorce, "casually repeating the threat men made so freely", underlining the gender binary in which Umm Hasan is held as 'captive wife'. Why she is so determined to travel to Ramallah is never made explicit, presumably because the Israeli occupation and her husband prohibit it; it is her mode of defiance and resistance: "to thumb her nose at Israel, and go—whether her husband, Abu Hasan, liked it or not" (Badr 2006, 39). This decision is part of her response to a man "demanding silence and obedience", who doesn't even know her name: "you just call me *ya mara*, 'wife'". We are not told her name. By making the journey to Ramallah, although with her six children (all without papers), she is metaphorically shedding both *yamara* (wife) and mother (Umm), marital 'properties'—secondary identifiers.

Umm Hasan prepares the children for the journey, having borrowed an ID card from a neighbour whose husband, in the telling phrase, "allowed her to lend Umm Hasan her ID card, for no more than two days. Umm Hasan was just a harmless woman, after all, he thought" (44). As they also had no ID, the children had been drilled in their assigned, false names. On the road, there was/is a constant anxiety about military patrols and 'flying checkpoints' set up by armed settlers. Umm Hasan is fearful that she will be dragged into a patrol car or that her small daughters will be run over by an 'extremist' settler. Despite her panic attacks, her journey was a rare one with no roadblocks encountered, but at the Qalandia checkpoint she had to find another driver to take them to Ramallah itself. They pass through the checkpoint in a crowd and are not asked for ID. The accommodation is expensive and the city is 'full of enticements' but they are free from the Israeli attacks and settler provocations of their home town, a place where "frequent settler attacks" and "rounds of army fire" meant that no relatives dared to visit. Even in this space of freedom, she is anxious about running out of money and worried about the return trip with her borrowed ID card and her children with their assumed names.

On their return, there is a long delay at the Qalandia checkpoint where they are allocated to the PA queue before the security search. Surprisingly, they are waved through but the journey back, in the same taxi, is punctuated by frequent delays by military convoys or at checkpoints, each time in intense heat. The point I made earlier about the control and frustration of movement is exemplified by this return journey as the Israelis at the checkpoint would "sit there and do nothing for a long while", and the car "sat immobilised among the stopped cars", waiting for up to an hour. Time is erased by the Occupation, mobility is cancelled.

With her baby in pain and with a dirty nappy, Umm Hasan, already overcome with anxiety about her children, opens the door of the car and gets out. Throughout her wait in the 'hellish heat' of the car, "all eyes were on the guards who stood blocking the long road ahead of them for no apparent reason"; the arbitrariness of this emphasises the power differential in the Occupation—"those soldiers controlled everything around". Shouted at by one of the soldiers, she walks over, "She had lost all sense of time and place, even of her children in the car behind her" (Badr 2006, 55). This disorientation is one of the aims of the Occupation. The contempt of the soldiers marks their power, gendered and political: "What was this woman with a scarf and a baby trying to do". She is not just a 'woman' but an Arab Muslim woman (scarf), it is implied; a person of no consequence in a colonial/masculinist world.

In the face of this hostility—one soldier spat in her face—"she lived in a different world", one outside of the Occupation, of patriarchy, transfigured by her humiliation and frustration into an active, agentive figure, the reverse of all her ascribed roles: "It's hot" she said, "The baby's sick. Let the cars go", addressing the Captain. This approach seemed to trigger something in the captain, an emergent awareness of the hostile wilderness in which he was operating, "this accursed prison". Not only is he momentarily unhinged in respect of the Occupation and his role, but, importantly "fascinated by her indifference to him as she turned her back", his gendered entitlement, his rank, is undermined; he is temporarily emasculated by her daring to speak, as a subaltern, beneath his rank and gender. Signalling the cars to move on, "He didn't waste a moment getting into his own vehicle, *mobilising his men* and clearing the way". He reclaims himself, after this temporary loss of power and meaning, by recovering his poise/possession "in his *own vehicle*" (not just a means of transport but also a means of restoring his masculinity) and, having been momentarily immobilised, he mobilises his men: recovers mobility, command and possession, perhaps fearing the men had lost their respect for his rank.

For Umm Hasan the journey to Ramallah is a temporary liberation; temporary because she returns to the 'absent present' of her domestic life in Old Hebron. However, her *interlude* of disorientation in time and dislocation in space opens up a future perspective/horizon in which her oldest daughter ("getting married in a few years' time"), although likely to be conscripted into a patriarchal culture, may end up "living in Ramallah, or perhaps some other city. When that happened, they would visit, *together*, the places that were now forbidden to them … They would eventually reach those other cities they dreamed of visiting. There were still plenty of ways" (Badr 2006, 57).

A key word there is "together" for, although Umm Hasan will return to her former life as wife and mother, her 'disobedience', her refusal to be confined in gendered and political submission, means that she is able to project a vision beyond the now, the possibility for her daughter of something other ('other cities') than being the other, a post-OPT world, a post-patriarchal world. Having found one way out of subordination, as the last line of the story says: "There were still plenty of ways".

Plan Dalet

This chapter has as its focus displacement and immobility with reference to Palestine. Although displacement is a continuing process in the OPT—the 'ongoing NAKBA'—attention in this section will be paid to what might be called the founding displacement in 1948, the eviction of 750,000 people from more than 450 towns and villages in Palestine, and the consequences of this displacement in the seventy plus years in what has become the spatial encirclement and enclosure of Palestinians by means of walls, fences, checkpoints and roadblocks, and a set of restrictions on what is permissible.

Without in any way seeking to excuse, or justify, the Nakba, much less so the 1967 Occupation, these have to be seen in the wider historical context of centuries of oppression and ghettoisation of Jewish people, the nineteenth-century pogroms in Eastern Europe, and, of course, the Holocaust. Many of those involved in the Haganah (the predecessor to the IDF) and Irgun were recently in flight from Europe, bearing in mind that most countries refused to take in significant numbers of Jewish refugees. These emigrants, their families and their descendants carried an ongoing memory and, later, post-memory (see Hirsch below) which shadowed perceptions and attitudes for many years and accounted for much of the defensiveness and insecurity of the Israeli Jewish population.

Starting with a recent novel, *Minor Detail* (2020 [2017]), which seeks to recall the moment in which the context is set for the later dispossession of the Palestinians in the form of the 1967 Occupation in terms of racialisation, feminisation and potential eradication, and which also traces the effects of occupation—spatial and psychological—on those residents excluded and contained by the limits of curfew and permit, I shall then conclude with a discussion of a text which focuses on displacements in one city brought about by the fifty years of the Occupation since 1967.

1948 marked the dispossession of Palestinians and the triumph of settler colonialism which produced the Israeli state and inaugurated a regime of domination based upon "a logic of social organization that produces regimented, institutionalized, and militarized conceptions of hierarchized 'human' difference" (Weheliye 2014, 37). This unequal power structure, sustained by violence, resulted in the subordination and disfiguration of the land and people of Palestine: "'Plan Dalet' or 'Plan D' was the name given by the Zionist High Command to the general plan for military operations within the framework of which the Zionists launched successive offensives in April and early May 1948 in various parts of Palestine. These offensives, which entailed the destruction of the Palestinian Arab community and the expulsion and pauperisation of the Palestine Arabs, were designed to achieve the military *fait accompli* upon which the state of Israel was to be based" (Khalidi 1988, 8). As will be shown, racialisation, dehumanisation and displacement are a set of cultural and sociopolitical processes delivered through violence, an ideology of masculinity, and, as discussed in Chapter 1, features of the coloniality of power. This is not a one-off process but something which requires frequent repetition and reinforcement to the point where, although not evenly, it becomes internalised by those under subjection: the objects of coloniality. I am using racialisation in the sense of 'racialising assemblages' as developed by Alexander Weheliye (2014, 8). It is this racialisation which enables a particular structure in dominance to categorise certain classes of people as less than human, to be disposed of with impunity. This withholding, or denial, of humanity is part of the process of disfiguration mentioned earlier. In Sylvia Winter's terms, discussed in Chapter 1, "racialization figures as a master code within the genre of the human represented by western man", and as such the western (white) coloniser is above racialisation because of the self-ascription 'Man' which means that the colonised are perceived as symbols of 'lack'. Race, then, is an organising narrative, "a set of classificatory regimes that seek to order subject populations differentially in pursuit of particular historical agendas" (Weheliye 2014, 27).

In a sense, following Patrick Wolfe's argument, if race is 'ideologically performative', Israel brought Palestinians into being as a social category with specific prescriptions: Arab, other, less than human, dirty, etc., in order to legitimise its expropriation and retention of territory by means of technologies of violence which have become increasingly sophisticated.

1948 was not, as has been argued, opportunistic or a spur of the moment action but the product of much deeper historical preconditions, the culmination of a long-gestated plan. It was thus the fulfilment of a fundamental transformation, something encapsulated elliptically in the first part of Adania Shibli's *Minor Detail*, as will be shown, which dramatically enacts the construction of a Palestinian Other. One of the recurring claims of settler colonialism is that the 'native' is unproductive, in the case of Israel "a rootless nomadic Bedouin rather than a settled *fallah*" (Wolfe 2016, 225).

This claim about the unproductive 'other' helped to justify the post-1948 shape and function of the Jewish settlements in Palestine, as Eyal Weizman and colleagues have shown:

> Planning and building in the West Bank is effectively executing a political agenda through spatial manipulations. (Weizman 2017, 19)

It is these 'spatial manipulations' together with the militarisation of the West Bank which combine to produce the alienation and anxiety of the woman in the second part of *Minor Detail*. The challenge for any writer attempting to construct a narrative about a topic saturated by fiercely contested political positions is, as Lena Jayyusi says, "What register does one speak in, when every register is contaminated? The concrete, the historical, the moral, the political, the quotidian, the existential … all these are inflected with the performance of power, and the cruelty that attaches to it. All these are distorted by the machinery of power" (Jayyusi 2003, 129).

Tracing History

Adania Shibli's literary response to the question posed here is to construct a narrative built upon the performance of power, the encratic language of power and the ways in which power is inflected with gender. It is an articulation of power which is contaminated by an ideology of masculinity expressed through violence. *Minor Detail* is a 105-page novella which uses a framework based upon an actual event in August 1949 during the Armistice period following the 1947–1948 war in Palestine (Shibli 2020 [2017]).[3] The book is divided into two sections and has a specular structure with images and events in the first part being echoed/mirrored in the second. Although their linguistic registers are very different, the division between the two parts is not marked, which suggests a continuity despite the gap in time: from 1949 to the present day, although no date is specified, apart from 13 August 1974, the date of birth of the female narrator of the second part.

The event in question was the gang-rape and murder of a young Palestinian female by soldiers and an officer of a small platoon of the Israeli army in Nirim, in the Negev area close to the border with Egypt. Although a number of the soldiers, and the officer, were later tried and imprisoned, the case received little attention and remained classified information until it became the subject of a *Haaretz* article in 2003 (Lavie and Gorali 2003).

The novella constructs the violation and murder of the girl as an example of Israeli war rape culture but also as an embodiment of a militarised masculinity as well as a metaphor of dispossession and displacement of Palestinians by the Israeli invasion. Even if the rape-murder can be seen as *allegorical*, to a certain extent, this in no way minimises the abuse of the girl but serves to underscore the role of race and gender in the invasive impact of the eventual occupation. The historian Benny Morris, in an interview with Ari Shavit for *Haaretz*, says that "he was surprised to find that there were also many cases of rape which usually ended in murder" (*Al Arabiya English* 2015, 2). In the same article, the professor of Law at the Hebrew university, Nadera Shalhoub-Kevorkian, confirmed what many have said in the context of other conflicts (Bosnia, for example), that rape of Palestinian women was used as a military tactic.

The girl is captured when an advance party of the platoon comes across a small group of Arab infiltrators (code for Palestinians) with their camels and a dog. The men and the camels are summarily executed by the soldiers, even though they found no weapons, and the girl and dog taken back to the camp. Previously, the officer had briefed the men on their mission which was to secure the southern border with Egypt and, tellingly, to *cleanse* (Shibli 2020, 8) the area of any remaining Arabs. The West Bank is now almost entirely constituted by 'borders' for Palestinians: "The borders imposed here between things are many" (57), and this action was a pioneering forerunner of this. The word 'cleanse' echoes Ilan Pappé's disputed phrase "the Ethnic Cleansing of Palestine". The camp itself is built on what appears to be the ruins of a destroyed Palestinian village—'two standing huts and the remains of a wall in a partially destroyed third' (Shibli 2020, 7).

The officer remains detached and distant, carefully stressing his performative command as he logs with precision each date. His approach is one of rationality, with attention to detail, method and procedure. Insect bites threaten to undermine him, almost 'feminise' him as he administers treatment to himself in the same kind of meticulous detail, anxious not to show weakness in front of his men. Not yielding to pain is part of the warrior mentality. The whole of the first section is related in the third person and in measured, affectless prose—in, what might be called 'man-made language'. The platoon, in accordance with military practice, has a hierarchical organisation along the lines of the homosociality of what Raewyn Connell calls 'relational masculinity', the place of symbolic authority (Connell 2005). The relationship is vertical until they bond horizontally around a shared contempt for the female. The embryonic Israeli state is a masculinist institution, and its military prefigures this in a sense. This was not, of course, something peculiar to Israel, as all settler-colonial projects were established on a similar basis. One difference is that the state of Israel "remains a settler colonial state, retains full sovereign control over the entire territory of Palestine/Israel, and continues to colonise Palestinian land and displace Palestinian people" (Clarno 2017, 1). In the introduction to his memoir of what many at the time considered terrorism, *The Revolt*, Menachem Begin says he had written the book for Gentiles, "lest they be unwilling to realise, or all too ready to overlook, the fact that out of blood and fire and tears and ashes a new specimen of human being was born, a specimen completely unknown to the world for over eighteen hundred years, 'the FIGHTING JEW'" (Begin 1979 [1952], xxv, capitals in original). Hegemonic masculinity is a *claim* and I see this 'event' as a rehearsal in microcosm for this emergent state predicated upon a race and gender hierarchy: a claim to the legitimacy of patriarchy and authority. The violence is a particular encoding of power. I am speaking throughout of men in a specific gender order.

If violence can be seen as a phenomenon of power, then this action can be seen as a metaphor of the originating violence at the heart of Israeli social symbolisation, laws and institutions. The rape and murder can be regarded as a *primal scene*, establishing and legitimising a command structure in dominance. The euphemism used by the actual officer, Moshe, at the trial, articulates this unquestioned power: "I saw fit to remove her from the world". The checkpoints, the roadblocks, the wall and the militarised occupation are all a legacy of this foundational violence, the inscription of power over Palestinian women's bodies, and of men also, through incarceration and torture. The whole of this opening part of the novel is this *inscription* of power, gendered and racialised. This is emphasised in the words of the judges of the appeals court shortly after the historical event, when reducing the sentence of one of the soldiers: "At the time there was a general feeling of contempt for the life of Arabs in general and infiltrators in particular … All this helped create an atmosphere of 'anything goes'" (Lavie and Gorali 2003).

This founding contempt is the primary source of a mentality which persists today as part of the justification for the expulsion of Palestinians. It has become part of the Palestinian historical narrative, the counterpoint to the Israeli narrative with its euphemisms and codes designed to eradicate the memory of the Nakba. *Minor Detail* is such a work of memory and narrative resistance.

In the actual trial, the judges believed that the platoon commander was subject to a "psychosis that seems to have taken root in the officer's blood" but I want to argue that this was not a condition isolated in a specific person but the result of a generic ideology of masculinity. I am relying here on an article by Zipi Israeli and Elisheva Rosman-Stollman: "Men and Boys: Representations of Israeli Combat Soldiers in the Media". This is a study of the ways in which contemporary media in Israel frame the representation of the combat soldier in the Israeli Defence Forces (IDF) but, I would argue, that a comparable representation could be constructed from the military 'architects' of Palestinian dispossession over seventy years ago. In *Minor Detail* we see how the platoon commander stoically copes with his insect bites and back pain: "adult men must overcome personal pain" and control their emotions.

The authors of the article argue that the warrior as the 'epitome of ultimate masculinity' was, in the 1940s, crucial in the shaping of Jewish collective identity, with the figure of the 'New Jew' "everything the diaspora Jew was not", "whereas Diaspora Jews were weak, studious, and passive, the New Jew was strong, farmed the land, and was ready to bear arms in order to protect himself" (Israeli and Rosman-Stollman 2015, 68). The Diaspora Jew was seen as having a 'more feminised identity', a characteristic later ascribed to the Palestinian male. In *Minor Detail*, the soldiers are embodiments of this extreme warrior masculinity, even if many of them were recent recruits from Europe and poorly trained. The commander set the warrior tone and disgust for the female body. As Hélène Cixous claims, "More so than men who are coaxed towards social success, toward sublimation, women are body" (Cixous 1976, 886). The commander's whole masculinist performance is a form of sublimation, achieving value by distancing himself from the sexualised body of the female. She had to be murdered because her rape was an instance of male sexual arousal (although primarily an act of violence), a weakening of the warrior, the emblem of the civilised male. The disgust is part of the distancing, the sublimation and this is embodied (literally) in the smell of the female: "disgust is the key to sublimation. In this anal logic, it is disgust with the smell of sex, which takes the female body particularly as its object, that is the ground for the founding of civilisation" (Kahane 1990, 413). At one point in the first part of the novella, it is said: "Her smell invaded his nose" (Shibli 2020, 26). This underlines the point made by Kahane, as do the words 'stink' and 'putrid smell' used at another point about the girl. The word 'invaded' is also significant, as if the female is a threat to the male: "A mixture of odours had collected in their weave: the scent of manure, a sharp smell of urine and genital secretions, and the sour stench of old sweat overpowering new" (Shibli 2020, 30). There is a clear sense that it is not only the geographical border which has to be secured. The cleansing activity is part of the Israeli civilising process, distancing from the barbaric Arab.

However, in the novella, this masculinity was not framed only by combat but in relation to race and gender, the Palestinian female 'other'. The platoon becomes a foundry in which a masculine identity is forged and then affirmed through the subordination and humiliation of the Arab girl. Her clothes and hair are seen as filthy so she is undressed ceremoniously by the officer in a display of power in full view of the whole platoon—itself an affront to Muslim modesty codes—showered publicly and her long hair—a symbol of beauty in Islam—cut. As she is clothed in an Army uniform and has very short hair she has an ambiguous and 'dangerous' androgynous identity which brings her visually closer in terms of race and gender to the members of the platoon: "By putting on her new uniform, the girl resembled the members of the platoon standing around her, apart from her long, curly hair" (Shibli 2020, 33). Her 'danger' is marked in another way also as she washes herself: "She straightened slightly, and began moving the soap in circles over her head, then her chest, which was soon covered with a fine layer of *white* suds, concealing, for a moment, the brown of her skin" (32, my italics) the danger is in that phrase 'for a moment' when her body could have threatened the 'whiteness' of the men. In contrast with this, is the officer's act of shaving: "He put a little shaving soap on his cheeks and chin, wet the brush with clean water from the bowl, raised it to his face and began moving it in circles until his skin appeared pure *white*" (28, my italics). The two actions mirror each other but how, the question arises, is she to be dissociated from the platoon and the cultural markers (uniform) of Jewish men and masculinity erased?

This dissociation is achieved in two forms, by treating her as a sexual object and by referring to her original 'dirty' state as a means of distinguishing them from her. In *Traces of History*, Patrick Wolfe briefly discusses Mary Douglas's *Purity and Danger* (1966) in which she argues that "dirt is matter out of place to the human domain: race denotes certain peoples as being out of place and therefore, dirty" (Wolfe 2016, 17). In this way, the Arab girl stands in for a whole population that, as mentioned earlier, had to be cleansed and displaced as 'matter out of place'. As Wolfe shows, this subordination and displacement was a characteristic feature of settler colonialism wherever it occurred. So the body of the Arab female is a danger, potentially contaminating to the Jewish male, and, having been cleansed in a way which placed her in temporary proximity to the Jewish men, has to be exterminated through the rape which makes her "dirty" again; she also has to be killed to remove her as her sexuality endangered the platoon. Another way in which she is *distanced* from the men is when: "in that moment after dusk, before complete darkness fell, as her mouth released a language different from theirs, the girl became a stranger again, despite how closely she resembled all the soldiers in the camp" (Shibli 2020, 37). There are several instances in the text where this *liminal*, in-between state (after dusk, before complete darkness fell), the possibly of resemblance menaces the 'necessary' difference of nationalist (with language a defining category) and gendered identity. Her being less than human is emphasised in: "Now the only sound was the muffled weeping of a girl who had curled inside her black clothes *like a beetle*" (25, my italics). Interestingly, during the court proceedings, the officer denied rape on the grounds that, "Morally speaking, it was impossible to sleep with such a dirty girl". It was this mentality which enabled the officer in the novel to dehumanise and objectify the girl with his offer to the men of two options for a vote: "either they send the girl to work in the camp's kitchen, or they all have their way with her" (Shibli 2020, 39). The men set about arrangements for the 'rape' as though it were a logistical exercise (and the prose enacts this) but the officer then commanded them not to touch her or he would use his gun on them. The officer exercises his right to rape but in the process his body is described in terms which suggest indecision and 'unmanliness'.

The first half of *Minor Detail* can be seen as an archetypical enactment, in elliptical form, of a founding moment in settler colonialism, with the terrain seen from his binoculars by the officer as the proverbial 'terra nullius'—barren land. At one point he gives the men a Zionist homily in which he speaks of the unproductive and uncivilised Arab who had neglected the land for centuries, whereas they are taking part in building their 'infant state', the homeland "where our forefathers passed thousands of years ago" (Shibli 2020, 37). This is straight from the 'textbook' of Zionist nationalism which is contrasted with the Arabs' "sterile nationalist sentiments" (37), the word 'sterile' implying infertility, the inability to give birth to anything, unlike the *infant* state.

An Infinity of Traces

"In the *Prison Notebooks* Gramsci says: The starting point of critical elaboration is the consciousness of what one really is, and is 'knowing oneself' as a product of the historical process to date, which has deposited in you an infinity of traces, without leaving an inventory" (Said 1978, 25).

After the impersonal clinical detachment of the 'masculine' account of the first part of Shibli's narrative, the second part is recounted in the form of a first person, interior monologue produced by a young woman who is preoccupied, obsessed with the fact that the 1949 traumatic event took place on a day twenty-five years before her own birthday, 13 August 1974. This coincidence, it is assumed, is the 'minor detail' whereas in terms of the masculinist narrative I have outlined, it is rape and the death of the 'sub-human' Arab girl which would be seen in this way as something of no real consequence, nothing unusual. It is the first of many resonances, connectives, continuities between the two sections of the narrative. There is no logical reason to connect the two dates but, for the woman, a strong emotional, affective identity is established. In this part of my analysis, I want to bring together the Gramsci quotation with Marianne Hirsch's concept of *postmemory* in order to understand the experience of the unnamed narrator. She undertakes a journey from her home in Ramallah to the site in the Negev where the original rape and murder took place in order to find out the truth for herself of what happened. As I have said, the second part of the narrative bears a number of traces carried over from the first. What her journey does is to discover/recover the historical process from that founding moment in 1949 through a cartography of the territory of the OPT in order to construct an inventory of the 'legacy' of which she has no memory but only a newspaper account. This inventory is a kind of alternative 'facts on the ground'. The mapping is not just of places but of the psychological and physical limits and enclosures placed on Palestinians by the militarised security technologies of the Israeli state; technologies which produce a range of insecurities in the occupied population.

These insecurities manifest themselves in the young woman in her restless, edgy discursive register and in the form of a psychopathology which includes anxiety disorders and symptoms which present as post-traumatic stress disorder. According to the Oxford Clinical Psychology site (June 6, 2020) psychiatric and psychosomatic conditions can be divided into two groups: proximate and ultimate (evolutionary) causes. The proximate is person specific, but it is the evolutionary which is of interest here. One of these causes is a mismatch between adaptation and her current environment. The dysfunction experienced by the narrator indicates this kind of *mismatch*. I would argue that the Occupation can be categorised as a 'diseased civilization' and that the woman's mismatch and anxiety disorder are not pathological but societal. In other words, although specified in personal terms, her condition is metonymic, 'representative' in a sense of a wider Palestinian experience.

Marianne Hirsch describes postmemory as the relationship that the 'generation after' bears to the personal, collective and cultural trauma of those who came before—to experiences they 'remember' only by means of the stories, images and behaviours among which they grew up:

As I see it, the connection to the past that I define as postmemory is mediated not by recall but by imaginative investment, projection and creation. To grow up with overwhelming inherited memories, to be dominated by narratives that preceded one's birth or one's consciousness, is to risk having one's own life stories displaced, even evacuated, by our ancestors. It is to be shaped, however indirectly, by traumatic fragments of events that still defy narrative reconstruction and exceed comprehension. (Hirsch, n.d.)

'Shibli's female narrator is of the third, rather than after, generation and her whole journey is a process of 'imaginative investment, projection and creation'. The challenge for the woman is to construct a narrative from the fragments of the traumatic event. Displacement is the defining characteristic of post-1948 Palestinian experience and she and others have had their life stories displaced. The 'minor detail' of the girl's rape and murder is in fact the occasion of the *major* detail of colonialism, invasion and dispossession through violence which formed the prelude to the later 1967 Occupation. Her attempt to constitute a memory of this originating violence defies narrative reconstruction as the archives museum she visits and the people she speaks to in the settlements have erased all traces as part of what might be called a larger historic denial. The memories which are constructed are not personal but what Hirsch calls 'affiliative' or cultural.

Not only does the woman attempt to memorialise the Bedouin girl and the extremity of her experience, but she, consciously or not, elects to inherit her trauma and, in the process, becomes a revenant, an incarnation. The girl had no name, no voice, no choice and the woman is similarly unnamed, struggles to speak, and, as a Palestinian hedged around by ID cards, permits, checkpoints and a perceived 'otherness', nor does she have anything but the most limited choice. She lives throughout the 'future' prefigured in the first section, as its consequence.

The woman's narrative begins with signs of her anxiety disorder, in respect of a concern with cleanliness and order but she acknowledges that she can't handle borders, although she lives in a world of many barriers. She says: "There are some people who navigate borders *masterfully*, who never trespass, but these people are few and I'm not one of them" (Shibli 2020, 57). It is significant that she uses the word 'masterfully' a reference back to the gendered realm of the first part, and also 'trespass' as she is a trespasser in a past time as well as in the territory from which she is excluded. In a society encircled by rigid boundaries, she is out of place and the source of ongoing anxiety throughout her journey is the fact that she is a 'trespasser' as she has had to borrow an identity card to make her 'quest', as hers does not qualify her to travel through her own land or *into Israel*. Every checkpoint, each roadblock causes a panic attack—symptomatic of the 'disease' mentioned earlier. As Raja Shehadeh says, in another context, "most of the stories he told me were about checkpoints, a Palestinian vein of narrative that is almost inescapable" (*New York Times* 2017). The woman goes into great detail of the regulations governing access to the various areas, to the point where she seems to inhabit an Alice in Wonderland absurdity. Because of this, her journey, like her narrative, is never linear but indirect, composed of fragments of Palestinian life—militarisation, impoverished children begging, the entitlement of the settler/coloniser, the indigence of villagers or bombing by the IDF. Living under siege is the everyday experience, and her tone is apologetic and diffident: "By the way [addressing the reader] I hope I didn't cause any awkwardness when I mentioned the incident with the soldier, or the checkpoints, when I reveal that we are living under occupation here" (Shibli 2020, 59–60).

Being haunted by the incident which occurred twenty-five years prior to the day of her birth she acknowledges may be considered as narcissism but, in fact, her self-absorption, her inability to evaluate situations 'rationally and logically' (unlike the discourse of power used by the platoon commander) reveals her as a lateral thinker, with a distinctive way of seeing. She uses the minor detail, of the gang rape coinciding on the date she was born in 1974, to magnify the 'forgotten' incident (in the Israeli narrative) and to link it with "what happens daily in a place dominated by the roar of occupation and ceaseless killing" (64). Her narrative is accompanied by the roar of occupation and consists of a series of 'coincidings'.

Part of the challenge of her journey is making sense of the maps she has brought with her—one a map of Palestine as it was until 1948 and the other issued by the Israeli ministry of tourism. In a sense, she is travelling through a palimpsest, of her land under erasure. Driving through a wilderness of obstacles, she becomes increasingly disoriented, one of the effects (and purposes?) of occupation. The journey is through absences as "little details drift along the length of the road, furtively hinting at a presence" (Shibli 2020, 79), among the absence of anything Palestinian.

Part of the inventory is constructed out of absences when she opens the Palestine map and recovers a whole host of villages destroyed after the expulsion of their inhabitants. This links with the first Governmental Names Committee set up a month before the 13 August 1949 incident, to "create a Hebrew map of the Negev". As Nadia Abu El-Haj explains "this work must be situated within that larger reality of spatial transformation and military conquest" (Abu El-Haj 2001, 91). The map of Palestine the narrator possesses was obliterated by the Names Committee which, in speaking of the Negev, stated: "Being half of our country, the foreignness of the names in the Negev evokes fear, nearly all of the names are Arabic, many are confused and distorted. Among them some lack meaning while others have negative, sad or degrading connotations. Through these names a foreign spirit blows" (ibid., 93). This was the 'rhetoric of settler nationhood' that helped to destroy the 'inventory' of the map of Palestine possessed by the narrator. What she is left with is the "unmapped and unmappable" (Solnit 2005, 161).

In the Israeli Defence Forces History Museum she feels anxious and out of place again but remarks cryptically that the polite, smiley soldier's "military uniform must be part of the exhibition" because of his lack of the expected aggression. She also comments on the "heroic and encouraging phrases" in the telegrams of soldiers in the late forties, the time of the rapes and murder. She also sees uniforms of the time which enable her to imagine a reenactment of the scene by detailing the exhibited items. She enjoys a moment of power when she watches, then re-winds a film of settler construction, and in the process of re-winding the film: "Again and again, I build settlements and dismantle them" (Shibli 2020, 83). She also examines a range of weapons, some contemporary with the incident, but this only agitates her mental state and she realises "Official museums like this really have no valuable information to offer me, not even small details that could help me retell the girl's story" (85). Everything she experiences—the roads, the checkpoints, the maps and the museums—bears the inscription of an Israeli narrative. She shuts the map of Palestine until 1948 "as a horror rushes over me", the result of an ongoing trauma, 1948–1949. What was the area of the originating trauma—Nirim—is now an Israeli settlement. Throughout this time she is overcome with fear, especially when she sees some leftover military huts, and she is gradually "becoming the girl of August, 1949".

When asked her name by a volunteer at the Nirim museum, she replied with the first non-Arab name that came to mind, as she is now both trespasser and imposter, the only spaces left for the Palestinian in her own land. The volunteer, an Australian immigrant, was not present at the time of the founding of the settlement or the war but proudly recites the story of that time according to the authorised Israeli narrative. Unlike her voice, his is calm and clear, the voice that is of 'the settled'. She asks if he knew of the August 1949 incident, as he said that he had volunteered in a military unit after the war. His measured response was that "one day, during a patrol, they found the body of a young Bedouin girl in a nearby well, and explains to me that when Arabs are suspicious about a girl's behaviour, they kill her and throw her body in a well. Such a shame, he adds, that they have such customs" (Shibli 2020, 93). The extraordinary distortion is underscored by the matter of fact way it is related as part of a seamless Israeli narrative of the period, highlighted by the banner, reprised from Part One: "Man, not the tank, shall prevail". Apart from this being the reverse of the truth, its gendered nature is actually true. It is of interest that the woman is addressed as if she were Israeli ('they have such customs') which recalls the anxiety in Part One caused by the Arab girl's temporary resemblance to the Israeli soldiers.

She realises that, for all her travelling, she has learnt nothing she could not have found out at home. At this stage, she travels on a road between "silent yellow hills trembling nervously under the heft of a mirage" (Shibli 2020, 94), reminding one of "the mirage-like qualities of the past—its haziness and its immateriality and the way, depending on one's angle of perception, it seems to assume a form one moment and slough it off the next" (Trela 2020, n.p.). Not only of the past, one might add, as the present also has this mirage-like quality, with illusions shaped by conflicting angles of perception.

Preoccupied with trying to find a clue, a thread to 'what the girl endured', she decides to go to Nirim again and experiences more explicit references, unknown to her, to the original crime—a barking *dog*, spilt *petrol*, the *hut* in the guesthouse where she stays, the shower where she doesn't have to worry about the use of water unlike in Ramallah. Even a book on Art which she reads in the hut brings her closer to the girl. These World War I German Expressionist paintings contained radical distortions of the human figure and its surroundings, one is a "painting of a naked girl lying on her stomach on the sand as if she had fallen into it; her body is yellow, like the sand, and her short, tousled hair is black" (Shibli 2020, 101). In the first part of the novel, the girl fell to the sand, "while the afternoon sunlight gathered on her naked bottom, itself the colour of sand" (53). Her hair, after it had been cut, would have been short and tousled. The narrator is gradually entering the original/originating narrative.

Within earshot of bombings in Gaza or Rafah, she is aware that there is no dust, unlike earlier at her office, and this makes her realise "how profoundly far I am from anything familiar, and how impossible it will be to return" (102). The process of defamiliarisation, and a destination from which there is no return, causes her anxiety and horror to increase. In psychoanalytic terms, she is driven by a compulsion to repeat the original traumatic incident/crime—her whole drive is towards death. She approaches an Arab village, of which there is no trace on the Israeli map, and, mirage-like, thinks she catches sight of a girl. She reaches a point and turns right into part of the Naqab, without a clear reason, "as if I am no longer able to leave the area" (108). Again, as if she is under some compulsion: "Now, the only movement belongs to the mirage". In keeping with her obsession, she gives a lift to a woman in her seventies, "the girl would have been around the same age now most likely, if she hadn't been killed. Maybe this old woman has heard about the incident, since incidents like this would have reached the ears of everyone living in the Naqab, terrorizing them all" (109). This summarises, and generalises, the common Palestinian experience of being terrorised by the omnipresence of violence. As she continues to search for the "incident as experienced by the girl. And finally arrive at the whole truth" she becomes aware of the way in which "the distance between us grows" and she changes direction: "I don't resist the urge to head in its direction, despite a sign indicating that this is a military zone" (110). At this point she has narrowed the distance between the girl and herself as the 'primal scene' is re-enacted, with the finding of a bullet case, the presence of camels, and a group of soldiers: "One of the soldiers shouts in my direction, and the others raise their guns at me" (111). Her anxiety takes on bodily form, aware that the Palestinian rental car has aroused their suspicions: "I have to calm down, I must be overreacting. Yes, just like usual" (112). At this climactic moment, she *completes her identification* with the Bedouin girl: "And suddenly, something like a sharp flame pierces my hand, then my chest, followed by the distant sound of gunshots" (112). Although the narrator says that the girl's death didn't *necessarily* belong to her—"the fact that the girl was killed twenty-five years to the day before I was born doesn't necessarily mean that *her death belongs to me* or that it should extend into my life, or that it should be my duty to retell her story" (Shibli 2020, 69, my italics)—she does finally retell, and relive, her story, and discovers the complete truth, that *violence*, originary and continuing, is the narrative which binds them, the enabling 'vocabulary' of dispossession, the signature of power. The death of the Bedouin girl belongs not just to the narrator but to every Palestinian girl, or woman, since, as it extends continuously into all of their lives.

A Jar in Ramallah

The colonial reality of the founding moment of Israel which shapes the narrative in *Minor Detail* was, at the time, anomalous as Eqbal Ahmed pointed out: "August 1947 marked the beginning of decolonization when British rule in India ended. It was in those days of hope and fulfilment that the colonization of Palestine occurred. Thus at the dawn of decolonization, we were returned to the earliest, most intense form of colonial menace … exclusivist settler colonialism" (Bengelsdorf et al. 2006, 301). In modern times, of course, the colonisation of Palestine began with the Balfour Declaration of 1917, and the establishment of the British Mandate in 1920, approved by the League of Nations in 1922. If, as Rashid Khalidi suggests, the Palestine narrative is a growing currency, I should like to conclude this chapter by a consideration of the most recent work of one of the writers who can be credited with having made a major contribution to this, Raja Shehadeh. Edward Said claimed that Zionism "won the political battle for Palestine in the international world in which ideas, representation, rhetoric and images were at issue" (Said 1988, 1). Throughout this chapter, I have been looking at writers who have refused the Israeli narrative and challenged it through radical ideas, forms of representation, and the rhetoric and images of resistance. What Shehadeh has attempted in eight works of memoir and autobiography is to provide a compass for the Palestinian narrative. I use 'compass' advisedly as his writings are, literally and metaphorically, works of navigation and exploration of spaces, orientation and direction, especially *Palestinian Walks* (2008) and, the most recent, *Going Home* (2019). Ramallah is made present as an experience in terms expressed by Derrida: "To experience is to advance by navigating, to walk by traversing" (Derrida 1995, 373). This book is a retrospective, an elegy and a self-criticism. It is subtitled 'A Walk Through Fifty Years of Occupation' and is structured around a single day, the fiftieth anniversary of the Israeli occupation of Palestine—5 June 2017. In a sense, the Occupation becomes the narrative, and the narrative becomes the Occupation except that Shehadeh is trying to locate temporalities other than those imposed by the society of control, the highly mediated spaces of the Occupation. The writing is a subversion of this control, a re-conceptualisation of Ramallah, a resistance to the present structure. Every street is multi-layered, both a physical presence and a resource for memory. The walk is from his house to his law office in the centre of Ramallah. I say 'house' rather than 'home' because, although he expresses the hope that he and his wife, Penny, will spend the rest of their days in their house, "And yet, despite this long-standing attachment, I continue to be troubled by a recurring dream in which, for what feels to be an agonizingly long time, I search for but cannot find my home" (Shehadeh 2019, 11). An epigraph to the book is a quotation from James Baldwin: "Perhaps home is not a place but simply an irrevocable condition". So, from an early stage in the narrative, 'home' takes on a complex and multi-layered meaning, with the word 'going' in the title suggesting a continuous process, never completed, with 'home' an ever-receding place, overlaid by time. As the writer, Ella Winter, said to the American novelist Thomas Wolfe, "Don't you know you can't go home again", and this is something which Shehadeh realises in the course of his walk, in the course of his writing (Godwin 2011, xix). The walk and the writing are fused into a single project.

The city he walks through is now a space of borders, checkpoints, and, in the distance, settlements or colonies (a term preferred by activists) which mean that the only walk available to him now is an urban walk: "When I look at the Ofer checkpoint I see both how it is now and what it was like before it was ruined. For me it was an open road, for them a border" (Shehadeh 2019, 34). The 'them' referred to is the younger generation. Shehadeh's walk becomes a journey through ruins, an ongoing exchange between 'open road' and 'border'. The walk through the city's spaces is also a walk through time, in his childhood, the period before the Occupation, the first and second intifada, and the Oslo Accords, all of which have shaped Palestine, Ramallah and himself. He bears the marks of time and of defeat (he says as much in his "Note to the Reader", ix), and the realisation that his generation, with their strategies, have to yield to a new generation and another phase of struggle. In the second chapter, Shehadeh recalls a time nineteen years ago that, when he was fitting an antique Byzantine jar to a new stand, it shattered into pieces. He gathered these up and placed them in a bag. Later, he re-assembled the jar by gluing the shards together, although there were gaps he failed to fill. Reflecting on this experience, he draws a fairly obvious analogy with Palestine, "once whole and lovely, now reduced to shards" (14). He doesn't labour the metaphor but what I think he does in the book is to gather together shards of time and place in an attempt to piece his city together again, to story it through transgressive meanings. De Certeau calls walking an "act of enunciation" (de Certeau 1984, 98), a mode of appropriation, and what Shehadeh is doing is bringing Ramallah into existence by mapping not just its spaces but the overlapping temporalities of these spaces, places, sites which are invoked as markers of experience. The writing produces a cartography of resistance, a defiance of the city's concealment of what is no longer visible.

A building passed or an image seen become part of a schemata for recall and reconstruction in which an episode, or moment, linked to that place is re-visited and is narrated as if it were happening in the present—almost like a *resumption*, but also a rupture.

Shehadeh is trying to repair what, in geological terms, might be considered a fault line or a discontinuity across which there has been a traumatic displacement. A fault line is a place where the fault can be seen or mapped on the surface. For him, the fifty years of Israeli occupation is such a fault line which, in the course of writing/walking, he is mapping through the Six-Day War (1967), the two intifadas, and the Oslo Accords—all of which have brought about a systematic effacement of his home. When we speak of home we think of a physical, and almost spiritual, space—a town, city or neighbourhood. In *Going Home*, there is a sense in which the larger space has gradually been eroded to a point where 'home' now is the "intimate surroundings" of a single dwelling: "I look around me at our intimate surroundings and now call out to Penny, 'I'm home'" (Shehadeh 2019, 196). The 'intimacy' of the Ramallah of his earlier years and of memory has been erased but, as Bachelard says, "all really inhabited space bears the essence of the notion of home" (Bachelard 1994, 5) and, in terms which capture Shehadeh's writing precisely, de Certeau says that "haunted places are the only ones people can live in" (de Certeau 1984, 108) and "it is this very haunting of space by stories that allows a place to become 'home'" (ibid., 106). So, the writer is not only going home but *making* it by the act of slowing down time to a walking pace.

The walk takes the shape of a doubly articulated narrative—that of the contemporary infrastructure and landscape, and what might be thought of as an archaeological narrative, an effaced earlier space on which the contemporary narrative has been superimposed. The walk is an act of recovery, of restoration, a tracking of the still visible traces of an earlier time and place. In an attempt to align the present with the past, Shehadeh uses a form of auto-ethnography in which he seeks to overcome the erasure produced by the Occupation (in which 60 percent of the West Bank is controlled by Israel). He does this partly by means of nostalgia—uncovering the palimpsest—but also by immersing himself, and by extension the reader, in the physical space of Ramallah, by locating/positioning the reader through signifiers of location—here, there—and direction—turn left, turn right and in the process producing a psychogeographic memory synchronised across time: then and now brought into simultaneity, what Bachelard calls 'topoanalysis.'

The overall theme is that of displacement and loss, with each of the chapters focusing on particular aspects of this loss—people, buildings, crafts, family, culture, flora and the memory of those killed by the IDF. Home is not just a house, but a locus of belonging, not only for those in the West Bank but for the millions of Palestinians wishing to return to the sites of their lost villages. Porteous and Smith have coined the term 'domicide' to describe "this deliberate destruction of home against the will of the home dweller" (Porteous and Smith 2001, 3), and this captures the essence of Shehadeh's book. Another coinage of theirs is 'geopiracy' to describe Israeli's actions in the West Bank and Gaza. Shehadeh's 'hauntings' or 'hacking' of these spaces produces an anti- or counter-narrative.

One of the questions posed frequently in the course of this book is how to find an appropriate form for the expression of the inexpressible, that which would seem to be beyond words. Shehadeh uses a range of different techniques, including auto-ethnography, participant (witness) observation, psychogeography and the method of loci or the memory palace.

The use of the walk, or journey, is a way of encoding the place in which Shehadeh lives with reference not just to physical locations but to signs or markers of places no longer present except in his memory—imprints of spatial disappearance. These imprints exist as loci where images are stored and can be stimulated by passing a building or meeting a person. As the Occupation is embedded as a narrative in Shehadeh's physical and mental landscape, he uses the local topography of his adopted home town to plot his journey, constructing a kind of memory palace which contains the Occupation, his memories of a time prior to it, and its impact on his personal and political life: Sheringham calls the city a "memory machine" (Sheringham 2010, 12) and this could be applied to this kind of writing.

The structure of the book is an attempt to tell the story of the walk as if from the perspective of the time when it was taken, as if the networks of his memory were active in the process of walking and not simply recalled in the act of writing. The writing re-locates and re-places what resulted from the displacement and relocation of a people, with Ramallah as a symbolic centre. The disfigurement of his home is linked with his own ageing process—the book begins with the writer looking in the bathroom mirror and charting the changes in his own hair, face and hands, the marks of time, and he realises that had he paid more attention to his father as he aged, he would have been more aware of the impact of the ageing process on himself. The author's uneasy relationship with his father—murdered in 1985—features prominently in the book and forms part of his self-awareness and self-criticism. The Occupation has not only scarred the city of his upbringing but, metaphorically, his own body and the failure to bond with his father. In many ways, the book is a kind of reckoning, a coming to terms, as he says in "A Note to the Reader", with "the political defeats, frustrations and failures that I have witnessed over the years of occupation and resistance" (Shehadeh 2019, ix). The walk and the writing are an act of witness as well as something of a confession, a recognition that the political strategies of his generation have not been a success—something underlined by the Oslo Accords (1993–1995)—and the realisation that the present generation needs to come up with entirely different strategies which they are doing through digital resources and BDS (Boycott, Divestment and Sanctions). It is this aspect of the book which brings it close to a lament, a text of mourning. In *The Two-State Delusion*, Padraig O'Malley (2015) speaks of a tale of two narratives but, arguably, the Occupation is designed to produce a people without its own narratives for, as Kubiak argues, "to disrupt narrativity … is to disrupt body and mind … to induce a kind of madness not merely to interrupt the story, or cause us to question the outcomes, or challenge our beliefs and suppositions" (Kubiak 2004, 297). De Certeau says, further, "deprived of narratives … the group or individual *regresses* toward the disquieting, fatalistic experience of a formless, indistinct and nocturnal totality" (de Certeau 1984, 100). There is a certain mood of fatalism in *Going Home*, but the point of the book is to give form and distinctiveness to Shehadeh's experience of his home over the fifty years of the Occupation which is a *pre*occupation of this narrative. My basis for saying that it is a text of mourning is an essay called "The Inability to Mourn—Today" by Margarete Mitscherlich-Nielsen which focuses upon post-Nazi Germany. She speaks of character deformations, mystifications, misinformation, denials and repressions in post-1945 Germany, and of traditions of authority and obedience, which have characterised mentalities. In "Checkpoint Jitters" (2012), Shehadeh speaks of how docile, submissive and obedient people have become, not just at checkpoints, but in the West Bank generally. Almost echoing Mitscherlich-Nielsen, he says "I must rebel against this, too, and against these new quiescent times. I must refuse to be beguiled, confused, mystified" (Shehadeh 2012, 3). Apart from his work as a lawyer, challenging the expropriation of Palestinian land for Israeli settlements, and in setting up the al-Haq Human Rights centre, Shehadeh's rebellion has taken place through his writing. *Going Home* is the eighth work of memoir-journalism since 2002.

The purpose of Shehadeh's writing is to reclaim that narrative which has been disrupted or interrupted by the Occupation, through the active process of *storying* which is both empowering and restorative. As de Certeau says, "Stories map out a space which would otherwise not exist" (de Certeau 1984, 115), and Shehadeh's writings are a work of reclamation, of restoration and of the mapping out of spaces which had been obliterated, either literally or metaphorically. In the words of Mitscherlich-Nielsen, Shehadeh has the ability to mourn as "he is able to part with open eyes not only from the lost objects but also from lost attitudes and thought patterns … The work of mourning, a process of leave-taking, is the prerequisite for being able to think new thoughts, perceive new things, and alter one's behaviour patterns" (Mitscherlich-Nielsen 1989, 408). *Going Home* is, in some ways, a leave-taking.

Much of the text is concerned with the visual, the act of seeing and witnessing, a gradual opening of the eyes as he re-situates lost objects and lost attitudes (parental/personal and political). Shehadeh has a kind of 'double vision', both seeing things as they were and in the way they are now. It is this dialectic of then and now, this dual vision, which forms the rhythm and framework of the book. The fact that the political and personal are so entangled is underlined by his acknowledgement that "I am doomed to feeling the need to justify my existence through writing and speaking … while assuming the burden of and responsibility for the failure of all I see around me as if it were my own" (quoted in Lindsey 2017). This is not a counsel of despair but a realisation of his role and responsibility as a writer: to bear witness.

The writing is an investment in the city—a preoccupation, bringing it into being despite the Occupation, an active involvement, 'a making present', even that which is past or absent. The narrative is produced in what Ricœur calls a "third time", a *now* which is not that of the walk itself, or its recall, but something generated by the narrative: public, shared time. At the level of narration, the walk already exists as a *story*, it is then brought into the time of narration which gives the story significance; its accumulation of signs and events is activated and made meaningful.

The walk is both a pre-text and a pretext as well as the source of speculation, reflexivity and interpretation: it is offered as a synopsis a 'single take' in cinematic terms, both conceptual and temporal. It is designed as a source of empowerment and resistance—an *embodiment* of something of substance.

The Occupation is likened to a prison, with the Palestinians as hostages to Israeli intransigence, and the walk is a relatively privileged form of mobility because the Occupation is very much about the control of movement through blockage—checkpoint, permit, gated entrances and blocked exits. Once open spaces are now closed, with little remaining of Palestine except symbols, with the Palestinian Authority seeming to have accommodated the Occupation, forgetting the liberation struggle now left to a younger generation with very different strategies from Arafat and Shehadeh's own generation, a digital resistance based upon international mobilisations: "a city claimed by the young" (Shehadeh 2019, 183), he says. His visit to the Arafat Museum and Mausoleum underscores this because of its selective presentation of the Palestinian story, marked particularly 'for what is left out'. What is left out is 'any presentation of sumoud' (steadfastness) that endurance which characterises those who live under the Occupation. Shehadeh describes the main story of the Museum as that of "the doomed armed struggle" (181).

In Chapter 11, Shehadeh metaphorically hands over the narrative to a woman, Maha, with her story of a visit to the Civil Administration at the edge of the Beit El settlement or colony, in order to gain a permit to enable her son to leave Palestine by the airport rather than face the humiliation of the Allenby bridge (referred to earlier by Barghouti). The Civil Administration is the Israeli governing body that operates in the West Bank, set up under Military Order 947 in 1981 and staffed by IDF soldiers. Maha's story adds further evidence of the story of 'spatial strangulation' through the medium of immobility: closed highway, blocked roads and hours of waiting. As Gershon Shafir points out, "Occupied Palestinians were required to apply for ID cards and permits to travel, to work, to relocate, to study abroad, to rezone land, and to open a business;

later, specialized personnel had to apply for authorization to move about under curfew. The Shin Bet [Israeli Security Service] holds the ultimate authority for the approval of permits" (Shafir 2017, 36). In each of the texts examined earlier, permits have played a controlling role.

Maha drove part of the way until the road was blocked, she then walked as far as an empty car park, from which West Bank residents are banned. Severed by checkpoints, all the exits from Ramallah have been closed. In a story of frustration and delay, this is just the first stage. Arriving at 9 a.m., she then gives a precise account of the time spent waiting for the permit, punctuated by a number of false alarms that the permits were ready. The soldiers administering the process were concealed from the applicants and seemed to be engaged in a performance of power as most of the applications were *marfood* (rejected). Each rejection was met with ironic applause, the only shred of dignity left to those waiting. Each moment when time is recorded by Maha adds to the sense of immobility, experienced here and in many of the other texts in this chapter. What is a Palestinian? A Palestinian is someone who *waits*. Eventually, Maha's application is rejected (and cheered) and she had wasted seven hours. As she leaves, she comes across a foreign woman picking up permits for her staff with no *delay* and rages at her. In condensed form, Maha's experience sums up much of what the book is about, the gradual erosion and enclosure of Ramallah, Israeli governance, and the ubiquitous presence of the military, with waiting the prerogative of privilege and power.

Disheartened by the fact that the national liberation struggle has been muted, replaced by consumerism, debt and religion, Shehadeh speaks at one point of the need for a revisionist history of the Palestinian struggle which has not yet been written. Seeing himself as someone yearning to belong but always an outsider with a "recurrent dream of searching for a home" (Shehadeh 2019, 190), perhaps his writing is a major contribution to that revisionist history of which he spoke. Being an outsider gives him a perspective, a lens, with which he has found an 'enabling vocabulary' to re-make Ramallah as his home by keeping time and place *in motion* against an occupying power which would render them static and frozen.

Postscript: An Incurable Malady

Throughout this chapter, numerous instances have been given of the negative effects of the Occupation's displacement, not only on land but also on the minds of those living in the West Bank. Shehadeh gives an example of this by quoting a poem written by his maternal Grandfather, Boulos Shehadeh, entitled "Despair", especially the last line: "I'm but a stranger in these lands who has outstayed his time" (Shehadeh 2019, 191). The separation wall, the blocked roads, the checkpoints and the near impossibility of getting permits are all designed to make the Palestinian feel like a 'stranger' and someone 'who has outstayed their time'.

However, shortly after quoting from his grandfather's poem, Shehadeh is able, after looking at his face in the bathroom mirror, "to smile back at the image I see" (196). To conclude, I should like to link this smile with what Darwish wrote: "We Palestinians suffer from an incurable malady called 'hope'". Nine times in the course of a brief paragraph, he repeats the word 'hope' and it is this insistence which forms the basis of his affirmation of resistance and could be said to sum up what sustains so many of those, examined in this book, who have been forced to flee and have been displaced as a consequence, either from their countries of belonging or within their own lands:

> But we have a incurable malady: hope. Hope in liberation and independence. Hope in a normal life where we are neither heroes nor victims. Hope that our children will go safely to their schools. Hope that a pregnant woman will give birth to a living baby, at the hospital, and not a dead child in front of a military checkpoint; hope that our poets will see the beauty of the color red in roses rather than in blood; hope that this land will take up its original name: the land of love and peace. Thank you for carrying with us the burden of this hope. (Darwish 2002, 2)

NOTES

1. There is an extensive literature on the annexation wall (Palestine), or the security barrier (Israel), depending on whose perspective is being represented. I have found the most illuminating accounts in Simone Bitton's film, *Mur* (2004) and, as far as I know, the only book-length study, René Backmann's *A Wall in Palestine* (2006). Bitton's film is subtitled "a cinematic meditation on the Israeli-Palestinian conflict" and she travelled to Jerusalem to film the construction of the wall, even visiting factories which produced the materials. She also interviewed people living on both sides of the division, including Palestinian labourers working on the wall, as well as interviewing the Director General of the Israeli Ministry of Defence who,

as representative of the ministry responsible for the building of the wall, not surprisingly defended the construction.
2. As I was completing this chapter, news came in of the demolition on 3 November 2020 of seventy structures and of seventy-three people displaced in the Jordan valley, with the use of six bulldozers and one hundred Israeli soldiers. The structures were in the rural herding community of Khirbet Humsa. According to ICAHD (The Israeli Committee Against House Demolitions), the demolitions were the largest operation ordered by the Israeli Civil Administration in the past ten years. The reason given for the demolitions was that the community did not have a residence permit and the area was designated a 'firing zone' (as is 18 percent of the West Bank). As indicated elsewhere in this chapter, residence permits are impossible to obtain, and the community has rented this land for generations from Palestinian owners (ICAHD UK, November 2020).
3. There is very little critical material on *Minor Detail* as yet but the essay by Robyn Creswell (2020) in the *New York Review* offers a very interesting analysis in which he draws upon Shibli's earlier works and some of the literary sources for the novella. While overlapping in some respects with my reading of the text, Creswell takes a different approach which sees it as less allegorical than I do and makes little or no comment on the gender aspects.

References

Abu El-Haj, Nadia. 2001. *Facts on the Ground: Archaeological Practice and Territorial Self-Fashioning in Israel Society*. Chicago: University of Chicago Press.

Amiry, Suad. 2005. *Sharon and My Mother-in-Law: Ramallah Diaries*. London: Granta Books.

Bachelard, Gaston. 1994 [1958]. *The Poetics of Space*. Boston, MA: Beacon Press.

Backmann, René. 2010 [2006]. *A Wall in Palestine*. Translated by A. Kaiser. New York: Picador.

Badr, Liana. 2006. "Other Cities." In *Dissat: Short Stories by Palestinian Women*, edited by Jo Glanville, 39–57. London: Telegram Books.

Barghouti, Maroud. 2005 [2000]. *I Saw Ramallah*. Translated by Ahdaf Souief. London: Bloomsbury Publishing.

Barghouti, Maroud. 2012. *I Was Born There, I Was Born Here*. Translated by Humphrey Davies. London: Bloomsbury Publishing.

Baroud, Ramzy. 2018. *The Last Earth: A Palestinian Story*. London: Pluto Press.

Begin, Menachem. 1979 [1952]. *The Revolt*. Translated by Samuel Katz. London: W. H. Allen.

Bengelsdorf, Carollee, et al. 2006. *The Selected Writings of Eqbal Ahmad*. New York: Columbia University Press.
Bishara, Azmi. 2006. *Yearning in the Land of Checkpoints*. Tel Aviv: Babel Press.
Cixous, Hélène. 1976. "The Laugh of the Medusa." *Signs* 1 (4): 875–93.
Clarno, Andy. 2017. *Neoliberal Apartheid: Palestine/Israel and South Africa after 1994*. Chicago and London: Chicago University Press.
Connell, Raewyn. 2005. *Masculinities*. Cambridge: Polity Press.
Creswell, Robyn. 2020. "The Body and the Border." *The New York Review*, October 22.
Darwish, Mahmoud. 1995 [1987]. *Memory for Forgetfulness: August, Beirut, 1982*. Berkeley: University of California Press.
Darwish, M. 2001. "Not to begin at the end." *Al-Ahram Weekly* 533 (online). Retrieved October 2020 from, http://weekly.ahram.org.eg/2001/533/op1.htm.
Darwish, Mahmoud. 2002. "On the Incurable Malady of Hope." *Women's World*, March 25: 1–2.
Darwish, Mahmoud. 2006. *Absent Presence*. Translated by M. Shaheen. London: University of California Press.
de Certeau, Michel. 1984. *The Practice of Everyday Life*. Translated by Steven Rendall. Berkeley: University of California Press.
Derrida, Jacques. 1995. *Points...Interviews, 1974–1994*. Edited by Elisabeth Webster. Translated by Peggy Kamuf and Others. Meridian: Crossing Aesthetics.
Fanon, Frantz. 2001 [1965]. *The Wretched of the Earth*. London: Penguin Books.
Freeman, Mark. 1998. "Mythical Time, Historical Time, and the Narrative Fabric of the Self." *Narrative Inquiry* 8 (1): 27–50.
Godwin, Gail. 2011. "Introduction: Thomas Wolfe." In *You Can't Go Home Again*. New York: Simon and Schuster.
Gregory, Derek. 2004. *The Colonial Present: Afghanistan. Palestine. Iraq*. Oxford: Blackwell Publishing.
Handel, Ariel. 2009. "Where, Where to, and When in the Occupied Territories: An Introduction to Geography of Disaster." In *The Power of Inclusive Exclusion: Anatomy of Israeli Rule in the Occupied Palestinian Territories*, edited by Adi Ophir, Michal Givoni and Sari Hanafi, 179–222. New York: Zone Books.
Herzl, Theodor. 1960 [1895]. *Complete Diaries*. Edited by Raphael Patai. New York: Herzl Press.
Hirsch, Marianne. n.d. "An Interview with Marianne Hirsch." Author Interviews. Columbia University Press.
ICAHD. 2020. "Urgent Action Bulletin: 70 Structures Demolished and 73 People Displaced in the Jordan Valley." info@ichaduk.org.

Israeli, Zipi, and Elisheva Rosman-Stollman. 2015. "Men and Boys: Representations of Israeli Combat Soldiers in the Media." *Israeli Studies Review* 30 (1): 66–83.

Jayyusi, Lena. 2003. "Letters from the Palestinian Ghetto 8–13th March 2002." *Open Edition Journals*: 125–29.

Kahane, Claire. 1990. "Freud's Sublimation: Disgust, Desire and the Female Body." *American Imago* 49 (4): 411–25.

Khalidi, Walid. 1988. "Plan Dalet: Master Plan for the Conquest of Palestine." *Journal of Palestine Studies* 18 (1): 4–33.

Kotef, Hagar. 2015. *Movement and the Ordering of Freedom: On Liberal Governances of Mobility*. Durham and London: Duke University Press.

Kubiak, A. 2004. "Spelling It Out: Narrative Typologies of Terror." *Studies in the Novel* 36 (3): 294–301.

Lavie, Aviv, and Moshe Gorali. 2003. "I Saw Fit to Remove her from the World." *Haaretz*, October 28.

Lindsey, Ursula. 2017. "The Lights in the Distance: The Peregrinations of Raja Shehadeh." *The Nation*, November 29: n.p.

Mansour, Camilla. 2001. "Israel's Colonial Impasse." *Journal of Palestine Studies* 30: 83–87.

Mitscherlich-Nielsen, Margarete. 1989. "The Inability to Mourn—Today." In *The Problem of Loss and Mourning: Psychoanalytical Perspectives*, edited by D. R. Dietrich and P. C. Shabad, 405–26. Madison, CT: International Universities Press.

Mur. 2004. Directed by Simone Bitton. A Cine-Sud (Paris)/Arna Productions (Jerusalem) co-production.

O'Malley, Padraig. 2015. *The Two-State Delusion: Israel and Palestine—A Tale of Two Narratives*. New York: Viking.

Ophir, Adi. 2002. "A Time of Occupation." In *Other Israel*, 51–66. New York: New Press.

Ophir, Adi, Michal Govini, and Sara Hanafi. 2009. *The Power of Inclusive Exclusion: Anatomy of Israeli Rule in the Occupied Palestinian Territories*. New York: Zone Books.

Pappé, Ilan. 2016. "Israel Is the Last Remaining Active Settler-Colonialist Project." Interview with Eli Massey. *In These Times*, May 5.

Peteet, Julie. 2009. *Landscape of Hope and Despair: Palestinian Refugee Camps*. Philadelphia: University of Pennsylvania Press.

Porteous, John Douglas, and Sandra Smith. 2001. *Domicide: The Global Destruction of Home*. Montreal: McGill-Queens Press.

"RE-EXPOSED: A horrific story of Israeli rape and murder in 1949". *Al Arabiya English*. August 17, 2015.

Said, Edward. 1978. *Orientalism*. New York: Pantheon Books.

Said, Edward. 1984. "Permission to Narrate." In *The Edward Said Reader*. 2001, edited by Mustafa Bayoumi and Andrew Rubin, 243–66. London: Granta Publications.

Said, Edward. 1988. "Introduction." In *Blaming the Victims; Spurious Scholarship and the Palestine Question*, edited by Edward Said and Christopher Hitchens, 1–19. New York: Verso.

Segal, Rafi, and Eyal Weizman. 2003. *A Civilian Occupation: The Politics of Israeli Architecture*. London: Verso.

Shafir, Gershon. 2017. *A Half Century of Occupation: Israel, Palestine and the World's Most Intractable Conflict*. Oakland: University of California Press.

Shehadeh, Raja. 2012. "Checkpoint Jitters." *The New York Times*, June 22: 1–3.

Shehadeh, Raja. 2017. "Life Behind Israeli Checkpoints." *New York Times*, May 20, 2017.

Shehadeh, Raja. 2019. *Going Home: A Walk Through Fifty Years of Occupation*. London: Profile Books.

Sheringham, Michael. 2010. "Archiving." In *Restless Cities*, edited by Matthew Beaumont and Gregory Dart, 1–17. London: Verso.

Shibli, Adania. 2020 [2017]. *Minor Detail*. Translated by Elisabeth Jaquette. London: Fitzcarraldo Editions.

Solnit, Rebecca. 2005. *A Field Guide to Getting Lost*. New York: Viking.

Trela, Bailey. 2020. "Minor Detail." www.blog.pshares.org. October 23.

Weheliye, Alexander. 2014. *Habeas Viscus: Racializing Assemblages, Biopolitics, and Black Feminist Theories of the Human*. Durham and London: Duke University Press.

Weizmann, Eyal. 2002. "The Politics of Verticality." *Open Democracy*, April 23. https://www.opendemocracy.net/en/article_801jsp/#.

Weizman, Eyal. 2017 [2007]. *Hollow Land: Israel's Architecture of Occupation*. London: Verso.

Wolfe, Patrick. 2016. *Traces of History: Elementary Structures of Race*. London: Verso Books.

Index

A
Absent Presence (Mahmoud Darwish), 17
Abu El-Haj, Nadia, 216
Abyssal thinking, 168
Adey, Peter, 12, 13
Affect
  close-up, 133
  inline, 133
  subject, 194
  subjectivity, 3, 176
Afghanistan (Afghans), 20, 28, 41, 88, 104, 122, 128, 130
  Kunduz bombing, 128
Africa, 1, 6, 23, 33, 39, 67, 68, 133, 141, 142, 145, 152, 153, 156, 158–162, 164, 165, 167, 168, 176, 177
  North Africa, 133
African Titanics (Khaal, Abu Bakar), 10, 14, 151, 166
Agier, Michel, 66, 70, 119, 120
Agnew, John, 33

Alcoff, Linda Martin, 5
Alioua, Mehdi, 154
Allen, Woody, 113
Al Nassiry, Khaled Saliman, 49
Alterity, otherness, 66
Amin, Idi, 156, 159, 162
Amiry, Suad, 187, 191, 199
Amnesty International, 30, 40
Anderson, Benedict, 21
Antisemitism (antisemitic), 146
Anti-structure, 95
Anzaldua, Gloria, 3, 9, 16
Apartheid, 66
Arab Spring, 59
Arafat, Yasser, 225
Armenia, 76
Ashcroft, Bill, 151
Asterix the Gaul, 115
Astley, Neil, 56
Asylum seekers, 3, 4, 13–15, 20, 21, 23, 27–29, 31–34, 36, 41, 47, 48, 54, 60, 61, 63, 65–72, 74, 75, 78–80, 82, 101, 103,

104, 113–118, 144. *See also* Immobility; Migration; Mobility; Refugees
asylum claimants, 65, 68
asylum legislation, 15, 67
asylum narratives, 23, 51, 66
Auden, W.H., 55
"In Memory of W. B. Yeats", 55
"September 1, 1939", 55
Augugliaro, Antonio, 49, 52
Australia
  Christmas Island, 79, 85
  Darwin, 79
  Melville Island, 79
  Migration Act, 1958, 79
Auto-ethnography (auto-ethnographical), 81, 83, 95, 222

B
Bachelard, Gaston, 221, 222
Backmann, René, 227
Badr, Liana ("Other Cities"), 201–204
Baek, Jiewon, 138
Baldwin, James, 160, 220
Balibar, Etienne, 8, 16, 35, 36, 48, 66
Banerjee, B., 105, 111
Bannon, Steve, 142
Barghouti, Maroud, 182, 184, 186, 189–193, 199–201, 225
  I Saw Ramallah, 189
  I Was Born There, I Was Born Here, 182, 199, 200
Baroud, Ramzy, 184
  The Last Earth: A Palestinian Story, 184
Begin, Menachem, 208
Bengelsdorf, Carollee, 219
Benhabib, Seyla, 62, 63
Bennett, Bruce, 48
Benvenisti, Meron, 184

Berlin conference (1884–85), 156
Berlin Wall, 1
Betts, Alexander, 11, 14
Bigger, Stephen, 95
Biodiversity, 3, 162
Biopolitics, 80, 102
Bishara, Azmi
  Yearning in the Land of Checkpoints, 195
Bitton, Simone, 188, 227
Black Lives Matter, 36, 146
Body organs, 10, 31
  global trade in, 31
  sale/trade in, 10
  trade in spare body parts, 45
Boochani, Behrouz, 8, 60, 63, 80–97
  No Friend but the Mountains, 8, 60, 95
  with Nazanin Sahamizadeh, *Manus* (play), 80
Borders
  border controls, 17, 102, 120
  border crossings, 16, 52, 65
  fences, 7, 10, 16, 20, 47, 102, 141, 153, 154, 157
  frontier(s), 14, 184
  grey zones, 134
  open/closed borders, 51, 132
  shifting borders, 184
  walls, 7, 16, 20, 141, 177. *See also* Immobility; Migration; Mobility; Movement; Refugees
Border thinking, 7, 16, 49, 55
Bosnia, 68, 76, 207
Brant, Clare, 166
Brexit, 21, 77
Brezhnev, 38
Bruner, Jerome, 29
Brussels, Belgium, 30, 143
Bulgaria (Bulgarian), 47
Butler, Judith, 5, 151, 169

C

Calais. *See also* Evans, Kate; George, Sylvain
  context, 121
  'the Jungle', 11, 119–121
  refugee camp, 121
  Sangatte, 41, 120
Camus, Renaud, 142, 145
Canning, Peter, 63, 64
Capitalism, 1, 6, 7, 13, 16, 19, 22, 28, 29, 32, 34, 35, 38, 39, 45, 49, 145, 146, 152, 162, 171, 172
Castro, Andrés Fabian Henao, 6, 14
Castro-Gomez, Santiago, 6
Cavell, Stanley, 91
Ceriani, Pablo, 153
Chakrabarty, Dipesh, 55, 152
Chaplin, Charlie (*Modern Times*, 1936), 110
  Chaplinesque, 113
Chaudhuri, Shohini, 46
Chauka, Please Tell us the Time (Behrouz Boochani, Arash Kamali Sarvestani, Directors), 80, 86, 96
Chrisman, Laura, 151
Chung, Kwangsook, 71
Chute, Hillary, 125, 138
Cixous, Hélène, 210
Clarno, Andy, 208
Clemens, Michael, 131, 132
Climate change
  as cause of migration, 2
  environment. *See* Environmentalism
Cold War, 33, 65, 120, 149
Collett, Mark, 146
  British National Party (BNP), 146
  "Patriotic Alternative (PA)", 146
Colonial Discourse and Postcolonial Theory (Laura Chrisman and Patrick Williams, 1993), 151

Coloniality. *See also* Decolonial; Geopolitics; Global North; Global South; Neocolonial; Postcolonial
  annexation, 227
  colonialism, 5, 78, 79, 96, 159
  colonial, 5, 55, 151, 152, 159, 166
  colonial encounter, 159
  colonial matrix of power (CPM), 6
  colonisation, 151
  colonised, 5, 159, 161
  displacement, 6, 96, 205, 211
  imperialism, 160
  settlement, 151
  settler colonialism, 181, 205, 206, 211, 212, 219
Columbia, 76
Comaroff, Jean, 152
Comaroff, John L., 152
Confederal Group of the European United Left–Nordic Green Left, 30
Connell, Raewyn, 208
Consumerism, 31, 45, 145, 168, 226. *See also* Capitalism; Globalisation
Counter Extremism Project, 147
Counter-hegemonic narratives. *See also* Decoloniality; Narrative
  asylum narratives, 51, 66
  counter-narratives, 1, 35, 165
  hegemonic narratives, 33, 49, 159
  radical/provocative narratives, 9
COVID-19 pandemic, 20, 141, 146
Creswell, Robyn, 228
Croatia, 149
Cuba, 68
Cultural imaginaries, 27, 29, 36
  alternative imaginary, 186

D

Dalal, F., 61, 62

Dalby, Simon, 34
Darwish, Mahmoud, 182, 183, 185, 227
  Absent Presence, 17
  Memory for Forgetfulness, August, Beirut, 1982, 182
D'Cruz, Vin, 79
de Benoist, Alain, 142, 144, 145, 147, 149
de Certeau, Michel, 36, 63, 185, 221, 223, 224
Decoloniality, 7, 9, 10, 19, 22, 55, 166. *See also* Coloniality; Counter-hegemonic narratives; Postcolonialism
  decolonial, 10, 166
  decolonial narrative, 151
Dehumanisation. *See also* Counter-hegemonic narratives; Empowerment, agency and human value
  discardable, 6
  disposable, 4
  disposable others, 6
  less than human, 4, 93
  racialised abjection, 163
  sub-human, 42, 102, 213
  those who do not count, 136, 137
Deleuze, Gilles, 44
Del Grande, Gabriele, 49, 50, 52, 56
Denmark, 149, 166
  Copenhagen, 51, 54
  Danish, 149
Derrida, Jacques, 35, 36, 219
Des Pre, Terence, 54
Diaspora, 210
Dirty Pretty Things (Stephen Frears, Director), 10, 30, 31, 45
Displacement. *See also* Asylum seekers; Migration; Refugees
  discontinuity, 65, 190, 221
  dislocation, 65
  displaced, 2, 141, 160, 162, 189, 190, 211, 214
  interruption, 65, 162
  naziheen, 190
Douglas, Mary
  Purity and Danger, 211
Dublin II Regulation (Dublin III), 52
Duncanson, Ian, 79

E
Earle, Harriet, 138
Eastern Europe, 204
Ecology. *See* Environmentalism
Egypt, 28, 207, 208
Ek, R., 110
The Empire Writes Back (Bill Ashcroft, Gareth Griffiths and Helen Tiffin, 1989), 151
Empowerment, agency and human value, 29
  agency, 29
  empowerment, 104
  grievable, 54, 150
  subjects of value, 30, 77
Environmentalism
  climate, 2, 14, 141
  environment, 3, 14, 95, 101, 103, 108, 111, 119, 121, 213
  pollution, 36, 39
Epistemic violence, 10, 18, 156, 166
Equatorial Guinea, 156
Eritrea, 13, 104, 166, 167, 176
Escape from Syria: Rania's Odyssey (Anders Hammer, Director), 30, 45
Escape to Paradise (Nini Jacusso, Director), 59, 66, 68, 69, 71
Eto'o, Samuel, 159, 164
EU Qualifications Directive, 71
Europe
  European hegemony, 161

Fortress Europe, 55, 75
Western Europe, 5, 19
European Parliament, 30, 55
European Union (EU), 3, 7, 15, 17, 21, 23, 27, 28, 31–33, 40–42, 48, 66, 77, 103, 135, 141, 149, 153
Evans, Kate, 119, 121–123
Everyman, 108
Extremism. *See* Far-right; Terrorism

F
Fabian, Johannes, 143
Famine (as cause of migration), 2
Fanon, Frantz, 7, 162, 187, 199
Farrier, David, 43, 44, 152
Far-right. *See also* Identitarianism
  'dark money', 148
  far-right narratives, 142, 143
  far-right rhetoric, 148
  fascism, 146
  the Great Replacement, 145, 146
  Nazi, 146
  neo-Nazi, 148
  the New Right (Nouvelle Droite), 142
  reconquest, 6, 145
  Reconquista Germania, 145
Faye, Guillaume, 143–145, 147, 151
Feminism (feminist), 84, 87, 145, 168
Film, 9–11, 23, 27–51, 53–56, 59, 62, 64–78, 80, 83, 96, 97, 101, 110, 119–121, 130, 132–138, 151, 153–155, 159, 175, 188, 191, 216, 227. *See also* Narrative
  cinema, 10, 40, 43, 44, 136, 227
  DVD, 40, 56, 133
  video, 40
Fiorenza, Elisabeth Schussler (the Kyriarchal System), 84
Floyd, George, 92, 97

Football, 155, 158, 160, 161, 163, 164
Foster, Michelle, 103
France. *See also* Calais
  Calais, 119
  Dunkirk, 130, 131
  French asylum system, 119
  the Jungle, 119
  Marseille, 51
Freeman, Mark, 185
Friberg, Daniel, 147
Fricker, Miranda, 163

G
Gauthier, David, 50
Gavroche, Julius, 49
Gender, 36, 84, 127, 146, 185, 201–203, 207, 209–211, 228
Geneva Convention (1951), 62, 101
Geoghegan, Peter, 148
Geopolitics (geopolitical), 1, 16, 32–34, 44
George, Sylvain, 119, 132, 137, 138
Germany, 28, 148, 156, 224
Ghana, 135
Giddens, Anthony, 196
Globalisation, 10, 11, 13, 16, 19, 27, 29, 33–35, 38, 67, 77, 145, 148, 152
Global North, 6, 18, 20, 22, 29, 49, 55, 137, 174, 175. *See also* Coloniality; Globalisation; Global South
Global South, 1, 6, 8, 11, 19, 22, 28, 56, 67, 141, 144, 151–153, 157, 158, 163, 166, 175
Godin, Marie, 119
Godwin, Gail, 220
Going Home: A Walk Through Fifty years of Occupation (Raja Shehadeh), 219, 221, 223, 224
Gorali, Moshe, 207, 209

Gramsci, Antonio (Gramscian), 56, 145, 212, 213
Grass, Günter, 60
Great recession, the, 2007–2009, 1
Greece, 46, 47, 77, 148
  Golden Dawn, 77, 148
  Lesbos, 46
Gregory, Caroline, 133
Gregory, Derek, 184
Griffiths, Gareth, 151
Grillo, Beppe, 150
Grisoni, Tony, 41, 43
Grosfoguel, Ramon, 5, 151, 159
Guardian (newspaper), 47, 81, 142, 150
Guatemala, 17
The Gurugu Pledge (Juan Tomás Ávila Laurel), 8, 10, 18, 151, 156, 160, 162, 163
Guthrie, Woody ("Deportees"), 53

H
Hage, G., 161
Haitian revolution, 9
Hall, Catherine, 4, 5
Hammer, Anders, 45–47
Hanafi, Sara, 194
Handel, Ariel, 195–197
Heaney, Seamus, 56
Heinrich, Tobias, 166
Heller, Charles, 175
Helton, Arthur, 65
Herzl, Theodor (*Der Judenstaat*/The Jewish State, 1896), 187
Hicks, Dan, 119–121, 133
Hirsch, Marianne, 204, 213, 214
Hollow Land: Israel's Architecture of Occupation (Eyal Weizman), 195
Holocaust, the, 54, 146, 204
Hope Not Hate, 146
Huffer, Lynne, 125, 127

Human rights abuse (rights abuse), 27, 29, 40
Human Rights Watch, 31
Hungary, 142

I
Identitarianism. *See also* Far-right
  Bloc Idententitaire, 144
  Generation Identitaire, 144
  Generation Identity, 146
  identitarian, 144
Identity, 31–37, 45, 60–64, 66, 72, 77–79, 83, 86, 92, 105, 107, 116, 125, 136, 143, 146–149, 153, 155, 156, 160, 162, 163, 165, 169, 171, 186, 191, 197, 200, 210–213, 215
  hierarchies of identity, 64
  transitional identity/identities, 65
Ideology, 4, 21, 28, 34, 50, 60, 66, 71, 78, 142, 145, 148, 154, 161, 185, 205, 207, 209
Immobility. *See also* Mobility; Movement
  arrest of movement, 3
  bureaucracy, 114, 117, 119
  checkpoints, 7, 11, 23, 226
  curfews, 11, 23, 186
  detention, 3, 7, 120
  internment, 62
  paperasserie, 113
  queuing, 87, 89, 115, 117, 135
  red tape, 113, 131
  refugee camps, 184, 185, 193, 194
  waiting, 7, 13, 120, 155, 172, 186, 196, 226
Indonesia, 78–81, 84, 87
Inequality, 5, 7, 19–21, 29, 32, 64, 103, 132, 172, 187
Ingold, Tim, 12

In This World (Michael Winterbottom, Director), 10, 28, 30, 31, 40, 41, 43, 44
Iran, 28, 41, 80, 81, 91, 113, 117
Iraq, 20, 68, 76, 91, 104, 122, 129
Irgun, the, 204
I Saw Ramallah (Maroud Barghouti), 189
Isin, Engin F., 67, 68
Islam (Islamic), 62, 143, 145, 211
Islamist terrorism
  Al-Quaeda, 143
  Daesh, 143
  ISIS, 143
  Taliban, 130
Israel. *See also* Jewish identity; Jewish refugees; Zionism
  Israeli, 182, 191, 193, 202, 208, 209
  Israeli Defence Forces (IDF), 186, 196, 197, 209
  Jerusalem, 194, 197, 227
  West Bank, 23, 141, 182, 183, 193, 194, 196, 197, 201, 222, 225, 228
The Israeli Committee Against House Demolitions (ICAHD), 228
Israeli Defence Forces (IDF), 186, 196, 197, 204, 209, 215, 216, 222, 225
Italy
  Lampedusa, 50, 52, 59, 168, 173
  Milan, 2, 50–52
  Ventimiglia, 53
Ivory Coast, 155
I Was Born There, I Was Born Here (Maroud Barghouti), 182, 199, 200

J
Jacusso, Nino, 96
Jara, Victor, 192
Jayyusi, Lena, 184, 185, 206
Jewish identity
  collective identity, 210
  collective memory, 149
  Holocaust, 54, 146, 204
  Jewish diaspora, 210
  pogroms, 204
Jewish refugees, 204
Jordan, 15, 28, 182, 201
Journey of Hope (Xavier Koller, Director), 40, 41
Judaism, 142. *See also* Religion

K
Kafka, Franz (Kafkaesque), 113
Kahane, Claire, 210
Kasparek, Bernd, 22
Kaufmann, Vincent, 12, 62
Kearney, Richard, 54
Khaal, Abu Bakar, 14, 166, 167, 169, 170, 172, 173, 175–177
Khalidi, Rashid, 187, 219
Khalidi, Walid, 205
Khosravi, Shamsan, 127, 132, 189
Khoury, Nuha, 199
Kinstler, L., 113
Kosovo (Kosovan), 120
Kotef, Hagar, 13
Kozole, Daman, 30
Krebs, Pierre, 149
Kubiak, A., 223
Kurdistan, 76, 91
Kyriarchal System, 84, 87, 88, 90, 91, 94, 95

L
La Forteresse (Fernand Melgar, Director), 59, 64–66, 68
Laïdi, Zaki, 149
The Last Earth: A Palestinian Story (Ramzy Baroud), 184

Last Resort (Pawel Pawlowski, Director), 30, 31
Latin America, 159
Latin American theorists, 4
Laurel, Juan Tomás Ávila
  Ahmed the Arab, or the Desert's Embrace, 163
  The Gurugu Pledge, 8, 10, 18, 151, 156, 160, 162, 163, 166
Laurie, Timothy, 153
Lavie, Aviv, 207, 209
Lear, Edward, 114
Lebanon, 15, 28, 182, 186
Lecadet, Clara, 158
Left, the (political), 145
Lenin, 38
Le Pen, Marine, 124
Levinas, Emmanuel, 37, 49, 50, 127
Liberalism, 62, 142, 145
Libya (Tripoli), 144, 166, 167, 170, 173, 176
Lilya 4-Ever (Lukas Moodysson, Director), 30–32, 37, 44
Lindsey, Ursula, 224
Lucht, Hans
  Darkness Before Daybreak, 67
Luckhurst, Roger, 75

M

Macedonia, 47, 149
Mahon, Derek, 56
Maldonado-Torres, N., 114
Mali, 153, 155
Mallet, Sarah, 119–121, 133
Mancuso, Marco, 49
Manea, Dragos, 127
Mansoubi, Moones, 81
Mansour, Camille, 183
Manus Island, Papua New Guinea, 23, 78
Maps. *See also* Borders; Geopolitics; Space, spatiality

cartography, 161, 183, 184, 213, 221
landscape, 32, 38, 42, 111, 133, 183, 185, 188, 221, 222
maplessness, 104
mapping, 33, 168, 183, 213, 221, 224
mental maps, 105
psychogeographic memory, 222
topoanalysis, 222
topography, 222
Marfleet, Philip, 5, 21
Markov chain, 118
Marvel comics, 126
Marxism (Marxist), 145
Maryns, Katrijn, 70
Matthews, Julie, 71
Mayblin, Lucy, 1, 2
May, Theresa, 124
May They Rest in Revolt (*Qu'Ils Reposent En Révolte*) (Sylvain George, Director), 11, 132
Mbembe, Achille, 6, 158, 160, 162, 169
McDonnell, John, 132
Mediterranean, 8, 14, 16, 19, 51, 53, 54, 59, 102, 150, 168, 175
Melgar, Fernand, 64, 73–75
Melilla, 15, 17, 23, 120, 141, 153, 154, 156, 157, 161, 165
Memory, 5, 70, 72, 77, 88, 153, 184, 185, 189, 190, 192, 204, 209, 213, 214, 220–223
Memory for Forgetfulness, August, Beirut, 1982, 182
Mexican-US border, 3
Mexico, 14, 17, 23
Mezzadra, Sandro, 16, 19
Middle East, 1, 6, 50, 133, 143, 191
Mignolo, Walter, 4–7, 19, 55
Migration. *See also* Asylum seekers; Immobility; Mobility; Refugees

INDEX

absence, 36
anonymity, 77, 96, 155, 169
criminalisation, 32, 173
deaths of migrants/refugees, 11, 128
defamiliarisation, 104, 218
economic migrants, 3, 31, 77, 103
erasure, 176
exile, 86
forced migration, 10, 56, 142, 151, 166, 182
hostile environment, 16
immigration, 17, 108, 141, 143, 144
mass displacement, 2
mental capital, 102, 105, 107, 109
migrant journeys, 13
migrants, 2–4, 10, 12, 14–17, 20, 28, 31, 32, 36, 37, 41, 45, 59, 67, 79, 101–104, 108–110, 119, 120, 131, 133–135, 141, 142, 144, 145, 147, 150, 151, 153–157, 163, 171–175
political migrants, 3
reactive migration, 3, 14, 101, 103, 104
scapegoating, 20
silenced deaths, 177
transmigration, 154
unbelonging, 45, 61, 104
undocumented migrants, 17
Western media narratives, 169
Mikes, George
  How To Be an Alien, 1946, 113
Militarisation, 14, 102, 153, 206, 215
Minor Detail (Adania Shibli), 193, 205–207, 209, 210, 212, 219, 228
Mirzhoeff, Nicholas, 62
Mitscherlich-Nielsen, Margarete, 223, 224

Mobility. *See also* Asylum seekers; Immobility; Migration; Refugees
  air travel, 11
  boats, 175
  cars, 51, 203
  cruise liners, 134
  desert crossing, 170
  ferries, 134
  forced mobility, 11, 19, 20
  journey, 23, 44, 104
  lorries, 134
  mobilities paradigm, 11
  movement, 11–13, 17, 67
  road, 194, 196
  sea, 23
  ships, 176
  trains, 134
  travel, 11
  voyage, 51
  walking, 12, 225
  wandering, 134
Morocco
  Melilla/Morocco border, 17, 120
  Mount Gurugu, 153, 156
Morris, Benny, 207
Morrison, Toni
  The Bluest Eye, 18
  Unspeakable Things Unspoken, 9
Motility, 12
Movement, 3, 10–13, 16, 19, 28, 29, 31, 36, 40, 44, 46, 51, 53, 60, 63, 67, 70, 86, 94, 96, 103, 105, 118, 123, 132, 134, 144, 146, 148, 162, 169, 186, 193–196, 199–201, 203, 218, 225
Müller, Beatrice, 171
Murdoch, Simon, 146
Mur (Simone Bitton, Director), 227

N

NAFTA (North American Free Trade Agreement), 14, 23

Nail, T., 104
Narrative. *See also* Counter-hegemonic narratives; Stories
  allegorical, 169
  analepsis, 167
  biographical, 23
  caricature, 117
  contrastive method, 114
  fable, 157
  fictional, 23, 28, 63, 166
  film, 9, 33, 45
  first-person, 157, 162, 165, 167
  folktale, 157
  graphic, 10, 42, 96, 101, 104, 105, 119–122, 132, 138
  immobility, 23
  irony, 75, 169
  irrealist, 157
  literary, 2, 6, 9, 10, 142, 207
  mobility, 8, 23
  myth, 72, 83, 168
  narrative of displacement, 106, 148, 183
  narrative voice, 33, 36, 56, 73, 133, 157, 217
  narrativity, 29, 223
  narrator, 18, 157, 162, 165, 166, 169, 213, 214, 218
  oral traditions, 157
  perspective, 5, 9, 70, 141, 161
  point of view, 161
  prolepsis, 167
  realist, 69, 71
  satirical, 114
  second-person, 157
  space, 33, 36, 42, 56, 73, 74, 82, 105, 121, 143
  surreal, 105
  temporality, 187, 189
  testimonial, 2, 6
  third-person, 175
  visual, 10, 122, 190

Nationalism
  authentic/inauthentic national identity, 60
  authenticity, 60
  citizenship, 60
  ethno-nationalism, 103, 149
  far-right nationalism, 61
  heritage, 149
  ideologies of nation, 5, 8, 60
  inauthenticity, 60
  national identity, 61
  nativism, 142
  Palestinian nationalism, 185
  populist nationalism, 4, 7, 61
  sovereignty, 15, 60, 61, 78, 148
  territorial imagination, 59–61
  territorialism, 59
  territoriality, 60
  white nationalism, 146
  Zionist nationalism, 212
Ndlovu-Gatsheni, Sabelo J., 158, 160, 162, 166–168
Neilson, Brett, 16, 19
Neocolonial, 151, 156, 158, 159, 162
Neoliberalism, 10, 19, 21, 23, 29, 31, 33, 77, 148
New York Declaration for Refugees and Migrants (2016), 3
New Zealand, 81, 143, 147
Neyestani, M.
  An Iranian Metamorphosis, 113
  Petit Manuel du Parfait Réfugié Politique, 104
Ngugi wa Thiong'o
  The Perfect Nine: the epic of Gikuyu and Mumbi, 168
  Something Torn and New, 152, 153
Nigeria, 76, 135
No Friend but the Mountains (Behrouz Boochani), 8, 60, 95
Norval, Aletta, 91
Nottingham, 13, 15

O

Occupied Palestinian Territories (OPT), 182
O'Malley, Padraig, 223
On the Bride's Side (*Io Sto con La Sposa*) (Antonio Augugliaro, Director), 48, 52, 56, 135, 137, 172
Ophir, Adi, 184, 194, 195
Orban, Victor, 142
Orientalism (Edward Said), 151
Orwell, George (Orwellian), 118
Oslo Accords, 186, 193, 202, 220, 221, 223

P

Pakistan, 28, 41, 43, 68
Palestine
  Gaza (Gaza Strip), 15, 193
  Hebron, 183, 201
  Intifada, 220
  Jerusalem, 193
  Nakba, 183, 204
  Occupied Territories, 191
  Operation Cast Lead, 186
  Palestinian Authority, 193, 225
  Ramallah, 189, 219, 220
  Sabra, 185
  Shatila, 185
  West Bank, 15, 23, 182, 191
  West Bank wall, 141
Palladino, Mariangela, 96
Pappé, Ilan, 181, 183, 193, 208
Pawlowski, Pawel, 30, 31
Patriarchy
  aggression, 216
  gendered power, 203, 204
  homosociality, 208
  male violence, 7, 209
  masculinist, 203
  masculinity, 203, 208
  misogyny, 165
  patriarchal, 201, 204
People trafficking/smuggling (human trafficking), 23, 28, 30, 31, 42, 130, 168
Perera, Suvendrini, 80
The Perfect Nine: the epic of Gikuyu and Mumbi (Ngugi wa Thiong'o, 2018), 168
Peteet, Julie, 183
Petit Manuel du Parfait Réfugié Politique (M. Neyestani), 104
Pezzani, Lorenzo, 175
Philo, Chris, 78
Picozza, Fiorenza, 135
Pitt Rivers Museum, Oxford, 121
Place and placelessness, 105
Poe, Edgar Allan ("The Purloined Letter"), 50
Poland, 149
Populism, 4, 7, 61, 148, 150
Postcolonial/Postcolonialism (post-colony), 6, 16, 151, 158, 166
Postmemory, 213, 214
Poverty
  as cause of migration, 2, 32, 42, 158
  economic deprivation, 103
  immiseration, 195
Precariousness, precarity, 8, 9, 20, 60, 146, 163, 171
Precup, Mihaela, 127
Pritchett, Lant, 131, 132
Pugliese, Joseph, 126
Putin, Vladimir, 147

Q

Qu'ils Reposent en Révolte/Des Figures de Guerre (May They Rest in Revolt/Figures of War) (Sylvain George, Director), 11, 119, 132

Quijano, Anibal, 152, 160, 161

R
Rabin, Yitzhak, 191
Racialisation (race), 1, 5, 16, 86, 92, 142, 162, 205
Racism
  racist discourse, 80
  racist rhetoric, 150
  racists, 164
Rajaram, Prem Kumar, 79
Rancière, Jacques, 66, 83, 137, 172
Rathzel, Nora, 36
Red Cross (International Red Cross), 52, 62
Refugee Rights Europe, 119
Refugees. *See also* Asylum seekers; Biopolitics; Immobility; Migration; Mobility
  agency, 8, 9, 153, 160
  anti-refugee rhetoric, 3
  anxiety, 120, 194
  autonomy, 8, 160
  exclusionary discourse, 27
  fear, 3, 7, 46, 79, 86, 101, 103
  independence, 71
  mental health, 102
  populist representations of refugees, 1
  refugee crisis, 22, 28, 160
  refugee journeys, 3, 13
  trauma, 13, 71, 109
  undocumented, 15, 22, 158
  unsettlement, 104
  welfare, 65, 102
  well-being, 3, 93
  wellness, 102
Refugee Week festival, Nottingham 2016, 13
Religion
  Christianity, 5, 19, 142

Islam, 143, 145, 211
Judaism, 142
Richmond, Anthony H., 3, 14, 101, 103, 104
Ricoeur, Paul, 37, 72, 73
Right, the (political), 20, 80
Rimbaud, Arthur, 176
Robinson, William T., 19–21
Roma, 77
Rosman-Stollman, Elisheva, 209, 210
Routledge, Paul, 33
Russia, 30, 39, 68, 147
Rygiel, Kim, 67, 68

S
Said, Edward, 143, 151, 182, 183, 189, 212, 219
Salah, Mohammed, 164
Salgado, Sebastião, 27
Salmela, Mikko, 146
Salvini, Matteo, 144
Sands, Bobby (*Prison Diary*), 81
Sangatte, Calais. *See* Calais
Santos, Boaventura de Sousa, 6, 17, 18, 22, 168, 174
Sarrazin, Thilo, 146
Schachar, Ayelet, 17
Scotland, 15
Sennett, Richard, 148
Sex slavery
  human trafficking, 28
  people smuggling, 30, 31, 42
Sexuality, 36, 211
Shafir, Gershon, 182, 225, 226
Shalhoub-Kevorkian, Nadera, 207
Shamir, Rouen, 12
Shapiro, Michael, 34, 44, 64
Sharpe, Christina, 168
Shavit, Ari, 207
Shehadeh, Raja

Going Home: A Walk Through Fifty years of Occupation, 219, 221, 223, 224
Palestinian Walks, 219
Shelley, Percy Bysshe, 176
Shibli, Adania (*Minor Detail*), 193, 206, 207, 209, 210, 212, 219, 228
Sidibe, Abou Bakar, 180
Siebert, Moritz, 180
Six-Day War (1967), 195, 221
Slavery and the slave trade, 5, 30, 41, 152. *See also* Sex slavery
Slobodian, Quinn, 19, 21
Slovenia, 149
Socialism (socialist), 61
Social media
  internet, 147
  weaponising internet culture, 147
Soeting, Monica, 166
Soguk, Nevzat, 33, 36, 60, 63, 64
Solnit, Rebecca, 216
Somalia, 75, 76, 104
Something Torn and New (Ngugi wa Thiong'o, 2009), 152, 153
Soto Bermant, Laia, 153
South Sudan, 104
Soviet Union, 32, 33, 38
Soyinka, Wole, 151
Space
  space-time, 116, 134
  spatial barriers, 184
  spatiality, 110, 167, 189
  spatial manipulation, 181, 206
  spatial power, 188
  territorial space, 33, 197
Spain (Ceuta, Melilla), 153, 157, 180
Spare Parts (Daman Kozole, Director), 16, 30
Spencer, Richard, 144, 147
Spivak, Gayatri Chakravorty, 12, 97
Squire, Corinne, 119

Steele, William, 79
Stoler, Ann Laura, 80
Stories. *See also* Narrative
  self-storying, 162
  storied, 30, 77
  story, 8, 13, 15, 29, 30, 38, 41, 44, 45, 47–50, 60, 65–67, 69, 70, 72, 73, 76, 81, 82, 96, 106, 109, 110, 113, 114, 123, 129, 142, 152, 157, 162, 166, 168, 174, 175, 181–183, 185, 191, 194, 199, 201, 216, 218, 225
  storying, 182, 224
  storytelling, 161
Storyselling, 69, 71
Subalternity, 7, 203
Sweden (Malmö), 39, 51, 54
Switzerland (Swiss, Swiss national referendum (2006)), 23, 62, 66–69, 72, 74, 75
Syria, 13, 20, 28, 45–47, 49, 51, 54, 102, 104, 119, 144

T
Tahir, Zaman, 119
Tan, Shaun, 104, 105, 108, 112, 138
Tarrant, Brenton, 147
Tazzioli, Martina, 12, 16
Terrorism
  terrorists, 45, 50, 143, 144, 171, 173, 195
  'war on terrorism', 35
Theatre of the Absurd, 90, 113
Third Baltic Sea Conference on WoMen and Democracy, 30
Thomas, Robert, 69, 71
Those Who Jump (*Les Sauteurs*) (Abou Bakar Sidimé, Estephan Wagner, Moritz Siebert, Directors), 151, 153
Threads: From the Refugee Crisis (Kate Evans), 11, 119, 125, 126, 135

Ticktin, Miriam, 119
Tiffin, Helen, 151
Time
  clock-time, 134
  duration, 11, 31, 40, 117, 118, 186, 200
  'temporal bombs', 134
  temporality, 10, 19, 108, 167, 187, 189
Tofighian, Omid, 81, 82
Togo, 76
Trela, Bailey, 217
Trilling, Daniel, 8, 151
Trouillot, Michel-Rolph, 9, 18, 19
Trump, Donald, 61, 144, 146, 194
Tsantsoulas, Tiffany, 159, 165, 166
Tunisia, 166, 167, 173
Turkey, 28, 41, 46, 47, 68, 70
Twin Towers, 1

U
UK
  Dover, 21, 43, 59, 130
  Essex, 59
  London, 31, 41, 43, 143, 150
  Morecambe Bay (Lancashire), 59
UKIP, 77
UN Development Programme's Human Development Index (HDI), 22
UNICEF, 30, 40
UN Refugee Convention (1951), 3
Urry, John, 11, 12
US
  Ellis Island, 108
  New York, 108
  Statue of Liberty, 108

V
Venice film festival, 55
Violence
  epistemic violence, 10, 18, 156, 166
  murder, 78, 93, 97, 149, 207, 209, 213, 214, 216
  rape, 10, 38, 39, 44, 125, 207, 209–216
  repression, 224
  repressive, 81, 154, 161
  sexual violence, 164, 210
von Scheve, Christian, 146
Vulnerable Persons Resettlement Scheme (VPRS), 15

W
Wagner, Estephan, 180
Wallerstein, Immanuel, 16
Walsh, Catherine, 19
War, as cause of migration
  conflict, 1, 20, 94
  infrastructural warfare, 188
  violence, 6
  warfare, 130
Weber, Cynthia, 64
Weheliye, Alexander G., 159, 205, 206
Weizman, Eyal
  Hollow Land: Israel's Architecture of Occupation, 195
West Bank (Palestine/Israel), 15, 23, 141, 181–184, 186, 187, 191, 193–197, 201, 206, 208, 222, 224–228
Williams, Patrick, 151
Williams, Robbie, 40
Wodak, Ruth, 148
Wolfe, Thomas
  You Can't Go Home Again, 220
Woolley, Agnes, 75, 96, 152
World Social Forum, 18, 23
The Wretched of the Earth (Frantz Fanon), 7, 162
Wynter, Sylvia, 4, 159, 166

X
Xenophobia (xenophobic), 66, 67, 77, 148

Y
Yearning in the Land of Checkpoints (Azmi Bishara), 195
Young, Iris Marion, 126

Yugoslavia, 33
Yuval-Davis, Nira, 65

Z
Zapatistas, 18, 23
Zetter, Roger, 20
Zionism (Zionist), 187, 205, 212, 219

Printed in the United States
by Baker & Taylor Publisher Services